My Daily Bread

A Summary of
The Spiritual Life

Simplified and Arranged
for Daily
Reading, Reflection
and Prayer

BY
ANTHONY J. PAONE, S. J.

1954

IMPRIMI POTEST:

JOHN J. McMAHON, S. J.
Provincial, New York Province.

NIHIL OBSTAT:

MARTIN J. HEALY, S. T. D.
Censor Librorum.

IMPRIMATUR:

THOMAS EDMUNDUS MOLLOY, S. T. D.
Archiepiscopus-Episcopus
Brooklyniensis.

Brooklyni, XXVII Februarii 1954.

ISBN: 978-1-61890-812-4

Published by:
TAN Books
PO Box 410487
Charlotte, NC 28241
www.TANBooks.com

Printed and bound in the United States of America

Foreword

THE CONFRATERNITY OF THE PRECIOUS BLOOD is privileged to present another in its series of basic books for the Catholic family. The Confraternity has endeavored, during a score of years, to popularize the Liturgy, Sacred Scripture and Theology by placing in the hands of millions throughout the world such books as My Sunday Missal, My Daily Psalm Book, Christ in the Gospel, The New Testament, and My Way of Life.

The work here presented "My Daily Bread" is a summary of spiritual doctrine so simplified and arranged that everyone can come to a knowledge and practice of the principles of the spiritual life. It is divided into three books which treat respectively of the three ways of the Spiritual Life. (1) Purification—we must reform that which has been deformed in us by sin. (2) Imitation—we must conform to Christ that which has been reformed. (3) Union—we must transform through Christ that which has been conformed.

This book must be read, not only with the head, but with the heart. We must think and pray. This daily exercise will transform belief into realization, theory into practice. This work has been authored by the Rev. Anthony J. Paone, S. J. May it prove a helpful guide to daily spiritual growth. May it help souls to persevere in the holy resolutions which they make at the time of confession, Holy Communion, missions, retreats, or any moment of grace. While written primarily for the layman in the language of the layman, it will prove helpful to the priest and religious.

(Rt. Rev. Msgr.) Joseph B. Frey
Feast of Our Lady
Dec. 8, 1953

How to Use this Book

EVERY MAN DREAMS, at some time or other, of the better person he might have been or may yet become. This book deals with that dream—self-perfection. True, there are different ideals and standards of self-perfection, but only one ideal, one standard alone, will stand the test at the judgment seat of God. The one and only standard of goodness and perfection is the standard which God Himself has given us. We do not have to establish an ideal for ourselves. Our Heavenly Father has already given us one— His divine Son, our Lord Jesus Christ.

If, like Mary, the sister of Lazarus, we had the privilege of sitting at the feet of Jesus and listening to His precious words of wisdom, peace, and joy, who of us would refuse to do so? Well, we can do so. Our Lord speaks to us far more often than we listen. He is much closer to us than we dream. Within one year, we would go far in self-perfection if we placed ourselves at His feet for a few minutes each day, and heard Him tell us how to improve our daily lives.

In this book we have some of the wonderful thoughts of Christ. Receive them, a chapter a day, as coming directly from Him. Often, between the lines, He will give you a message which is meant for you alone. This will be the grace of that chapter. God's grace will show you how to live a better life today, and it will also bring you the strength to do so. If you use these graces well, God will grant you greater ones. Daily you will grow more like Christ and less like your old self.

Each chapter follows this simple plan: (*a*) listen; (*b*) think; and (*c*) answer Him.

BOOK ONE

The Way of Purification

PART ONE: Conversion
- **A.** A Thoughtful Glance at Human Life
- **B.** The Four Last Things

PART TWO: After Conversion

Facing the Old Routine with a New Spirit

PART THREE: Temptation
- **A.** Nature, Value and Control of Temptations
- **B.** Certain Temptations in Particular

PART FOUR: Conquering Bad Habits

PART FIVE: Self-Conquest Through Mortification

BOOK ONE

The Way of Purification

THOUGH A MAN may disregard God's holy commandments during his earthly life, he will have to account for them sooner or later. The greatest catastrophe which can befall a man is an unprovided death. At present he can help himself by admitting God's truth and obeying His law. After death, however, he will no longer be able to save himself. Though he had a lifetime to take advantage of God's love and mercy, he now faces God's justice. The Divine Justice will reward him according to his earthly life, and he will go to Heaven or hell.

A spiritual man is one who seeks to make the best use of this brief earthly life. He seeks to live in such a way that he may never sacrifice his greatest success for smaller and less important successes. He strives to place first things first. Therefore, he endeavors to follow God's holy Will in all things.

The first stage of a successful spiritual life consists of self-purification. Though self-purification is a life-long task, one in this stage of spiritual development makes it his outstanding daily goal. He strives to rid himself of all serious sins and any predominant venial faults which may lead to mortal sin. In so doing he lays a foundation for virtues which he will later practice in a more positive manner, and not just as the opposites of his present faults.

PART ONE
Conversion

A. A Thoughtful Glance at Human Life

CONVERSION means "turning to God", whether it be for the first time or whether it be after a period of sluggish and half-hearted service. In this first part, one must honestly strive to see himself as he really is—weak and selfish, but loved by God, and made for the eternal glory and happiness of Heaven. Man must be deeply impressed with the true purpose of this earthly life, and do everything possible to make that purpose the main goal of his future actions.

CHAPTER 1

Man's Purpose on Earth

CHRIST:

MY CHILD, the highest goal of your life is union with Me in Heaven. Let your intentions throughout the day be guided by this truth. In all things be sure to stay on the path which leads to Heaven. Do not become too deeply interested in the passing desires and brief enjoyments of this earthly life.

2. I have given you everything that you are and everything you have. All things come to you from Me, the Supreme Good. Whatever comes, accept it, use it, enjoy it, as I wish and as much as I wish.

3. If you think only of satisfying yourself, without considering My approval, your mind becomes confused and your will becomes weak. Mistakes and sins will rob you of peace on earth and of unending happiness in Heaven. In all things, therefore, keep your eyes on Me.

4. Happy are those who desire only what I want, trying steadily to do My Will. Such people do not let themselves become completely

absorbed by their daily activities. They frequently offer their activities to Me. They see the brevity of human contentment on earth.

5. Examine your motives in your daily words and actions. Find out how you may please Me more, and avoid everything which may draw you away from Me.

THINK:

I was created for eternal happiness with God in Heaven. Everything else must take second place in my life, because if I lose Heaven, I will be losing everything. The sure guide to Heaven is God's holy Will. If I follow it in my daily life, every moment on earth will be a sure step toward the perfect happiness which my heart craves.

PRAY:

My God and loving Father, grant me the wisdom to think, speak, and act each day as You want me to. May I never be such a fool as to disagree with Your supreme goodness and wisdom. Nothing on earth can bring me any lasting happiness. Therefore, let me never sin for the sake of anything. I want to live for the perfect happiness for which You created me. *Amen.*

CHAPTER 2

The Purpose of Created Things

CHRIST:

MY CHILD, if you directed your desires according to My Will, you would learn many a holy lesson from the events of daily life. Nothing is so small and unimportant that it does not, in some way, reflect my wisdom and goodness. When you have become as good and unselfish as you should be, you will find it easy to understand the deeper meaning of the events in your daily life. An unselfish heart sees much more than what appears on the surface.

2. I created Heaven and earth for the service of man. I have even appointed angels to help man. In fact, I Myself am continually serving and helping man. If he lives as I desire, he shall one day share with Me the perfect happiness of Heaven.

3. What are you doing in return for My numberless favors? You should serve Me every single day of your life. Yet, you fail to give Me unselfish service even for one single day. I deserve all possible obedience, all

possible honor and eternal praise. To Me you owe each breath and second of life. Without My continued support, nothing could please nor help you. All assistance and relief is the work of My hand.

THINK:

If I ever wrote down a list of God's gifts to me, I would have to compose a book. Everything and everybody, whatever I may mention, is a gift of God for a definite purpose. All things, not just some things, are in my life for God's good reasons. In one way or another, they are meant to help me earn the unending happiness and glory of Heaven. I must reject any person or thing that leads me away from this goal by sin. All things are to be used wisely, that is, to help me live a good and useful life. By an intelligent use and control of life's daily needs and activities, I prove my sincere desire for God's eternal love and friendship in Heaven.

PRAY:

My God, the good things that attract me on earth are only tiny reflections of Your perfect attraction and goodness. Let them never turn my thoughts aside from You, the Perfect Good. I hope to turn away from anybody or anything which draws me away from You. The good things of earth will pass away all too soon, but You will remain forever. I choose You now by a sincere daily battle against sin. Grant me the glorious favor of pleasing You on earth and loving You in Heaven. *Amen.*

CHAPTER 3

A Right Intention in All Things

CHRIST:

MY CHILD, in all things I want you to have a light intention. That means that I want you to have a supernatural purpose in whatever you think, do, or say. Whether you seek to avoid hell, diminish your purgatory, or gain Heaven, such motives are supernatural, and therefore they are right intentions. True, you are often unaware of your motives, but as long as you are not in mortal sin, and your action agrees with My law, you have a right intention.

2. A right intention, however, may have different degrees of perfection. Thus, when you do something simply to please Me, your

intention is higher than if you think of your own advantage. Still, whatever be the degree of your right intention, it always seeks to fulfill My Will, and it always brings you a greater good than any intention which seeks only your earthly welfare.

3. Regardless of feelings, moods, prejudices, or preferences, strive to maintain a right intention at all times. As soon as your natural desires contradict My Will, check them as you would check any other foolish intention.

4. Do not let life's daily events disturb nor affect you too much. Seek to know My Will and to accept it in all things. With this pure intention, you will have a deep interior peace. This is My gift to those who let Me govern their lives.

5. A person's intention tends to become dim as he proceeds through his daily occupations. Gradually he is influenced more by pleasure or self-satisfaction. Therefore, renew your pure intention at different times during the day. Offer Me each activity and avoid anything which might lead you into sin.

6. Recall your heavenly goal from time to time. Let there be nothing great, nothing

high, nothing pleasant, nothing acceptable to you unless it helps you to follow My Will. Consider all useless consolations and sinful pleasures as so much worthless money.

7. One who truly loves Me, hates everything which holds him back from Me. I alone, the eternal, infinite God, the Perfect Joy of the soul, can bring true peace and unending happiness to your heart.

THINK:

Where are the pleasures and joys of last year? Gone and forgotten. If they made me worse, I shall find death and judgment a little harder to face. Why do I fail to value things according to God's way of thinking? He wants me to live a sinless and useful life. Even my pleasures should improve me in some way, and make me better able to do my work. Heaven is far greater than I can ever deserve. Still I should try each day to be a little less unworthy of it.

PRAY:

Lord, what You say is true. Grant that I may follow Your words in my daily life. Your truth shall teach me, guide me, and protect me. May it deliver me from all evil desires and foolish love. Let me esteem nothing as great, or valuable, or wonderful, except insofar as it makes me better and more pleasing in Your eyes. In this way I shall never be a slave of this earth, but shall walk daily towards Heaven with a holy freedom of heart. *Amen.*

CHAPTER 4

Holy Indifference

CHRIST:

MY CHILD, let Me do with you as I please. I know what is best for you. You think as a human being, so that your judgments are often influenced by your feelings, moods or prejudices.

2. I take better care of you than you could ever take of yourself. Anyone who does not give Me his whole-hearted attention and loyalty, is taking a great risk. I alone can lead you to eternal life. Let Me do with you as I please. Whatever I do will always be best for you.

3. Knowing all things, I know your most important needs. I want you to gain the perfect and unending joy of Heaven. For this reason I will place you at times in a spiritual

darkness of doubts and confusion. Then
again I will let you enjoy the light of My
truth and joy. One day I will console you,
and on the next day you may find life hard
and sorrowful. But through all these changing conditions, remember that My hand is
leading you on toward Heaven.

4. Follow My Will in all things. Be just
as ready to experience suffering as to have
joy, just as glad to be poor and needy as to
be well off. If you prefer My Will in all these
things, you will be preferring the Perfect
Wisdom and the Highest Good.

THINK:

God made me for the perfect life of Heaven.
Whatever He sends me is sent with this goal
in view. Some things I can remedy and improve in my daily life, while other things are
beyond my control. After I have done my best,
I should accept the results as God's Will for
me. Be it hard or easy, pleasant or disagreeable, I can always be sure that God knows,
wants and permits what is good for my soul.

PRAY:

My God and my All, You made and control all things in my daily life. How can I

forget this truth and complain about anything? Grant me the holy dispositions which you mentioned a moment ago. Make me equally willing to receive from Your hand the sweet and the bitter, the joy and the sorrow. I thank you now for whatever You decide to send me. Only keep me from sin, and I shall fear neither death nor hell. As long as You do not separate me from You forever, nor blot me out of the book of life, whatever suffering comes to me will not hurt me for long. Grant me the grace to see, love, and prefer Your Will in everything that happens to me today. *Amen.*

CHAPTER 5

Looking Away from God

CHRIST:

MY CHILD, the person who esteems anything for itself alone, forgetting My goodness and love, will always be small and inferior like the things which he values. Whatever does not help you to please Me, has no true value in your life. You should therefore consider it as nothing.

2. Unless you see Me in your daily life, you will sooner or later become discontented, wherever you are and wherever you turn.

3. If any man tries to enjoy anything as though it were his alone, he will not have a lasting joy nor true freedom. In many ways he will find himself tied down and shut off from Me.

4. He who thinks more of earthly things than he does of Me, will find nothing but insecurity, trouble and sorrow. He may not realize it, but he is planning his own destruction.

5. Be it ever so little, if anything is loved and valued more than it deserves, it holds you back from Me, the Highest Good, and it weakens your soul. The man who looks only for worldly satisfactions, becomes blind to the loving presence of his Creator.

THINK:

One who seeks only pleasure, ease, honor, or profit is a worldling, that is, he lives only for this life. Gradually he becomes a slave of his earthly desires, so that he cannot even think of God. He will believe in Heaven too late—when he finds its gates forever closed to him.

PRAY:

My God, I rely on Your assistance to keep myself free from the slavery of earthly attractions. I shall use my possessions and daily enjoyments as things which You have lent to me. May I never offend You with these gifts of Yours. As yesterday's enjoyments passed away, so too will those of today. I want to live for the greatest Good—for You, my God and my All. You alone are best and highest. Only You can satisfy my heart's longings forever. *Amen.*

CHAPTER 6

The Last and Highest Goal

CHRIST:

MY CHILD, My true friends refuse to pursue things simply because they are pleasant. They do not want anything which has only temporary value. All their hopes and ambitions aim at the success which I give, the success which will never pass away. They know that too much love for earthly things can draw them away from the only lasting joy and glory. So in all their daily activities, they keep an eye on Me and My commandments.

2. Among all the wonders of heaven and earth, there is no one like Me. My works are supremely good and My judgments are perfectly true. By My providence the universe is ruled.

3. Let others seek whatever else they desire besides Me. As for you, let nothing please you except Me alone, your Hope, your Eternal Salvation.

4. Daily look for Me above all things. Try to find Me in all things. I alone am the Giver of true peace and lasting happiness.

THINK:

No tongue can describe the peace which God gives to those who sincerely want His Will above all else. Many never find this peace because they lack the trust and courage to live entirely God's way. They try to obey God's law only in part. God loves the man who is honest enough to want first things first.

PRAY:

My loving Saviour and merciful God, can I be so foolish as to think that I can find happiness without You? Can sin ever bring me true joy when it separates me from You, the Fountain of lasting joy? No. I hope, with Your help to keep my eyes fixed on You throughout my daily life. I hope to avoid whatever displeases You, and to live as You wish me to live each hour of the day. Your Will shows the way to undying peace and happiness. Let me love Your Will in all things. *Amen.*

CHAPTER 7

Vanity in Daily Life

CHRIST:

MY CHILD, vanity is another name for foolish expectation and for useless pretense. Some people expect too much from the good things of this world. Others pretend to be bigger than they really are and try to attract more attention than they deserve.

2. Vanity of vanities, and all is vanity for those who do not love Me, or refuse to follow My commandments. Nothing is permanent under the sun. When you love anything for its own sake, and not because it helps you do My Will, you are a victim of vanity. Death shall take all these things away from

you, and nothing will be left. How wise is the man who appreciates this truth!

3. It is vanity to strive too intently for perishable riches and to fix your hopes on them. It is vanity also to be over-eager for honors, or to consider your self better than others. It is vanity to follow blindly the desires of the flesh and to want things which will bring a great penalty later on.

4. It is vanity to wish for a long life while caring little about living a good life. It is vanity to give your entire attention to the present life without thinking of the life which will come later. It is vanity to love only what is speedily passing away, instead of fixing your heart on Heaven—the home of endless joy.

THINK:

If the dead could relive their lives, how differently many of them would value things! Now they know how foolish are many things for which they lived, and worked, and even sinned. The good, however, now enjoy perfect joy and happiness with God in Heaven because they refused to offend Him for any worldly comfort or glory. My life is my choice. Will I try to please God in all things, or will I prefer some earthly satisfaction against His holy Will?

PRAY:

Lord, grant me heavenly wisdom, so that I may learn to seek You above everything else. May I find You, enjoy Your presence in my life, and love You above everything else. Let me understand all things according to their importance in Your eyes. Grant that I may prudently avoid the flatterer and patiently bear with those who make my life more difficult. It is great wisdom to fight the undue influence of human words and to keep my eyes on Your holy law. In this way I shall go safely onward along the way that leads to eternal life, unending happiness, and the only lasting success. *Amen*.

CHAPTER 8

The Voice of Conscience

CHRIST:

MY CHILD, refuse to do wrong for anything in the world. It is better to have the whole world against you rather than have Me against you. Whoever loses Me, is losing more than the entire world. Whatever you love on earth is but a reflection of My goodness. If you fix your attention and interest only on worldly things or people, you will soon shut Me out and lose My grace.

2. As soon as you become too interested in worldly pleasure and ease, your conscience objects. You are your own worst enemy when you act against your conscience. The wrong which you do becomes worse when you try to excuse yourself or justify your actions.

3. No man can safely enjoy life except the man whose conscience is clear. The wicked never have true joy nor real interior peace. They may say that they have peace and that they neither expect nor fear any harm from above. Either they are lying or they are fools. My justice will suddenly strike them and put an end to their deeds. They will think differently then.

4. A bad conscience is afraid and disturbed. A good conscience has peace even in time of hardship. The good man's glory lies in the testimony of a good conscience.

5. There is no true freedom nor profitable joy without a clear conscience and a holy fear of all sin. Blessed is the man whose eyes are on Me and who keeps his earthly desires within My law. A good life follows My wisdom and brings a deeper appreciation of this earthly existence.

THINK:

God made man intelligent enough to see that he should do what is right. And so the sinner knows that he is a sinner. He knows that his life is not going well. If he wants to cling to his sins, he will try to excuse himself in some way, but he cannot fool himself for long. Either he loses his peace of soul or he succeeds in dulling his conscience. The man with a dull conscience will find distractions and interests in many things, but he has not the abiding peace of those who live for Heaven.

PRAY:

Dear Lord, grant that I may never be insincere in my daily life. Let me always have the strength, the courage and the loyalty to follow what is right. I do not want to choose any temporary satisfaction or relief which is displeasing to You. Let me live for eternity by always choosing what You want me to choose. May death never catch me by surprise. I hope to live each hour of the day in loyalty to Your holy Will and at peace with You. *Amen.*

CHAPTER 9

Frailty of Human Nature

CHRIST:

MY CHILD, all human beings are weak. Do not think that you are stronger than others. Circumstances do not create the weakness of a man. They simply draw it out and show what he really is. You must be convinced of this fact. Your will is weak, and your blind human desires are strong.

2. It should not be too hard for you to admit your frailty. See how often you are troubled by a small matter! At times you resolve to become a better man. Then along comes a small temptation, and away goes your resolution. Just when you think you are safe, when you least expect it, you find yourself pushed over by a slight temptation. Even when you do not give full consent to it,

your feelings and desires confuse you. Hateful imaginations rush in on you and refuse to leave.

3. Before you can become serious about self-perfection, you must be convinced of its necessity. See how weak you are! You often tend toward what is wrong. You confess your sins today, and tomorrow you commit the same faults again. You resolve to be on your guard, and an hour later you act as though you had never made the resolution. You are so weak and unsteady. It is only right, then, that you should humble yourself and refuse to think too highly of yourself.

4. You are more inclined to go backward than forward. You do not remain in the same state of mind for any length of time. Your moods and attitudes change with the changing hours of the day. If you would only turn to Me! I can help you rise above these changing moods. Let your heart turn to Me and find its rest in Me.

THINK:

My human nature is like a spirited horse. It must be controlled at every step. It would like to run free and uncontrolled. Therefore,

I need not be surprised at my changing feelings and moods. They are not the higher self within me. God will honor me only for what I am trying to be. I would improve much faster if I begged His help more frequently by prayer and the sacraments. Too often I fail to put up a fight against my unreasonable feelings and blind desires. At other times I try to fight them alone. Only with God's help can I make any permanent progress. With the knowledge He gives me through His holy Church, and with the strength He offers me in His sacraments, I can live a holy life in spite of the restless lower self within me.

PRAY:

Dear Lord, my smallness and weakness are perfectly known to You. Have pity on me. Pull me out of the mud of self, so that I may not be stuck in it forever. Consider the labors and trials of my daily life. Please stand by me in my efforts. Strengthen me in my resolutions. I have often failed because I depended on myself alone. Now, however, I shall seek advice and direction as often as I need it. Only in this way can I hope to make progress in true and solid virtue. Make me wise and honest in my daily efforts, so that I may no longer waste valuable time. I hope to become at last the kind of person You want me to be. Without You I can do nothing. Lord, help me! *Amen.*

CHAPTER 10

Daily Renewal of Intention

CHRIST:

MY CHILD, progress in virtue depends on My grace and your own determination. My grace is always at your disposal. It is your determination that wavers and changes. Your intention would be more firm if you obtained more grace to help you. By prayer and sacrifice, and with an increased use of My sacraments, seek more grace. Then you would find your will stronger to follow your intention throughout the day.

2. It is not always enough to make good intentions in the morning. You must also recall and renew them during the day. Examine how faithfully you are following your intention, and seek to improve yourself in this effort. When you break your resolution,

begin again. This is far better than abandoning your good intention altogether. Anyone can make good resolutions, but keeping them and renewing them is the work of a real man.

3. If you are afraid to start again or are discouraged by failure, it is because you do not understand what goes on in your daily life. Without Me you can do nothing. Put your trust in My help. Then confidently do your best to follow your resolutions. If you fail, renew your intention at once and begin again. I will judge you more by your efforts than by your failures. It is your natural pride that makes you afraid to begin, or discourages you when you fail. Pride wants immediate success.

4. Be honest, and you will be humble. Make a sincere effort, but do not be surprised at your weakness and unexpected failures. Beg for My grace, and go on trying. Leave all else in My hands. He who keeps trying to please Me will never be abandoned by Me.

THINK:

Am I brave enough to renew my intentions and good resolutions each day, and to make an honest effort to follow them? God's help will not fail me. My old faults will slowly disappear as I advance in the practice of the opposite virtues. Thus, if I have a fault of laziness, I can best conquer it by seeking more opportunities to perform good deeds. And so will it be with my other faults.

PRAY:

Lord, let me do whatever is necessary to fight my faults and to advance in the opposite virtues. If I need to avoid some person or place, if I have to take some particular step, let me do so without any foolish delay. It is for Your glory and for my own greater good. Lord, now I begin, and shall keep on beginning again and again because I desire to please You. *Amen.*

CHAPTER 11

An Honest Daily Effort

CHRIST:

MY CHILD, so often your thoughts are on unimportant things. You do not center them enough on Me nor on your greatest need. After a few moments of recollection, your thoughts go right back to useless distractions. As a result you rarely get a good look at yourself and your actions. You hardly know your real worth because you take so little notice of your desires, motives, and intentions. You fail to be impressed by your many faults because you are blind to what is going on within your heart. Your interior motives are often selfish and corrupt. Consequently, your external actions are very imperfect and unsatisfactory. From a pure heart come the fruits of a good life, but from an imperfect heart there can only come an imperfect life.

2. External activity proceeds from internal vigor. If you serve Me only by external observances, you are no true follower of Mine. You must apply the ax to the root of your troubles. Learn to control this selfish nature of yours, and you will possess My peace. I daily offer you My grace for this divine purpose. Do not keep looking at your weakness. Do not be afraid to make the attempt. Nothing is impossible to Me. Fix your eyes on Me and make a sincere effort

to follow My Will. Your difficulties will gradually vanish.

3. Try as you will, you will always make a number of unavoidable mistakes. Still, with a little violence to yourself, you will gradually be able to serve Me with more ease. If you rooted out of your life one single fault each year, you would soon become a perfect man. Nowadays, however, people seem to be at their best at the beginning of their conversion. They consider it a great accomplishment if they do not become worse with time.

THINK:

Many admit that they have faults. When, however, any particular fault of theirs is pointed out to them, they will immediately justify themselves. They simply refuse to come face to face with any particular fault of theirs. As a result they live a lifetime with little progress in virtue. To better my life I must see and admit what is wrong. Then I can proceed to improve myself.

PRAY:

My God, make me brave enough to face my faults, honest enough to acknowledge them, and strong enough to fight them. I think of many things each day, but so many of my interests are unimportant and useless. Give me the strength and the generosity to make definite resolutions against definite faults. May I never be so selfish as to stop trying to please You more each day. Though my faults seem to continue, still my efforts must remain firm and I must go on trying to become daily a better man. If I will go on trying, I cannot help becoming better each day. A continued effort will slowly destroy my selfishness, and my faults will gradually weaken and die. Lord, on You I depend for the light and strength for this daily battle. *Amen.*

CHAPTER 12

Extreme Love of This Life

CHRIST:

MY CHILD, learn wisdom from the folly of worldly people. See how hard they take their worldly losses! For an earthly gain men will labor and suffer so much, but their spiritual losses are so easily forgotten. They are often interested in matters which have little or no value, and they negligently pass over matters which are important. Their entire attention is often absorbed by external affairs. Unless you fight to control your thoughts, you too will be enslaved by the passing events of the present moment.

2. How foolish are those who do not realize their miserable condition, making this passing earthly life the only object of their desires! Some cling so to this life that, if they could remain here forever, they would not care at all for the Kingdom of God. They would prefer to stay on earth even though they might have to strain and struggle for the bare necessities of this earthly existence.

3. How foolish and blind these people are! They lie buried so deep in earthly things that they enjoy only the pleasures of the senses. In a short while, they will come to the end of their earthly life. Then they will have a bitter realization of the uselessness and nothingness of what they loved.

THINK:

The best way to realize the quickly-passing value of earthly attractions, is to look at them in the past. Where are the enjoyments of last year? What became of the glory for which I struggled so hard five years ago? What's left of last summer's pleasures? Gone! All finished and gone! Do I want to go on living for that kind of happiness or do I want perfect, all-satisfying-never-ending happiness? Only a fool would hesitate in answering this question.

PRAY:

Lord and Father of all intelligence, may I never be guilty of the supreme folly—the folly of those who believe in living for today's earthly pleasures, without bothering about their eternal salvation. In the Gospel You speak of the man who sat back and prepared to think only of the pleasure and enjoyment of his earthly possessions. To him You said: "Thou fool! This night will they require thy soul of thee!" He died that night, unprepared to face his Judge. Let me always face life's greatest fact—I live for Heaven or for hell. My earthly life will show what choice I make. My God, give me the strength to live a holy life on earth so that I may receive the eternal reward of Heavenly life with You. *Amen.*

B. *The Four Last Things*

FEW THINGS in this earthly life are absolutely certain. The most undebatable of these is death. Every man, even the atheist, will admit this much. Death, however, is not the very last event in this life of ours. Right after death, we shall be judged. Our private judgment will be repeated on the Day of Judgment, when all men will know us for what we are.

Our judgment will depend on how we live this earthly life of ours. If we have honestly done our best and followed the commandments of Christ, we shall be rewarded with the perfect life of Heaven. If, however, we have disregarded His loving directions and refused to make use of His generous help, we shall be condemned to hell.

Death, Judgment, Heaven, and hell— these are the four last things toward which we are moving each hour of the day and night. They will never frighten us if our conscience is clear. If we love God in our daily life, that is, if we are sincerely trying to know and follow His holy Will, we have no reason to fear.

By keeping this eternal goal ever before us, we shall think straight when life's problems and difficulties face us. In making the following meditations, we must strive to become *eternity-minded*. We must seek to guarantee to ourselves, as far as is in our power, the unending success and unmarred happiness of Heaven.

CHAPTER 13

Nearness of Death

CHRIST:

MY CHILD, in a little while this earthly life of yours will be over. Just how ready are you to enter into the next Life? Man exists today, and tomorrow he is seen no more. When he is out of sight, he is quickly also out of mind. The human heart can be so dull and hard! It fixes its attention on things present. It often fails to provide for the things that are to come.

2. In the morning consider for a moment the fact that you may not live till evening. When evening comes do not be too confident that you will see the next morning. These thoughts should not make you gloomy, but

practical. Live in such a way that death will never find you unprepared. Live each day as you would want to live the last day of your life. Too many die suddenly and unprepared. I have warned everyone: "The Son of Man will come at that hour when He is not expected."

3. How many have deceived themselves into thinking that they still had plenty of time. They were snatched unexpectedly from this life. How often have you heard that someone was killed in a fight; another was drowned; another fell and broke his neck? This man died while sitting at table. That one passed away while enjoying a game. Some die by fire; some by violence; some are destroyed by disease; some are killed at the hands of robbers. Thus death brings an end to all, and man's life suddenly passes away like a fleeting shadow.

THINK:

Why should I refuse to face facts? Will I die any sooner if I think of death? Or am I going to escape death if I never think of it. The most terrible death which can come to me is the death which will find me in mortal sin. Every other aspect of death is a passing thing, but this last phase—the unprovided death—will hurt me forever.

Death, with all its uncertainties, is a fact. I should face facts and see what can be done about them. What can I do about death? I can live in such a way that no matter when death comes, it will find me in sanctifying grace.

PRAY:

Lord, for those in mortal sin, death is the gateway to hell, but for those in sanctifying grace, it is the pathway to Heaven. Let my greatest desire in life be to live in such a way that I can die fearlessly at any moment. Let me fear sin more than death or any other earthly harm. *Amen.*

CHAPTER 14

Man's Last Moments

CHRIST:

MY CHILD, when your last hour arrives, you will see this earthly life in a new light. If you were neglectful and careless about My law, you will have great regret. If you lived as I desire, your heart will be full of joy.

2. The time is coming when you would like to have another day, or even one more hour, to make up for the past. Take your day and your hour now that you have the time. Who can guarantee you another hour when you feel life slipping away?

3. Death may come at any time. Always be ready for it. In this way you will be free of fear or danger, no matter when My angel calls you from this life. Live in such a way that the hour of death may bring you joy rather than fear.

4. Never love any earthly thing too much. Place your confidence in Me and look to Me as your greatest Treasure. I am far more to you than you can even suspect. A weak soul is enslaved by its earthly desires and loves. The prayerful man gains a heavenly liberty from this life, a liberty which is not understood by worldly men.

THINK:

No matter what my interests may be, or how important they may seem, when death comes, I will leave everything and go to my judgment at once. Others will take my place and assume my importance and my activities. Few people know that their death is near. Most men are surprised by the arrival of death. To those who love God, it is a cause of joy. To those who love this earthly life too much, it is a painful parting.

PRAY:

My God, make me wise in my esteem for the work, the pleasures, the honor and the successes of this earthly life. Let me want nothing that might separate me from You. My first interest shall be to please You, to do everything as You desire. In this way, I hope to be ready for eternity every moment of the day. *Amen.*

CHAPTER 15

The Peace of a Good Conscience

CHRIST:

MY CHILD, if you have a good conscience, you need not have any fear of death. It is better to try to avoid sin than to try to escape death.

2. A wise man reflects often on the hour of death, so as to be prepared for it at all times.

3. If you want to please Me, try to become today the kind of man you would like to be at the time of your death. Make this effort, and death will find you full of confidence and peace. For this must you daily strive: a healthy contempt for worldly comforts, a burning desire to advance in virtue, a love of right order in your actions, a spirit of penance, readiness to obey authority, self-discipline, and patience to bear adversity for My sake.

THINK:

A good conscience means that I have honestly tried to learn what God desires of me, and I have sincerely tried to do what He desires. Without these two efforts there is no good conscience. A man who knows that he has really made those two efforts, has a good conscience. To such a man, God gives His peace. Others may be distracted with earthly activities and interests, but they do not have that interior peace which can remain calm even in the face of death.

PRAY:

My God, I hope to obtain Your holy assistance so that I may never avoid learning Your holy Will, nor ever fail to follow it in my daily life. I may find a little less pleasure if I follow Your Will, but I shall enjoy Your peace, which is greater than any pleasure. If ever I become selfish enough to avoid Your Will, let my conscience disturb and annoy me until I return to You. *Amen.*

CHAPTER 16

Being Ready for Death

CHRIST:

MY CHILD, your actions and thoughts should always be as orderly as though you expected to die this day. If you are unprepared today, how will you be prepared tomorrow? Tomorrow is uncertain. How do you know that you will be alive tomorrow? If you have ever seen a person pass away, just reflect that you too must pass away as he did.

2. You can do many good works while you enjoy good health, but when you are sick, who knows what you will be able to do? Few

people are improved by sickness. So too, those who have too many worldly interests seldom increase in holiness, because they are full of distractions. Recollection and prayer are the seeds of a good life; and a good life is the path to a holy death.

3. It is better to provide for yourself while you are still here in this life. Do not rely on the prayers and help of others after your death. The present time is precious. Now is your opportunity. This is your day of salvation. Spend today profitably. Send your prayers, sacrifices and good works to Me before you come to Me to be judged. It is within your power to earn eternal life by a wise use of this present time.

4. Think often of death, and remember that time lost will never return. You have not a lasting dwelling on this earth. In this life you are like a traveler. You will never have rest until you are united with Me, your Saviour.

THINK:

Few things are certain in this earthly life. The most certain fact of all is that I am to die. When? Where? How? I know not. That

I shall die, however, is certain. Many people are dying at this very moment. I am too busy with my own life to give much thought to them. So will it be when I am dying. That moment will be very important to me, but the world will go right on about its business. If I do not prepare for death by a good life, I am a fool.

PRAY:

Lord, let me not fear death with an empty fear, but with a wise and holy fear. An empty fear does not make men any better, but a wise and holy fear urges them to improve their lives. I will prepare for death by trying today to please you more and more in my thoughts, desires, words and actions. If I live this day as You desire, I shall be ready at any moment, and death will be nothing worse than Your loving call. *Amen.*

CHAPTER 17

The Coming Judgment

CHRIST:

MY CHILD, you must one day give a full account of your earthly life. How will you stand before Me, the just Judge, from Whom nothing is hidden? I take no bribes and accept no excuses. At present you can take advantage of My Divine Mercy. When this earthly life is over, you will receive strict justice.

2. Can you be so great a fool as to go on putting off your good resolutions, when pardon can be so easily obtained now? If you go on postponing your resolutions, how will you face My Divine Justice—you who are sometimes frightened by an angry fellow-human?

3. Why not begin today to prepare for the day of judgment? You will find it far less terrible if you begin now to live as I command. On the day of judgment no man can be excused or defended by another. Each one will find it difficult enough to answer for his own sins.

THINK:

While I am on earth, my efforts are useful, my tears are acceptable, my sorrow has power to purify my soul. God desires to forgive me here and now. It is better to wash away my sins and correct my bad habits now, rather than leave them for purification after death. I am deceiving myself when I follow my feelings and put off my repentance and resolutions.

PRAY:

Lord, let me think of my sins and be sorry for them, so that on the day of judgment, I may enjoy security with Your angels and saints. Teach me to do penance in little things now, so that I may not be subjected to worse sufferings hereafter. True, I should do all of this in loyalty to You. Yet, I am so selfish that I must have some fear to spur me on when my love for You fails. *Amen.*

CHAPTER 18

The Day of Judgment

CHRIST:

MY CHILD, those who are loyal to My commandments in this life, will not be in terror on the Day of Judgment. The sign of the cross will appear in the sky when I come to judge the world. Then all my loyal followers, the followers of the cross, will come with great confidence to Me, their crucified King and Judge.

2. On that day, the Just shall stand against those who annoyed and persecuted them. Those who humbly bore the judgments of their fellow-men, will rise to judge the rest on that day. The poor and the humble will have great confidence and joy, but the proud and the selfish lovers of this world will have many reasons to be afraid.

3. In that hour everyone will see that the wisest people were those who preferred to follow My commandments and live My way. They will no longer be considered fools by the worldly-minded. All wrong-doing will be silenced and condemned, while every suffering endured with patience, will bring joy and gladness. The unreligious will be sad, but My devoted followers will be filled with happiness. Many will thank Me for the hardships and trials which they bore on earth. That day will show forth My power, wisdom, and majesty.

THINK:

Like a river that flows ever onward toward the sea, the current of daily life moves ever onward toward the Day of Judgment. That day will correct the wrong standards and foolish ideals of worldly men. It will be the Day of Truth, the triumph of holiness. Will I drift along on my daily course or will I regularly check my direction by an intelligent self-examination? I prepare for a joyful judgment or a fearful one by the kind of life I live today.

PRAY:

O Jesus, My Judge and King, I refuse to drift along each day until death takes me by surprise. I want to follow Your standards as You speak to me today through Your Church. Tell me how You want me to live and I hope to follow Your every wish. I need not fear the Judgment if only I will be loyal to You in my daily life. *Amen.*

CHAPTER 19

God's Standards

CHRIST:

MY CHILD, on the Day of Judgment the rags of the poor will shine more brilliantly than the fine clothes of those who loved this earthly life too much. The homes of the poor will be honored more than the comfortable mansions of the rich. In that hour the patience of My loyal followers will have greater merit than the human might of this world. Simple obedience to My laws will be more highly praised than all earthly cleverness.

2. In the Day of Truth a pure and good conscience will bring more joy than mere learning. The man who refused to sin for earthly gain, will be the envy of those who lived only for this world. You will have more consolation for having prayed devoutly than for having enjoyed earth's pleasures and comforts.

3. Then you will be glad of the prayerful silence you observed, rather than for having talked a great deal. Good works will be of greater value than good words. Self-control and healthy penance will be more pleasing to you than all the delights of earth.

THINK:

How different are God's standards from those of worldly men! Is it any wonder that those who live God's way seem to live a foolish life? Yet the real fools are those who disagree with God's standards. Christ is sure to triumph at the Judgment, and those who follow His standards are certain to triumph with Him.

PRAY:

My Jesus, can I be fool enough to live by any other standard than Yours? Let me embrace Your standards in my daily life. Though I may find life harder, I will not complain as long as I know that Your Will is guiding me. Through the Church and the Scriptures, You promise to lead me to a happy judgment and a joyful eternity. I hope to be a loyal follower of Yours each day of my earthly life. *Amen.*

CHAPTER 20

The Pains of Hell

CHRIST:

MY CHILD, I have proved My goodness by My numberless gifts to men. They cannot mention a single good thing in their daily life which does not belong to Me. My love for them was proved by My earthly life of labor, work, suffering and prayer to obtain forgiveness for their sins. Anyone who takes time to think of what I deserve, cannot deny that he owes Me more than he can ever repay. Yet, in spite of My goodness and love, some people choose to walk away from Me. They refuse to follow My directions. As a result they fall into sin. Though I made them for Heaven, they shall never see it because they are refusing to do what it takes to get there.

2. Hell was made for the devil and his rebel angels. Man was made for Heaven. In refusing to live for Heaven, a man chooses to exist without Me. He shall have his wish—he shall join the rebel angels in hell. In refusing to follow My law, a man actually turns his back on Me as the fallen angels did. If he dies in this condition, he condemns himself to hell. The jury which convicts him is his own sinful life. I merely pronounce sentence on what he himself has chosen.

3. There is nothing on earth which can compare with hell. It is beyond all description. One must see it to know it. Though I may try to give you some small idea of it in this chapter, remember, this is a tiny and very imperfect idea of the real thing. Words

fall far short of the reality which is hell. I make no threats here. I simply want you to face this fact: Unless you live for Heaven, you shall one day be in hell.

4. All the sufferings known to man are as nothing in comparison with the sufferings of hell. The wise man would rather bear any trial on earth than place himself in danger of hell. One single hour of hell will be harder than a hundred years of suffering on earth. In this earthly life people have some rest from their labors and trials. They get some measure of consolation from their friends. In hell, however, there is no rest, no consolation, and no friends.

5. The fires of hell will never die. There will be no end to suffering. One will find no comfort in knowing that he has been there a thousand years. He can never hope for an end to his tortures. All the other sufferings would be bearable if only the damned could hope for relief. Despair is hell's bitterest pain.

6. In hell a man will be punished through the same faults by which he sinned on earth. Each sin will have its own particular torment.

The lazy will be forced to work continuously. The gluttonous will be tormented with extreme hunger and thirst. The proud will be filled with confusion, and the greedy will feel the pinch of miserable want.

7. And yet, the worst pain of hell is none of these. The people in hell would gladly bear all of this and much more if only they could hope for My friendship and love, no matter how long it might take, be it even a billion years from now. Their keenest torment is that they have forever lost Me, the Source of all true joy and perfect happiness. This suffering makes hell the home of despair and undying hatred.

8. My child, follow My Will in your daily life, and you need never fear hell. In fact you have every reason to be joyful and merry if you are following My commandments and using My sacraments. Do not condemn yourself to hell by refusing to obey My directions. I love you dearly. Do not prevent Me from taking you to Heaven.

THINK:

Hell is a fact. Christ, Our Lord, pointed this out time and again during His earthly life. Whoever rejects this fact is simply denying the word of Christ. He is God. He proved His divine power many times during and after His earthly life. His word is truth. He preached the truth of hell and continues to preach it today through His Church and Holy Scripture.

PRAY:

My Jesus, many find too hard a command in the words: "Deny yourself, take up your cross, and follow Me." Yet a much harder command will be: "Depart from Me, you cursed, into everlasting fire." If I become so impatient with a little suffering now, how can I ever stand hell? I cannot expect to have unrestricted enjoyment on earth and still rejoice with You in Heaven. Therefore, dear Lord, that I may be safe from eternal punishment, let me do my best in bearing the burdens of this earthly life. Let me prefer to suffer on earth or even die now rather than commit a mortal sin. *Amen.*

CHAPTER 21

Holy Fear of God

CHRIST:

MY CHILD, if you desire to make progress along the way to Heaven, keep in your heart a holy fear of the Divine Justice. It is only reasonable that you should be afraid to hurt yourself. When you bring sin into your life, you are making yourself an object of My justice. I, the Eternal Truth, cannot accept you as good if you have become bad by sin. Therefore, keep your earthly desires under control and refuse to surrender yourself to unnecessary or dangerous pleasures. This holy fear of My justice will help you to stay free of the slavery of earthly attractions.

2. It is not very wise to think only of having a pleasant time and to forget your spiritual needs. It is reasonable and good for you to be afraid of losing My graces. Without them you can never reach the perfect life and happiness of Heaven.

3. If your love of Me is not yet strong enough to hold you back from doing wrong,

then let your fear of hell keep you from sinning. A man who lacks this wise and holy fear, will not go on doing good for long. He will soon fall into Satan's snares, as he becomes more careless in avoiding temptations. This fear is a holy thing because it is given by Me. It makes a man strong in the daily battle against his unreasoning and selfish desires.

4. Even the saints, with all their confidence in Me, had this fear of Divine Justice. They knew the weakness and blindness of human nature. They were not less careful, nor less humble, because of their great virtues and many graces.

THINK:

If my love of God ever fails to hold me back from sin, it will be because my self-love is strong at the moment. Yet, even then I can make a last effort against this misguided love by the thought of God's justice, which will deal with me as I deserve. It is a foolish man, indeed, who will refuse to consider the harm that can overtake him if he follows a certain path. This holy fear of

God's justice is "the beginning of wisdom" because it guides men on to a holier life.

PRAY:

My God, I do not want to presume so much on Your love as to forget Your justice. You will some day deal with each man according to his works. I desire to make good use of all the gifts which Your love daily sends me. May I never forget that I must one day account for my misuse of these gifts. This thought will help me to fight sin and to please You more in my daily life. *Amen.*

CHAPTER 22

Compunction of Heart

CHRIST:

MY CHILD, how can any man abandon himself to the pleasures of this earthly life? Such people do not appreciate the miserable condition of their souls, nor the rapid passing away of this brief experience. They do not stop to think and to look beneath the surface of their daily activities. They laugh when they have many reasons to weep. Happy is he who can overcome the distractions which hinder him from straight thinking.

2. As for you, strive to develop within yourself a genuine compunction of heart. Compunction is a deep and lasting sorrow for your sins. It is not a gloomy nor depressing sorrow, but an intelligent admission of your sins and a sincere determination to do something about them. Since compunction comes from a realization of how you have failed so good a God, it brings with it a readiness to accept anything from My Hand.

3. Compunction opens the way to many blessings and precious graces. When compunction fills your soul, the world will lose its magic attraction and will become more distasteful to you. Compunction will help you realize how quickly earthly joys pass away, while eternity goes on forever. You will see clearly that your sins have offended Me. One who has genuine compunction, is honest enough to admit his sins, and is truly sorry for them. His sorrow is proved by his sincere efforts to be rid of his faults.

THINK:

Compunction is a great grace by which God helps me to face the truth about my sins. It also helps me to prove my sorrow for my faults. By compunction a man begins to attack his faults and to practice the opposite virtues. I can be sure of my sincere sorrow only when I have begun to do something about my faults. Compunction is a lasting sorrow because it is not an emotion, but rather an intelligent admission of facts. It shows me my faults, God's goodness, and my own need to change for the better. Then it helps me undertake the daily task of abandoning my faults and acquiring the opposite virtues.

PRAY:

Lord, I want to live a cheerful life, but I do not want that kind of cheerfulness which refuses to admit the truth. I can admit my sins and still be cheerful, as long as I am doing my best to overcome and make up for these sins. I do not want any gift or talent which might make me proud, or worse in any way. Not everything that is high is holy; nor is every pleasant thing good. Good desires are not always unselfish. You, my Lord, are not always pleased with the things that we prize. It is far better to have compunction than to be able to talk about it. Grant me genuine compunction, so that I may hate my sins and daily fight against them. *Amen.*

CHAPTER 23

Striving for Compunction

CHRIST:

MY CHILD, unless a man tries hard to acquire a holy sorrow for his sins, he is not worthy of My heavenly consolation. Are you doing your best to acquire this compunction?

2. This grace will reach you more easily if you will turn your back, for a while, on your daily distractions. Come aside more often, to be alone with Me. Reflect on My gifts and your misuse of them. Be honest and face the truth. Reading and reflecting will help you to realize the wickedness of all sins, even smaller ones. Do not look for new theories and mere curiosities, but stick to solid everyday truth, truth which will improve your daily life.

3. In solitude and quiet you will discover the hidden treasures of Holy Scripture. As

you become more intimate with Me, your Creator, you will make great progress. You will find tears to wash and purify your soul. You will also have a deep interior joy as My holy angels and I draw near to you. Learn to pray and labor unseen by the eyes of men.

4. Slowly, as the gift of compunction fills your soul, you will be filled with fresh vigor. As you become more eager to make up for your sins, you will find hard things becoming easier.

THINK:

Jesus said that certain devils are driven out only by prayer and fasting. This shows that some of God's gifts are given only if we do our part to prepare ourselves for them. Compunction will be lasting and fruitful only if I make a sincere personal effort to receive it worthily and apply it wisely. Through solitude, prayer, reading, and meditation, I will understand how I can best receive and use compunction in my daily life.

PRAY:

O holy and merciful Father, fill my soul with true compunction. Make me honest in admitting my sins, and determined in

overcoming them each day. I need Your assistance, so that I may not be a coward, but
may make a sincere daily effort to please
You more in all my activities. Help me to
abandon anything in life which is opposed
to Your holy gift of compunction. *Amen.*

CHAPTER 24

Purgatory Here or Hereafter

CHRIST:

M Y CHILD, do not expect to find peace
until you have overcome a variety of
troubles and opposition. If you say that you
cannot bear much suffering now, how will
you be able to endure the purifying pains of
Purgatory hereafter?

2. The patient man finds a cleansing
purgatory in this earthly life. When others
wrong him, he is more sorry that evil is done
than that he has been wronged. He forgives
the evil-doer from the bottom of his heart.
He is not slow to ask pardon when he himself
has hurt others. He is more easily moved to
pity than to anger. He frequently disregards
his feelings and tries to live above them, according to his intelligence and My grace.

THINK:

Either here on earth or hereafter in Purgatory I must make up for each fault I commit. Nothing tainted will be allowed to enter Heaven. I can purify my soul now by following the example and words of Christ, my Redeemer. He gained for me the grace to conquer sin and error. Now I must do my part by living a holy life. If I refuse, and die in venial sin, I'll have to make it up in Purgatory. If I die in mortal sin, I shall condemn myself to hell forever.

PRAY:

My Jesus, you fulfilled Your Father's Will largely by Your patience during Your earthly life. Therefore, it is only right that I, a miserable sinner, should be patient in my own daily life. Even though this present life may feel like a burden, still, by the help of Your grace, it is a great opportunity to earn heavenly merit. Your holy example and the lives of Your saints, make this life lighter and more bearable for those who take time out each day so as to see more clearly Your way to Heaven. *Amen.*

CHAPTER 25

Man's Greatest Treasure

CHRIST:

MY CHILD, only in Me will you find what is best and most precious for you. God is far greater and better than all things created. I am the Most High. No one else is all-powerful. God alone is perfectly charming and full of consolation. In Me you will find perfect beauty and all-satisfying love. Most noble and most glorious above all things is the Maker of all.

2. Beg often for the grace to find your joy in Me above all things created; above health or beauty; above glory and honor; above power and dignity; above all knowledge and cleverness; above all praise and admiration; above all arts and enjoyments; above all material comforts and wealth; above all hopes and promises; above all human consolation and appreciation. Treasure Me more than the gifts and rewards which I bestow on men. In Me you will find more than in everything else.

3. Whatever I give, whatever is not God, is too little and insufficient for you. I made you for Myself, the Perfect Good. Your heart will not find true rest until it rests in Me, the Perfect Giver and the Perfect Gift.

THINK:

No matter what I like or love, unless it is God Himself, it can never give me the perfect happiness which my soul desires. So many who reached earthly success, finally took their own life. Why? Because they came to realize that nothing on earth could give them the happiness which they wanted. They should have turned at last to God, but they had forgotten Him in their foolish quest for earthly joy.

PRAY:

Dear Lord, I cannot live for a joy that is doomed to fade away. Though I hope for a reasonable joy on earth, I shall never turn my back on You by sin. Earth's good things only reflect Your beauty, Your goodness and Your power. I will never abandon the Glorious Reality for the sake of Its reflection. When I am tempted to sin for some earthly attractions, give me the grace to remember Your goodness, greatness and love. *Amen.*

PART TWO
After Conversion

YOU MUST BE deeply impressed by the fact of your great weakness, your complete dependence on God, your blind selfishness, your need of frequently renewing your good resolutions and of daily expressing sorrow for your sins. Do not be afraid to face the truth: you must die and must receive a just sentence to either Heaven or hell. Far from being depressed, you should be determined to cooperate with the all-loving God, Who desires to show you the way to a holy life on earth, and a perfect, all-satisfying life in Heaven.

Having seen your complete need of God, and of His loving attention and generosity, try to realize that He deserves the best love and loyalty which you can offer Him. How can you please Him more in your daily life? Part of this question is answered in this section.

CHAPTER 26

Beginning a New Life

CHRIST:

MY CHILD, do not lose the hope of making spiritual progress. You still have time. Your chance is not over yet. Why put off your good intentions until tomorrow? Now is the time for action! Begin this very moment! Here is your opportunity to make a new start. Begin your new life with the help of My grace.

2. Always keep a steady hope of achieving success. Do not let your failures discourage you. Beware also of over-confidence, so that you may not become a victim of pride or laziness.

3. Whenever you have to omit your prayers or some daily spiritual exercise, because of some urgent duty or for the sake of your neighbor, try to make up later what was omitted. Do not be too ready to omit spiritual exercises because of weariness. This can easily become a habit which will hurt you.

THINK:

It is easy enough to start again. All I have to do is: (1) to examine my life, (2) face what needs to be done, (3) pray for strength, and (4) start doing it. I may fail on this occasion or that, but the main thing is that I have begun and am determined to go on trying in spite of any failures which may occur.

PRAY:

Lord, now I begin! Help me to live as You desire. If it is Your will, I can do it. If You want this of me, I ought to do it. Let me not be a coward and run away from Your Will. You know what is right and best. I must begin now. Lord, help me. I do not expect to become a different person overnight. Just as my faults developed slowly over a period, so too will the opposite virtues grow within me. I will not be discouraged when my old faults catch me by surprise. My love for You will be proved by action, that is, by a steady, patient effort to get rid of my faults and to practice the opposite virtue. Now I begin! *Amen.*

CHAPTER 27

Holiness in Everyday Life

CHRIST:

MY CHILD, at times you hear people say that they are too busy to bother with religion. People who say such things do not understand Me, nor themselves, nor their daily life. They do not realize that religion is as necessary an activity as eating, sleeping and working.

2. I am far more than the air you breathe, the food you eat, and the rest which brings you renewed strength. All of these things, and everything else, come to you from My hand. Without My loving support each moment, these things would fail you, and you yourself would vanish from the face of the earth.

3. I am the center of your existence. You depend on Me more than you dream. Just as you give due attention to the people who come into your daily life, so too is it normal for you to give due attention to Me. To speak to Me, to try to please Me, to ask for My help, to express sorrow for your offenses, and to

love Me for My goodness—these are normal acts for any intelligent human being. The more I show Myself to him, the more should he strive to please Me in his everyday life.

4. Religion is the bond which unites you to Me. To neglect it is as foolish as refusing to breathe, or eat, or rest. In fact, it is worse. These other things keep your body alive, but religion is necessary for the eternal life of your soul.

5. The man who neglects this part of his life is abnormal, that is, he is not what he ought to be. He is neglecting something which is natural and normal for him, something which perfects him more than he realizes.

6. There is no real opposition between laboring for your earthly needs, and laboring for Heaven. You have to work each day, but this work can be a glorious prayer. You must eat, work, sleep, and have recreation, but all of these can become holy actions, actions done for eternal life.

7. Whatever you do, do it as I want it done, and you will be doing it as perfectly as possible. Be reasonable in whatever you do,

or say, or think. Refuse to violate My commandments, regardless of any earthly advantage or disadvantage. I made the things of this life for you, so that you may perfect yourself by using them intelligently. Let My words and example guide you in whatever you do. In doubt consult My Church. Do this and you will be working for success on earth and an all-satisfying glory in Heaven.

THINK:

Once I get a full view of this earthly life, I will see how all-important a part God plays in it. Instead of living for the moment or for the next few years, I'll live for my highest and most important goal. I will see the unending importance of what I am doing today, I will understand how each act of this day helps me become a little more perfect, a little more ready for Heaven. Only sin is foolish. Only sin is bad. All else is good and pleasing to God, because it helps me in one way or another.

PRAY:

My Father in Heaven, I desire to make the best use of this earthly life of mine. I want to live as full a life as possible. Therefore, in everything I think, do, or say, I want You to be my Partner. Since You support me in all my thinking, speaking and acting, I want to please You in them. By living this way, I will be following Your wisdom and my own highest good. I now join this daily life of mine to the earthly life of Jesus, Your divine Son. With His example and with the strength of His holy sacraments, I hope to please You every moment. Thus, my daily life will be my best preparation for eternal life. *Amen.*

CHAPTER 28

Closer Friendship with God

CHRIST:

M Y CHILD, I have said that the Kingdom of God is within you. Turn to Me with your whole heart. Do not think too much of this world, and your soul will find rest in Me. Do not let this earthly life take all of your attention. Think often of Me and of My Will in your life. Then you will become more conscious of My presence within your soul. I bring you the gifts of peace and joy in the Holy Ghost. These gifts are not given to those who pay too much attention to this earthly life.

2. One who loves Me and lives My truth, is a supernatural person. By My grace he becomes free from sinful and dangerous desires. He can freely turn to Me. He is able to rise above the visible world around him and enjoy My friendship.

3. As iron, cast into the fire, loses its rust and becomes bright with the flame, so too a man who turns his whole heart to Me, is purified of all sluggishness and changed into a new man.

THINK:

If I take this step and concentrate more on God's place in my daily life, I shall find the peace of Christ. Earthly worries and distractions become small in the presence of God. The more I am impressed by Him, the less shall I be impressed by everything else.

PRAY:

My God, I want to be deeply impressed by You and Your holy Will in my daily life. Teach me to live this life of mine in Your presence, sharing with You my thoughts, desires, and every activity throughout the day. Let me recognize and follow Your Will as it comes to me through people and events in my daily life. *Amen.*

CHAPTER 29

Man's Interior Conflict

CHRIST:

MY CHILD, when I created the first man and woman, I gave them many gifts to make their earthly life as easy and peaceful as possible. They were free from pain, labor, sickness, and death. They immediately knew the answers to whatever problems came along. They had complete command over the appetites and desires of body and soul. Over and above these gifts, they were given grace to live a supernatural life. Dwelling within their souls, I gave more than natural light to their minds, and more than natural strength to their wills.

2. None of these gifts really belonged to human beings. I added them over and above the gift of human life along with the natural human powers of body and soul. At any time I could take away these extra gifts, and man would still have all that naturally belonged

to him. I left it up to Adam to decide whether he and his children were to keep these extra gifts forever. As the representative of the human race, Adam was to make one intelligent and free act, an act of obedience to My Will. By this act he would be acknowledging the supreme truth of his existence—that he is a creature completely dependent on Me, his Creator.

3. In disobeying My command in the Garden of Eden, Adam refused to acknowledge the supreme truth. The external act of eating the fruit was a small act, but the interior rebellion against My Will was a serious matter. Adam wanted to be equal to Me, as the rebel angels did in Paradise. As a result of Adam's disobedience, I took away My extra gifts. Man was left without the aid of My extra gifts, except that he might still obtain grace to earn Heaven.

4. Man now has to bear an inner conflict, a conflict quite natural to him. His animal appetites now go after their wants without regard for his better judgment and free will. Even when man wishes to follow his intelligence and strive after better things, he

has to fight for control of his unreasoning appetites and blind desires. He no longer has infused knowledge, but must learn the answers to his daily problems by labor and experience.

5. So often this interior conflict brings confusion to the mind and indecision to the will. Yet man's natural reason is still able to judge good and evil, still able to distinguish truth from falsehood. To save you from all serious doubts, I have given you My Church to guide your mind and strengthen your will.

6. As long as you have a human body on earth, you cannot be entirely free from venial sins, nor can you live without some sorrow and weariness. Yet you must do your best with patience and determination, regardless of failures. All too soon this present state of disorder will pass away. Then will your earthly life melt away into the perfect life which I have promised to those who keep My commandments.

THINK:

Adam passed on to his descendants the human nature which he himself possessed—a nature that was weakened by his disobedience. A large part of man's weakness lies in this, that after the Fall, man's animal nature retained its normal strength and appetites, but was no longer under the perfect control of man's higher power of reason and free-will. God, however, made up for this weakness by giving us His grace. By the use of God's grace, man can avoid fully deliberate sins, and thus become once more the master of his life.

PRAY:

My God, I am glad to have Your law guide me through life. With Your help, I want to correct the evil in my life and avoid, as far as possible, those temptations which will face me in the future. True, I often follow the law of sin, obeying my feelings instead of my reason. I want what is good, but I do not always know how to achieve it. Time and again, I make good resolutions, but in my weakness I quickly fall back and give up after a feeble resistance. At times, I know what I should be doing, but I simply fail to rise up and do it. With Your help I shall begin to act—I want to do all I can to live a life of loyalty to Your holy Will. *Amen.*

CHAPTER 30

Man's Lower Nature

CHRIST:

M Y CHILD, unless you learn to control your feelings, you will always find it hard to obey those who have authority over you. Your feelings do not reason. They simply turn away from what is unpleasant, be it right or wrong. Feelings can be calmed in some degree by an intelligent outlook. Still, you will never have a more troublesome and dangerous enemy than your own unreasoning feelings and blind desires.

2. By prayer and meditation you will acquire a grander outlook on life. You will see the unreasonableness and mean selfishness of your feelings and moods. I will show you the glorious goal which I have set for you. When you have grasped the higher purpose of your earthly life, you will acquire a holy contempt for whatever opposes that purpose. This heavenly knowledge and eternal goal will bring unity and order into your life. You will then find it easier to guide your lower nature according to My Will.

3. At times you will have to use stubborn resistance and even violence against the unreasoning tendencies within you. Sometimes you need to disregard your likes and dislikes, and follow your better judgment. With My truth to guide you and My sacraments to strengthen you, you cannot fail in this daily combat for Heaven.

THINK:

An obedient horse can help man in his daily tasks, but a stubborn mule can do more harm than good. So is it with man's own nature. His reason and will, strengthened by grace, must guide his unreasoning appetites and desires to right action. A good life is one which follows God's law. Only God's Will can lead me to Heaven.

PRAY:

Lord Jesus, I hope to follow You each day of my life. With Your help, I hope to have strength to be firm against my blind tendencies and desires. You are my King and Leader. Make me a loyal follower. I desire and hope to live the kind of life which You desire of me. Grant me Your grace. You have shown me how great it is and how necessary for salvation. Grant it to me so that I may overcome this weak nature of mine, which draws me on toward sin and eternal death. In my flesh, I feel the law of sin contradicting the law of my mind, and in many things making me a slave of my feelings. I can not resist these feelings unless You help me, by pouring into my heart the grace of ardent loyalty to You. I am in continual need of grace to overcome this nature which, from its youth, always tends to evil. I hope in Your help. *Amen.*

CHAPTER 31

The Honest Admission of One's Defects

CHRIST:

MY CHILD, let my infinite wisdom teach you what is best for you in your daily conduct on earth. Think of your sins with great displeasure and sorrow. Never consider yourself big because of your good works. The simple truth is that you are a sinner. Too often your actions are controlled by emotions or feelings rather than intelligence and grace.

2. If I leave you to yourself, you tend to what is wrong and fall into sin. You are easily overcome by selfishness. Your self-control falls apart in a short time. You are much weaker than you think. You have little reason to take pride in yourself and many reasons for humbling yourself.

3. Fear nothing so much as your disorderly tendencies and your sins. Run from them more than from anything else. They should displease you more than any other trouble. Be afraid of My judgment and fear the anger of the Almighty. Do not presume to criticize the works of the Most High. Look to your faults. Consider the wrong you have done and the good you have neglected.

4. Be angry with yourself, and do not let pride control you in anything. Foolish heart, what have you to complain about? Can you not accept the trials which come to you, when you have so often offended Me and deserved hell? My love has spared you. Still, you must be honest with yourself. Face the truth about yourself and be patient with your defects and limitations.

THINK:

God loves an honest man. Why should it be so hard to admit what I am? If I hide the truth from myself, how can I ever become pleasing to God? I need not become depressed and discouraged as I look at my many faults. All that God expects of me is that I begin today to fight against them. Being a sinner is not the worst thing. The worst thing is to remain a sinner. God loves the repentant sinner, that is, one who detests his sins and makes an honest effort to be rid of his faults.

PRAY:

Dear merciful God, at last I understand. I will no longer become paralyzed with sadness or discouragement, over my faults. I shall do what You desire of me. I will prove my genuine sorrow for my sins by fighting against them in my daily life. Show me which fault displeases You most, and I will at once begin a campaign against it. I may never get rid of it, Lord, but at least I can keep on trying each day. I cannot offer You much in my life, but this honest daily effort against my main faults I can offer as a proof that I am truly sorry for offending You. *Amen.*

CHAPTER 32

The Predominant Fault

CHRIST:

MY CHILD, I give strength to those who make an honest effort in fighting against their faults. The harder they try, the more will they advance in virtue. The self-control which I give is a man's greatest glory because he approaches closer to My perfection.

2. No two men have the same combination of faults, nor have they the same amount of grace. I give more grace to those who make good use of what they have already received.

3. As you make progress against your main fault, you will find your other faults easier to control. Once you are the master of your heart, you will be the master of your life. Your intelligence will be guided by My grace and your will, will follow My wise and holy law.

4. Begin at last! Attack first your most frequent fault. When you fall back into that

fault, instead of becoming sad and discouraged, prove your sorrow by beginning again. You will find selfishness at the bottom of every fault. Your feelings will rebel, but you must fix your eyes on Me, and let your will stand firm on My law.

5. Prayer, penance, and My sacraments will help you to see Me near, and will give you the strength to follow My Will.

THINK:

Every man has a predominant fault, that is, an outstanding one, because of which he commits most of the sins in his daily life. Conquering that fault means overcoming many different sins. This fault will not die easily, but a sincere and continued effort will weaken it more and more. Our Lord will not let me fight in vain. He will give me strength to make true progress against this fault. I need only to continue trying, doing whatever is necessary to overcome this fault.

PRAY:

Lord, make me wise in using the means which You have provided for my spiritual victory. Let me never become careless or lazy in following the guidance of Your

Church, nor in frequently using Your sacraments. The victory of this daily battle will bring me eternal glory in the wonderful life of Heaven. The reward which You have prepared is far greater than my effort can ever deserve of itself. Let me never become tired of fighting for Heaven. *Amen.*

CHAPTER 33

Necessary Care of Oneself

CHRIST:

MY CHILD, everyone must take a reasonable care of himself. In time of temptation arouse yourself, warn yourself, guard yourself and avoid idleness. No matter how much you do for others, do not neglect yourself altogether. Beware of too much talking. Whenever possible, try to be alone with Me. Take advantage of My presence. Every moment of your life is lived in My presence. You possess Him Whom the whole world cannot take from you. I am worth more than everything else put together.

2. If you neglect yourself, you can lose in a short time the spiritual strength which was acquired slowly and with great effort

over a long period. Reflect often on the eternal purpose of your earthly life. You have to be a spiritual man to reach this goal. I tell you through My Church how to live this earthly life. There is no other way. Examine your progress each day. In a short time your present life will be over. If you have been faithful, you will never again know fear nor sorrow. For the little labor which you do on earth, you will gain a glorious reward and unending joy. I shall not fail those who have been faithful to My Will.

3. The man who has learned to pray and reflect, looks on self-perfection as his first and highest business. One who studies himself honestly, finds it easy to be silent about others. Learn to hold your tongue about the affairs of others unless your duty obliges you to speak. Fix your attention on your own faults and do something about them. If you are a true man of God, the doings of others will not make you worse than you are. If you can remedy a bad situation, do so. Many times, however, you can do nothing but pray over the misdeeds of others. Do this as one sinner praying for another, not as a superior

being, praying for inferiors. When you have learned to fix your attention on your own affairs, you will find great peace of soul.

THINK:

As far as I can, I should strive to help others. In many things however, I can help only by prayer, good example, and silence. Prayer gives grace to me and others. Good example reminds others of what they should be doing. Silence prevents the spreading of scandal and the flaring of tempers. Minding one's own business is a great virtue. My first task is to save my soul. As far as I can, I must also try to help others live a holier and happier life. Many things, however, are not in my power. After I have done what I can to help matters, I should leave them in God's hands.

PRAY:

Lord, give me the courage to look at myself, the honesty to admit my faults and limitations, the sincerity to try self-improvement, and the love for You that will keep me at it for the rest of my life. Let me not be concerned about matters that are beyond my control, except to petition Your help. For the rest, let me really live the words: "Thy will be done." *Amen.*

CHAPTER 34

Helps and Hindrances to Holiness

CHRIST:

MY CHILD, there is one thing that stops many from making spiritual progress and keeps them from improving themselves. It is a fear of the difficulties or of the work required by their effort. The people who rise highest in holiness are those who are brave enough to fight against whatever holds them back from Me, no matter how hard or disagreeable the effort may be. The more you try to master your feelings and blind desires, the greater are the graces which I offer to you. If you keep on trying, you will gain as much success as I desire of you.

2. Different men have to face different obstacles. Yet, a diligent and zealous person will make greater progress in virtue, even though he may have to fight more defects than others. Some people have fewer defects to overcome, and still they do not

advance in holiness because they are less fervent in the pursuit of virtues.

THINK:

Many are frightened by the thought of changing their ways in daily life. Yet the way can be quite simplified if only they will make the effort. First, they need a spiritual director to guide them along and to help them see themselves without prejudice or fear. Second, they must be honest in striving for the virtues opposed to their main faults. Third, they must realize that their feelings and blind desires will go on rebelling and making their daily efforts more difficult. Lastly, they must learn to gain spiritual profit from all occasions, imitating the virtues which they see in others and avoiding the defects of their neighbors.

PRAY:

O Holy Spirit, my God and Sanctifier, grant me the light to see what a glorious opportunity I now have of beginning a better life. Help me to take whatever steps are necessary to purify my soul by a sincere daily effort. You will not deny me the strength which I need, if only I will try to develop

the virtues which I need most, in my daily
life. *Amen*.

CHAPTER 35

Variety in the Spiritual Life

CHRIST:

MY CHILD, not everyone can make use
of the same spiritual exercises. One
devotion suits this person, while another
suits that person. At times a change of spiritual exercises will do you good. Some devotions will help on ordinary days, and others
will be more helpful on holy days. You may
need one type of spiritual activity in time of
temptation and another in time of peace. A
man likes certain thoughts when he is sad,
but in time of spiritual joy, he prefers other
thoughts.

2. Variety in your spiritual life will help you
live a richer life and a holier one. Make your
spiritual goals and your resolutions according to the spirit of the different seasons of
the church calendar. Plan your interior life
as one who is eager to give Me better service.
Live as one who looks forward to Heaven.

3. Think of death as the gateway to Heaven. Learn to look upon your earthly life as a great opportunity to make a worthy preparation for Heaven. If I have not called you yet, consider that it is because you are not yet well enough prepared to receive the heavenly glory which is being reserved for you. Then plan how to prepare yourself for that heavenly reward. Never forget the words: "Blessed is that servant whom the Lord shall find watching when He comes. Indeed, I tell you, He will place him over all His possessions!"

THINK:

It is so easy to fall into a routine and stick to it. Many go on day after day, doing the same old things in the same old way. Variety makes life interesting, yet too few have the ambition and energy to put variety into their daily lives. In prayer, I shall try to learn various methods in case I should need them to avoid the dullness of routine. I can read the lives of the saints and see where I may make a few changes in my own spiritual life. My spiritual director can give me ideas on how to freshen my zeal for God's glory and for the help of my neighbor.

PRAY:

O Holy Ghost, my God and Sanctifier, grant me light to see how I can make my daily life more fruitful in doing good. Let me not fall into a rut and stay there. Life is a glorious opportunity to do great things—to become more like You, my God, by the good and love which I can give to others. Help me to see more ways of increasing the good in my daily life. Give me the unselfishness and strength to do good for Your sake. *Amen.*

CHAPTER 36

Frequent Communion

CHRIST:

MY CHILD, you should come often to Me, the Giver of grace and divine mercy, the Fountain of all goodness and holiness. In this way you will gain greater control over your passions, faults, and defects. In Holy Communion I will make you wiser and stronger against the temptations and deceits of the devil.

2. When I come to You in this Holy Sacrament, I offer you interior light and strength. These gifts are known only to my faithful ones. They are not enjoyed by unbelievers, nor by those who love sin. In this Sacrament, the soul receives the grace to regain lost virtues and the beauty which was lost by sin.

3. The blind desires of man tend to evil from his youth. Unless this divine Medicine assists him, he will quickly slip from bad to worse. Holy Communion withdraws you from what is evil and strengthens you in what is good. You need Me. Make full use of the wisdom and strength which I offer you in Holy Communion.

THINK:

To fight sin, I need a strength greater than my own. Jesus promises to give it to me in Holy Communion. I must not pass up this marvelous invitation. As often as possible I will go to receive Him. I will lay before Him my hopes, plans, and ambitions. He will give me the strength to do what is best for me.

PRAY:

Lord, this heavenly gift is certainly necessary for me. I become sluggish so easily, and

I fall into sin so quickly. I need to be spiritually refreshed, cleansed, and inflamed once more by frequent prayers, confession, and a loving reception of Your Sacred Body and Blood. By staying away too long, I may fall away from my good intentions. Make me wise enough to come to You as often as possible, so that I may have Your grace to work for eternal life. *Amen.*

CHARTER 37

Invitation to Holy Communion

CHRIST:

M Y CHILD, often ponder My words: "Come, all you that labor and are burdened, and I will refresh you." These are My words, and you ought to receive them gratefully and faithfully. They are Mine because I spoke them; but they are also yours, because they were spoken for your salvation. Receive them joyfully from My lips. Let them be deeply carved upon your heart. In these holy words, you see My loyal and tender consideration for you. Do not let your conscience stop you from rushing into My arms. I know how unworthy you are of My friendship, but I love you in spite of that.

2. In spite of your nothingness and your sins, I command you to approach Me with confidence. It is actually My Will that you should receive Me, the Food of Immortality. Through this heavenly Food, which is truly My own Body and Blood, you shall gain unending life and eternal glory. I say, "Come, all you that labor and are burdened, and I will refresh you!" These are consoling words in the ear of a sinner. I your Lord and God, invite poor and needy you to receive My holy Body. Do not say, "Who am I, that I should presume to approach You?" I command you to come and receive Me, for without Me you are lost.

3. Prepare your soul with confession, if necessary, and with prayers. Then approach My altar with confidence and with a burning desire to please Me in your daily life.

THINK:

God is so powerful, so great, so perfect, that we are as nothing compared to Him. The angels and saints in Heaven see God face to face and realize how very, very small they are in His presence. As a result they feel a deep indescribable respect for Him. Yet God, in His goodness, loves His creatures beyond all telling. He did many things to convince us of His love. He even sent His beloved Son to show His love in a human way. After living and dying for love of us, Jesus invented a way to remain with us in the Holy Eucharist. In this wonderful Sacrament He makes Himself the Food of our souls. Lest anyone refuse to receive Him in Holy Communion, He commanded that we should do so. It is His express wish that I receive Him in Holy Communion.

PRAY:

Lord, why are You so gracious to me and so concerned about me? You know how full of defects I am. I offend You so often by my faults and my negligence. How dare I welcome You into my heart? I have often been selfish with You in spite of all Your generosity to Me. The angels and archangels stand in deep respect before You. The Saints and the Just have a holy fear of You. Yet, You say, "Come to Me." Were it not You that say this, Lord, who could believe it, and who would dare approach this holy table? At Your loving command I will come. I will think of Your Will and forget my unworthiness, and I shall eat the Bread of Angels. *Amen.*

CHAPTER 38

The Man of Faith

CHRIST:

MY CHILD, My loyal follower is not rebellious at the unpleasant things which I permit in his daily life. He is a man of faith, that is, he believes My words and follows My teachings in his daily life. He sees My wisdom guiding his life at all times.

2. This supernatural faith helps him keep his peace of soul, even when humans seem to complicate his life by their meddling and interference.

3. What I send is not always easy to understand. It may even seem unjust or foolish to those who are living only for this world. The man of faith takes all from My Hands, knowing that I plan all things for the best.

4. Do not depend on your natural judgment alone, but learn to consult Me and My Church in all matters of importance.

THINK:

I must be a man of faith, with a bright vision of God in my daily life. He is ever near, ever interested, ever helping me. With such an interior vision I will not be disturbed by the sayings and doings of those around me. The supernatural man is not fooled by external appearances. He knows only too well that what looks good may sometimes be wrong, and what seems undesirable is sometimes the only thing to do. He sees clearly that God sometimes chooses the foolish things of this world to confound the wise.

PRAY:

Father of wisdom and goodness, my God, when will I see things with Your glorious, eternal outlook? Let me not be influenced by the wrong standards of worldly people. I will dare to be different when the humans around me disagree with You. Though they may mock and criticize what You have commanded, give me courage and strength to follow what You want of me. Your wisdom will conquer the foolish wisdom of this world. The folly of sin will one day be condemned and put to shame. Let me hate what is wrong and fear all sin in my daily life. *Amen.*

CHAPTER 39

Man's True Good

CHRIST:

MY CHILD, often it is safer for a man not to have many consolations and pleasures in his earthly life. Try to grasp this truth, so that you may not become sad and depressed when you cannot have what you desire.

2. If you had all the satisfactions and enjoyments which this world can offer, how long would they last? The knowledge that they must certainly end, would only make death more bitter and disagreeable to you.

3. The fact is that your soul can find full and lasting joy only in My friendship and love. True happiness and lasting peace come from Me alone. Foolish lovers of this world think that they know the meaning of peace and happiness, but what they enjoy is imperfect and short-lived. Genuine peace and happiness is given only to My loyal followers,

those who are unselfish in doing My Will
and generous in imitating My example.

THINK:

God desires that I should labor for my
daily bread and enjoy the rightful pleasures
of daily life. I must not, however, become so
entangled in these things that I would sin
for them. Each day is a step toward the true
and perfect life of Heaven. I need to put complete trust and confidence in God's wisdom
and love for me. This virtue will give me
the freedom of true charity. I will come to
see more clearly each day how to please God
more in everything I do.

PRAY:

My Jesus, please do not let me think too
much of my earthly needs. They can crowd
my mind and make me too busy to think of
You and Your holy words. Save me from the
blind love of pleasure and from the enslav-
ing worry about earthly security. Grant me
the freedom of those who live for Heaven.
Nothing on earth must hold me back from
doing Your Will. *Amen.*

CHAPTER 40

Heavenly Desires

CHRIST:

MY CHILD, be not too impressed by appearances. Foolish people think that a man cannot help being happy if he is rich, or powerful, or if he has fame and influence. Be wise with My wisdom. Fix your heart on heavenly riches. Then you will see that passing glories and unsteady contentment are not as desirable as they seem. In fact, they are often a burden of work, worry and fear.

2. Man's happiness does not consist in having a great deal. A moderate amount of this world's good things is enough for you if you are daily working for Heaven. The more you see life from My viewpoint, the more you will realize that this earthly life is a cross. It has its trials, burdens, disappointments, and sorrows, all of which must be borne patiently. It is not easy to be a spiritual man, because the good things of this world continually appeal to your feelings. Learn to govern your feelings with the reins

of reason and grace. Control them with your intelligence and My commandments.

3. As your desire for spiritual perfection grows, you will find yourself thinking more definitely of Heaven. Your desire for Heaven will become stronger and stronger. You may even have to control a dislike for the needs and obligations of daily life.

THINK:

The more one thinks of his eternal destiny, the more he will realize that his earthly life is a journey toward something far grander than this world. He sees each day as a step toward Heaven, and he looks at himself to see whether he is on the right path. Slowly he comes to value the events of his daily life according to God's Will and Heaven's eternal happiness.

PRAY:

Lord, nothing on earth can give me the joy and happiness of Heaven. In fact, there is no lasting joy apart from You. May I never be without Your holy grace. I desire to see the real value of the earthly things which I love. May I never love any person or thing more than You, that is, may I never sin because of them. *Amen*.

CHAPTER 41

Earning the Reward

CHRIST:

MY CHILD, for reasons which you cannot fully appreciate at present, I made your earthly life a time of labor and trial. Each and every time that I permit you to suffer pain, grief or disappointment I do it for your own good. These trials help you to come closer to Me in one way or another. I made your earthly life a time of labor and trial. Do not think too much about pleasure and rest in this life. Be prepared to exercise patience rather than enjoy comfort or consolation. Think more of carrying the cross of daily life rather than of avoiding everything unpleasant.

2. Do you expect to enjoy interior consolation whenever you wish? Not even My saints could do that during their earthly life. They had to face many troubles, temptations, interior misery and desolation. They went on, however, in spite of all these obstacles, trusting in Me more than in themselves.

They were fully aware that the sufferings of this life are not worthy to be compared with the glory that is to come.

3. Do you not see how selfish your desires are? You want to obtain quickly the peace and holiness which others achieved only after many trials and labors. You are more interested in enjoying My gifts than in earning them. No, you must do things My way if you want to live the best way.

4. Wait for the light and strength which I will send in due time. In the meantime have courage and be patient. Do not give up the fight against your faults and defects. Do your best to become the kind of person I want you to be. Leave the results to Me. I am near you at every moment. Be unselfish enough to go on trying for My sake. I will someday reward you far beyond anything you can imagine.

THINK:

Heaven is a reward—a thing to be earned. Though I can never really deserve it by my poor human efforts alone, Jesus has made it possible for me to work for it with His help. Strengthened by His grace, I can strive for Heaven. An honest daily effort against my faults and a faithful attempt to do God's Will in all things, will bring me the glorious reward of Heaven. Earthly life has its labors, trials, and difficulties. Each day I show by my actions, words, thoughts, and desires, how sincerely I am working for Heaven.

PRAY:

Holy Spirit, my God, help me to see Your guiding hand in time of trial, and let me follow humbly and loyally whatever You desire of me. I want to do the best that is in me, be it ever so little. Heaven is more than I will ever deserve, but at least I can do my best to make myself a little less unworthy of it. My God, I hope in You, for the grace to go on trying each hour of the day. *Amen.*

CHAPTER 42

Unselfishness with God

CHRIST:

MY CHILD, do not look for spiritual consolation or interior good feelings in your prayers and good works. Serve Me for My sake, as I deserve. Let your service depend on My word, and not on any pleasant feelings which I may send you. If I gave interior consolation and joy for every good work, many a worldly man would follow My commandments for the sake of these gifts.

2. As long as you are in this life, you will be tempted by the blind selfishness of fallen human nature. Turn frequently to Me and let Me guide your self-interest. I desire your self-interest to be intelligent and well-ordered. Place Me above all persons and things created.

3. I am far greater than all My works. I am your greatest Treasure! Seek Me above all else. Consider what I mean in your life. What do I deserve of you? What have I a right to expect of you? Can you draw your next breath or take your next step without My consent and assistance? Could you exist another instant if I withdrew My support? Only by facing these facts, and living on them each hour of the day, can you give Me the intelligent service which you owe Me.

4. Spiritual consolation is only a temporary gift to encourage one who is earnestly trying to serve Me. This gift is not at the command of any man, and it will not be

given to anyone who seeks it for itself. Such a person is too much like the man who seeks his entire happiness in the pleasures, satisfactions, and honors of this world. A frank and intelligent remembrance of your unworthiness, will help you perform your prayers and good works without expecting spiritual consolations in return.

THINK:

Jesus is right. I do not deserve the least of His gifts. I already owe Him so much that I should be glad to do His Will, without looking for further gifts. He owes me nothing, and I owe Him everything. If He chose to leave me in misery and sorrow, He would be doing me no injustice, since all that I am and have belong to Him.

PRAY:

Lord, I know that You will never treat me as poorly as I deserve, as long as I am truly trying to improve my daily life. You will never be outdone in generosity. Each holy desire and every good deed of mine will be rewarded a hundredfold. You will not leave me in my misery and troubles any longer than is necessary for my real good.

I have deserved little, but I need You and hope in Your help. Let me follow Your wise and holy Will by seeking You first, and Your gifts only as far as You want me to have them. *Amen.*

PART THREE
Temptation

GOD tells us that man is born imperfect and that he must use the opportunities and events in his earthly life to perfect himself as far as possible. He must use them according to the directions of his intelligence and according to the wisdom of God's law.

It is not, however, easy to act always with this holy moderation. Man's feelings, moods, sentiments, appetites, and desires are not always willing to obey his intelligence. He sometimes feels too strong a love for some things and too weak a love for other things. This continual tendency to go to extremes is called temptation. Temptation is not sin. It tends to draw a man to do what he knows is wrong, or seeks to hold him back from what he knows is right.

Temptation simply brings out what is in a man. One knows himself better when he has dealt with temptation. It proves his faults and tests his virtues. Just how much he really desires to earn Heaven, is seen by what he does to reach it. How much he really loves God, is seen by how much he is willing to do for God. The first safeguard against temptation is to recognize it, to see it as it really is without its attractive camouflage.

A. Nature, Value, and Control of Temptations

CHAPTER 43

Man's Daily Trials

CHRIST:

M Y CHILD, one who does not know My plan might easily be discouraged by the trials of this earthly life. Life on earth is so short. Hardly ever is it free from grief and troubles. Men on earth are stained with many sins, deceived by many desires, enslaved by many fears, endangered by many snares, distracted by many curiosities, entangled with vanities, surrounded by errors, tired with labors, troubled by temptations, exhausted with pleasure, tormented with many wants.

2. Afflictions and sorrows are seldom absent. You are surrounded by so many traps and enemies. Scarcely does one trouble or temptation go, when another arrives. Often enough, the first trouble is still with you when others come. You may wonder that anyone can love this earthly existence with its misfortunes, bitterness, and miseries. Yet, in spite of all this, many love this earthly life and seek all their delight in it.

3. Yet, My loyal follower can smile and be glad through all the darkness and trials. He does not fix his eyes on the present trial, but on the main purpose of his earthly life. He looks beyond the present darkness to the horizon where the light of the eternal day will soon break forth. Then will you be freed from the miserable slavery of your unreasonable desires and selfish ambitions. Then will you find your perfect joy, your all-satisfying life. You will possess at last the true liberty of Heaven without any hindrances, without pain of body or mind—the liberty which I alone can give.

THINK:

Life on earth is short and full of dissatisfactions and necessities. Yet God is a wise and loving Father. Every parent seems stern when he is training his children. When they have grown up strong in virtue and firm in character, only then do they appreciate their father's wisdom and love. So, too, with us. We little dream how weak we are until we feel the call to ease, selfishness and pride. We might never suspect what we really are if God had not given us a life of trial on earth. God made me for Heaven, a reward I cannot even begin to imagine. He asks that I do what I can, to be less unworthy of Heaven, by striving on earth for some of His goodness and holiness.

PRAY:

My loving God, what good is it for me to think myself better than I really am? Lord, if it were not for my earthly trials, I might never have known how selfish and proud I really am. I thank you, my God, for giving me this chance to become in fact what I desire to be in theory. Actions are the proof of true virtue. Every trouble and sorrow on earth was placed here, or permitted, by Your infinite wisdom. You know what I need, to make me a truly holy man. Some day I shall thank You for many a trial which now weighs me down. Make me unselfish enough to follow Your commands, whether my life be filled with prosperity or misery. Treat me as You wish, and it will be best for me. *Amen.*

CHAPTER 44

Temptations Come to All

CHRIST:

MY CHILD, the devil is never asleep, nor is your flesh dead yet. This means that you must always be on guard for a battle, since on every side you have enemies who are never at rest. Your old enemy is opposed to everything that is good. He is never tired of tempting people to sin. Day and night he lays snares, with the hope that some unsuspecting soul may fall into his trap. Be on your guard against temptations. Pray often for the grace to overcome them.

2. No man is entirely safe from temptations here on earth. You have within you

the source of temptation, since you were born with concupiscence. Concupiscence of the body is the blind tendency of your feelings and animal appetites to seek satisfaction, regardless of intelligence and reason. Concupiscence of the soul consists in an unreasoning and unreasonable self-favoring, without considering what is true or what is right.

3. When one temptation or trouble is over, along comes another. While you are on this earth you will always have something to suffer, because man has lost the original happiness which I had planned to give him even in this world.

THINK:

Every man gets his share of temptations. How he deals with them shows what he really is. If he tries his best to lessen the occasions for temptation in his daily life, he is a wise man. The fool takes chances with temptations and falls into sin. Man's greatest enemy is his spontaneous, unreasoning self. The devil's greatest ally against my true welfare, is this foolish self within me. He appeals to it by promising or offering what looks good. If I know God's way of thinking, I shall recognize Satan's bait, and with God's help, I shall control my unreasoning desires and foolish self-favoring.

PRAY:

My loving Father and all-wise God, I long to reflect Your holy honesty by recognizing myself for what I really am. Let me not be blind to my weaknesses and faults. I do not want to favor myself except in the highest way—that is, I want to win eternal life for myself by following Your holy commands in my daily life. I wish to avoid or contradict whatever endangers my eternal salvation. In fact, I desire to practice self-control and self-mortification so as to gain a greater command over my blind passions and unreasonable self-favoring. Only with such control, can I hope to overcome the many temptations, big or small, which daily come to me. *Amen.*

CHAPTER 45

No Time or Place Free from Temptations

CHRIST:

MY CHILD, in this world no one is so perfect or so holy that he does not, at some time or other, experience temptations. You never be entirely free from them. None of My saints was ever so sublimely held in prayer, or so illuminated by My grace that he did not suffer temptations at some time or other.

2. My saints passed through many troubles and temptations, and they profited by these experiences. Those who are unwilling to stand up and fight temptations, will quickly fall away from Me. Do not be disturbed that things are not going as you would like them to go. Look upon your trials as part of your daily life. Bear patiently with what you cannot remedy. Thus will you prove yourself a true follower of Mine.

3. Temptations may come to you at any hour of the day or night. You will meet them within yourself, or again they may come from the persons and things around you.

No time nor place is free from temptations, and every person has his share of them. Through all of this, however, I am close at hand, ready to give My heavenly strength to those who are willing to fight.

4. In time of temptation you have a chance to prove a more unselfish love for Me. It is then that you have your best opportunity to rise above your puny self and to reach out to Me.

THINK:

Temptation is the lot of every man. No one is free of it. No place in the world, no time of day is secure against temptation. Human nature is never fully satisfied, and the devil never sleeps. Between the two stands Jesus with arms outstretched toward me. I will walk straight toward Him by guiding my thoughts and controlling my desires, words, and actions. In Him alone shall I find my all-satisfying joy and happiness. This continual tugging, inside of me and outside of me, toward Jesus and away from Him, this it is that makes life a daily warfare.

PRAY:

Dear Heavenly Father, of all the things I choose this day, none is more precious than Your holy Will. You alone can show me the way to Heaven's eternal happiness. Help me to be a loyal follower of Jesus, Your divine Son. I want to make Him the King of my heart by my loyalty to His holy example. Let me become better acquainted with Him so that I may think, speak, and act more like Him every day. No goal can be higher, yet I must not aim any lower. My true welfare demands this. His boundless generosity with me demands it. I hope, with Your help, to give Him at least the loyalty of an honest daily effort. *Amen.*

CHAPTER 46

Two Interior Causes of Temptation

CHRIST:

MY CHILD, serious temptations can come from a lack of determination, or from too little confidence in Me. A ship without a rudder is driven to and fro by the winds and waves. So too, when a man does not bother to work at the virtues he needs, or if he abandons his good intentions, he is soon tempted by his own faults and weaknesses.

2. I am the Lord, and I give strength in time of trial. Come to Me when things are not going well with you. Heavenly light and strength are often held back from you because you are so slow to make use of prayer. How frequently, before you get down to serious prayer, you look for peace in worldly consolations, and seek your happiness in natural enjoyments or earthly occupations.

3. You will find little relief in anything until you realize that I am ready to help those who trust in Me. There is no perfect assistance, no helpful advice, no lasting remedy unless it is blessed by My love and strengthened by My presence.

THINK:

Lack of determination! How often I fall back into the same old faults because I am not determined to overcome them! A half-hearted resolution is little better than none at all. I must be fully determined to fight my faults with definite action, not merely with a vague resolution. I should keep trying, regardless of repeated failures. Insufficient confidence in God's help, is another reason for my lack of progress in virtue. God will not help a man of little confidence. I must earn His help by humble prayer, firm confidence, and a sincere effort to fight my failures.

PRAY:

Lord, where is my true confidence in this life? Of all the persons and things on earth, where is my greatest consolation? It ought surely to be in You, my Lord and God, Whose mercy has no limit. Was I ever really well off apart from You? Was I ever poorly off when near to You? Where You are, there is Heaven; and where You are not, there is death and hell. Let me live in close contact with you throughout my daily life. In union with You, I shall make my resolutions together with an honest effort to follow them. *Amen.*

CHAPTER 47

The Progress of Temptations

CHRIST:

MY CHILD, watch yourself especially at the beginning of a temptation. You will find it easier to overcome the enemy if you resist him at once. Stop him at the threshold, at the very moment when he knocks. He spoke wisely who said, "Resist beginnings; all too late the cure when ills have gathered strength by long delay." Though it is never too late to turn to Me, you will find it harder to do so, the longer you linger with a temptation.

2. First a simple thought will slip into your mind. This is followed by a strong imagination. Then comes delight, then an evil inclination, and lastly, consent. Thus, little by little, the enemy gains full entrance into your soul, when he is not resisted in the beginning.

THINK:

Many a ruined life could have been prevented, if only one had been wise enough to follow this advice. Too many take chances and linger too long at some pleasure, trying to enjoy as much as possible without falling into the evil that is there. People are so afraid of missing something. And so, they step closer and closer to actual sin, until, like a waiting spider, it reaches out and entangles them.

PRAY:

O Holy Ghost, my God and Sanctifier, in You I hope for the wisdom to recognize sin before it overcomes me. Grant me strength to resist whatever would draw me into sin. I would have less faults and sins today if I had turned away from temptation at its very start. With Your help, I hope to do whatever is necessary to lessen the temptation in my daily life. *Amen*.

CHAPTER 48

Facing Temptations

CHRIST:

MY CHILD, with My help you will gradually overcome these temptations which annoy you in your daily life. You are never entirely safe from them. As long as you are in this world, you will have to protect yourself from them. All around you there are people or things which may appeal to your weakness. When you cannot avoid them, meet them with patience rather than with anxiety or thoughtless severity. Correct and remedy what you can. As for things which cannot be remedied, bear them patiently for My sake.

2. Unless you keep your eyes on Me, you cannot stand up under the strain of this daily warfare. Without My help you will never earn the reward of the Blessed in Heaven. Face life bravely. With a firm determination, take definite measures to overcome the temptations in your daily life. I will grant heavenly strength to anyone who makes an honest effort. The sluggard is doomed to miserable failure.

3. Some try to run away from all temptations, and still they go on falling into sin. Flight alone will not conquer all temptations. Wherever you go, you will always find some occasion of sin. By humility, patience, and definite action, you will become strong against the enemies of your soul.

THINK:

Patience will help me to keep calm in my troubles and difficulties. It will help me think more clearly. As a result, I shall find it easier to turn to God when I need Him.

Humility will help me admit my weakness and nothingness. It will make me less irritable and resentful of my distasteful experiences. These two virtues will help me have peace in the middle of my troubles. Then with a definite plan in mind, I can proceed against my faults and conquer my temptations.

PRAY:

My Jesus, with Your help, I hope to do my best each day to overcome my faults and increase my virtues. When matters are beyond my efforts, and I can only suffer pain or disappointment, then let me see Your Divine Providence arranging my life in that way. Let me accept my cross with patience and humility. I will never stop trying to do my best. As for results, I leave them in Your loving hands. *Amen*.

CHAPTER 49

Temptation as a Teacher

CHRIST:

MY CHILD, when a man of good will is bothered by evil thoughts and inclinations, he understands more deeply how much he needs Me. He is impressed by his natural weakness in trying to live a good life.

2. He realizes that perfect security and peace are not to be had in this world. Then he finds this life less attractive. Death seems to frighten him less because it is the doorway to Heaven. He may even pray for it to free him from the temptations which surround him.

3. Fear not! Have confidence in Me! After such a storm you will be as strong as ever. I am always near, to help you grow ever more in goodness and holiness. You will come out of your trial a better and wiser man.

4. Is anything difficult to Me? Will I fail to keep My promises? Stand firm and keep fighting against your temptations. Have patience! Be brave and wait for My grace. Your fears will be conquered by a strong faith and confidence in Me. When you are ready for it, My comfort and consolation will come to you.

THINK:

Temptations tend to sadden and discourage a good man. Yet, he needs simply to turn to God for help, and then do his best. As long as he is doing his best, he should not fear, nor worry, nor be discouraged. His wisdom and peace will grow as he sees the passing nature of his trial.

PRAY:

My Lord, in all my trials and temptations, may I keep my eyes on You! Then it will be much easier to see the falseness of earthly attractions. I will refuse to be saddened, frightened, or discouraged by temptations. Nor will I be surprised at the rebellion of my own blind appetites and desires. For You I hope to fight and conquer all evil tendencies. *Amen.*

CHAPTER 50

Temptations Prove Man's Worth

CHRIST:

MY CHILD, temptations are often very profitable to you, distressing and troublesome though they be. They help to lessen your foolish pride by showing you your weaknesses. Without temptations you could deceive yourself into a dangerous self-confidence. They teach you many things which can help you come closer to Me in your daily life. They can purify your soul by forcing you to resist evil and practice virtue. Troubles, afflictions and opposition bring you opportunities for heavenly merit.

2. Temptations prove the real worth of your virtues. Often you do not really know yourself until you have faced various temptations. They make your virtues shine out, and they help you to see what spiritual gain you have made. Anyone can act virtuously when things are going as he desires. The man who keeps his patience in time of adversity, can rightly hope for a lasting reward from Me.

THINK:

Were I never tempted, I might never know my real self. I cannot be sure of my own sincerity and motives until I have proved them by action. Anyone can talk about a good life, but the only real proof of goodness is living a good life. I would hate to find out too late that I am completely unworthy of God's gifts. My temptations give me a chance to prove how truly I mean it when I say that I want to please God in all things.

PRAY:

Father of all truth and goodness, let me be loyal to Your holy Will. Your way is the best and only way to live. Grant me grace to see my many faults and to overcome them for Your sake. In all temptations, I want to prefer to die rather than offend You by sin. *Amen.*

CHAPTER 51

Variety of Temptations

CHRIST:

MY CHILD, some have to bear serious temptations when they resolve to turn to Me. Others have to fight great temptations towards the end of a good life. There are some who are bothered by temptations throughout most of their lifetime.

2. Some persons are tempted lightly, in accordance with My wisdom and justice. I have consideration for the condition and

merits of each man, and I plan all things for the salvation of those who love My law.

3. Some persons are spared from serious temptations and they are often overcome by light ones in their daily life. I permit this, so that these people may be humbled in their own eyes. Being aware of their weakness, they will not presume on their own strength and fall into serious sin.

4. When you experience temptations, do not fear nor despair. Pray for My help and then do what you can to remove the temptation. Remember the inspired words, "God is faithful and will not permit you to be tempted beyond your strength, but with the temptation He will also give you a way out, that you may be able to bear it."

THINK:

May I never become so self-centered as to think that I am the only one who suffers temptations. There is no more pitiful sight than to meet someone who feels that he has greater trials than everyone else. Every man has his cross and some people have to bear far more than I ever could. And yet, this is not a Christian motive for patience and perseverance in time of trial and temptation. The true follower of Christ has higher reasons for fighting temptation. His reasons are supernatural. He wishes to avoid hell, or a longer Purgatory than he now has. He desires to make reparation for past sins by his present efforts. He wants to please God by overcoming his faults or increasing his virtues. He seeks to help the holy souls in Purgatory. He is striving to obtain a particular favor for himself or some other person on earth. He may even be working to insure or increase his glory in Heaven. Finally, he may have the highest motive of all to give God an unselfish proof of love, by simply embracing his trials because they are a part of God's all-wise plan.

PRAY:

My Jesus, let me do my best to live my daily life in loyalty to You, my King. I do not want to complain nor pity myself. I desire, with Your help, to face each task or trial and to handle it as You desire. Life's daily temptations can make me a real saint. I will not look for trouble, Lord, but I will do my best to face each hour's duties and trials for You.

May I work, rest, play and suffer as You desire of me. *Amen.*

CHAPTER 52

Prayer, First Remedy for Temptations

CHRIST:

MY CHILD, face the truth and never turn your back on facts. As long as you are in this world, you cannot be free from trouble and temptation. My written word tells you that. "Man's life on earth is a trial." Therefore, do not take temptations too lightly, but guard against them by frequent prayer and self-denial. In this way the devil will never take you by surprise. He is never asleep, but he goes about like a hungry lion, seeking someone whom he may devour.

Prayer for Light

Enlighten me, O good Jesus, with the brightness of eternal light, and let all darkness depart from my heart. Let me see through my wandering thoughts and help me to replace them with good, healthy thinking. Defend me against the evil beasts that come to me in the shape of attractive desires.

Bestow on me true interior peace through Your power, so that Your praise may echo within my soul as in a holy temple. Command the tempests and storms. Say to the sea, "Be still!" Call to the raging wind, "Blow not!" And there shall be a great calm within my soul. *Amen.*

Prayer Against Temptations

O Lord, my God, do not depart far from me. Please look upon me and help me. Evil thoughts have risen up against me and great fears afflict my soul. How am I to pass on without being harmed by them? Show me how I may crush them. You have said, "I will go before you and will humble the great ones of the earth. I will open the gates of the prison and will make known to you hidden secrets." Dear Lord, do as You say, and let all wicked thoughts and desires flee before Your face. *Amen.*

CHAPTER 53

Seeking Advice

CHRIST:

MY CHILD, those who are still beginners and lack experience in the daily way to holiness, may easily be deceived and lost unless they follow the advice of wiser men.

2. When temptation upsets your interior peace, seek advice from a spiritual director. Prefer to follow the counsels of a more experienced man rather than follow your own ideas. Satan can quote Scripture to his own purpose. He can also imitate My inspirations in many things. It is not always easy to discover his deceit. Good intentions alone are not enough to make you holy. You must be right in the course you are following.

3. I left you My Church as a sure guide to My Truth. I have also left you My own example, and the example and words of My saints. Do not be too proud to follow these helps. Do not despise the proverbs of the past. They are filled with the wisdom of experience.

4. After you receive advice, be wise and humble enough to follow it. Try to discover the source of your temptations, so that you may root it out of your life. A man who offers only external resistance to temptations, without removing their causes, will make little progress in virtue. These temptations will return to him in a short while, and his condition will be the same, if not worse.

THINK:

Pride or fear prevents many from seeking needed advice. As a result they are hurt more seriously as they go along in life. It takes humility to admit my faults and my limitations. It takes courage to do something about them. Will I be a fool and avoid the aid of those who can help me? Secondly, may I never refuse to others the sympathetic understanding and assistance which I would want if I were in their trouble.

PRAY:

Dear Father of Wisdom, Lord of Mercy, grant that I may never be so proud and so foolish as to refuse advice. I want to live an intelligent life. If the advice of others increases my wisdom in action, give me the humility and courage to follow it. In this way, I hope to avoid or defeat the temptations of my daily life. *Amen.*

B. Certain Temptations in Particular

CHAPTER 54

Temptations against Faith

CHRIST:

MY CHILD, some persons are seriously tempted to disbelieve what My Church teaches. Such temptations are often caused by the devil, the enemy of Truth. He disturbs My followers because he hates and fears their way of life. He does not bother habitual sinners in this way because he captures them through other sins. Satan inspires many wrong doctrines among those who do not know My Church. Under the appearance of good, these errors appeal to many. Keep close to My Church, and you will never fall into Satan's trap. Whoever disagrees with the word of My Church, disagrees with Me.

2. If you are tempted in this manner, do not become anxious and troubled. Do not let

doubts rob you of your peace. Simply put your trust in My Church, and the enemy will be put to flight. Believe My Apostles and their successors. I have guaranteed them from error. "He that hears you, hears Me" I told them. Their work is to continue to the end of time.

3. Submit yourself to Me by faith. I want you to know My truth. I will add knowledge to your soul by grace whenever it is necessary for you. I do not require great learning, nor a deep understanding of My holy mysteries. What I ask of you is a strong faith in My words and a virtuous life.

THINK:

An honest and humble inquiry after truth is a good thing, as long as I am not trying to depart from the traditional and sound doctrine of Christ's Church. I must, however, remember that reason and natural investigation can never penetrate far into the mysteries which God has revealed. I have to submit my reason to His word. It is foolish for me to believe only what I can understand. Can not God know and do things which are far beyond my puny understanding? Will the Author of Truth lead me into error? Sound reason demands that I believe whatever God reveals, no matter how little I understand it.

PRAY:

Lord, If there are so many things here on earth which I cannot understand, how can I understand heavenly things? Human reason is weak and limited. It can be so easily deceived, but true faith can never be deceived. Such faith depends upon Your word, and Your word is Truth. If Your works were such that they could easily be understood by my puny human reason, they could hardly be called wonderful and divine. As long as I know that You speak through Your Church, I shall never doubt what She tells me. *Amen.*

CHAPTER 55

Faith in the Holy Eucharist

CHRIST:

MY CHILD, beware of a curious and useless inquiry into the reality of My presence in the Blessed Sacrament. At the Last Supper I changed bread and wine into

My body and blood. I then gave My Apostles power to do what I had just done. They in turn passed their powers and their work on to their successors. And so, today you have the privilege of receiving Me in Holy Communion. What I did is a historical fact, but it is also a fact that is far above your understanding, and too wonderful for you to grasp fully.

2. No human can appreciate completely the glory of My works. God, the Eternal and All-present, the Fountain of boundless power, does things which are too grand to be understood by men. Pray for an increase in faith and love. These two virtues are most powerful to help you draw closer to Me in the Blessed Sacrament.

3. Blessed is that simplicity which is not tormented with an endless questioning of what it fails to understand. Is not My word enough for every man? Some have been lost by the inquiries of pride. You will be wise to make frequent use of this sublime Sacrament. You will come to know Me better by the graces flowing from Holy Mass and Communion.

THINK:

I ought to live my life with a simple and undoubting faith in God's word, reverently and humbly approaching Jesus in Holy Communion. There will I find Him waiting for me. Whatever I cannot understand, I will leave to Him. He can do all things, and He cannot deceive. Christ, my God and Saviour, walks with the simple, reveals Himself to the humble, and gives understanding to those who are little in spirit. He teaches the deeper meaning of His words to pure minds, but hides His favor from the curious and the proud.

PRAY:

My Jesus, give me the grace of simplicity, so that I may receive Your words with trust, and without the opposition of unnecessary inquiry. You proved Your divine power during Your earthly life. Therefore, Your word is the word of God, and I believe it, no matter how little I may understand it. You are the Fountain of all truth and goodness. In You I put all faith and trust. *Amen.*

CHAPTER 56

Putting Off Holy Communion

CHRIST:

MY CHILD, do not doubt your readiness to receive Me in Holy Communion. It is not necessary to have holy sentiments and devout feelings. Just do the best you can, and come to Me. Follow the advice of wise counsellors and lay aside all anxieties and scruples. Too much thinking can stop My grace from helping you. Reject all anxiety. It can take your attention away from Me, so that you no longer hear My voice within your soul.

2. Then again, avoid the other extreme of receiving Me without a reasonable preparation. do not expect you to be perfect, but I do expect you to aim at perfection by doing your best. Be it ever so poor, if you are doing your best, I am pleased with you.

3. Some people are so half-hearted in dealing with Me that it makes little difference to them whether they receive Me or not. They think nothing of putting off Confession and Holy Communion. They are not particularly

interested in coming closer to Me. Some of them deliberately stay away from Me, for fear of learning their obligations better. They do not want to change their ways too much. If they go to hell, it will be because they refused to let Me help them. Do your best, but be sure that you are not deceiving yourself. Do your real best, and fear neither man nor devil, for I am always with you.

THINK:

If I am wise I will follow this wonderful advice. As long as I am trying my best, I have no reason to be afraid or anxious. I can not afford to stay away from Christ in the Mass and in Holy Communion. It is dangerous to stay away from Him for any length of time. Then again I must guard against self-deception. He deserves my best. If I think of my own convenience and inconvenience, I will fail Christ and avoid His Will in many things. He knows and wants only what is best for me.

PRAY:

My Jesus, You went to the trouble of leaving me Your Holy Sacraments. In them You forgive my sins and give me greater wisdom and strength. I will not neglect this spiritual medicine and food. Nor will I do anything unworthy of these gifts, by carelessness or half-heartedness. With their help, I hope to overcome my faults and increase my virtues in daily life. *Amen.*

CHAPTER 57

Missing Holy Communion

CHRIST:

MY CHILD, Satan knows what great light and strength I give to those who receive Me devoutly in Holy Communion. Therefore, he tries, by every trick he knows, to keep people away from Me. He aims his worst attacks and illusions at some persons just when they think of going to Communion.

2. I have revealed in the holy book of Job that the wicked spirit has been allowed to go among men and to tempt them. So it is that he annoys My followers with his wickedness. He tries to make them fearful and anxious, or even over-confident and careless. In this way he intends to lessen their loyalty to Me. By keeping them away from

Holy Communion, he hopes to corrupt their faith and their love for Me.

3. You need never fear Satan nor any of his followers. Pay not the least attention to any of his tricks and suggestions, be they ever so shameful and hateful. Turn them back on his own head. He deserves only contempt and scorn. Never be so foolish as to omit Holy Communion because of unholy imaginations and feelings. Do your best to think of other things, and come to Me with confidence.

THINK:

My will and my continued efforts show my real self. Imaginations and feelings do not belong to the real "me," except when I accept them and want them. By keeping close to Christ in Holy Communion, I shall receive the strength to overcome all temptations. As often as possible I will go to Jesus in Mass and Communion.

PRAY:

O Jesus, ever-present in the Blessed Sacrament, You wish to come to me as often as possible, so that You may grant me light and strength for life's daily battle. I shall

not hesitate to come to You. Keep my will
free of all sinful desires. With Your help I
hope to overcome or at least disregard, the
unreasonable imaginations and blind appetites of my lower nature. I do not want them.
I want only You and Your holy Will. *Amen.*

CHAPTER 58

Spiritual Tepidity

CHRIST:

MY CHILD, spiritual tepidity is another
name for halfhearted service of God. A
tepid man does not usually avoid his duty,
but neither is he enthusiastic about it. He
does as little as possible, and often does
it through habit. He has lost the joy of serving Me.

2. When you start to grow lukewarm in
serving Me, consult your spiritual director.
You are slipping into a dangerous condition
of soul on which your future may depend.
The tepid soul is afraid to exert itself. It begins to look for consolation from the worldly
things around it. The tepid man has con-
tracted a disease which brings spiritual

death. The germs that will kill his soul are laziness and worldliness.

THINK:

Tepidity, as a mood, comes to most people at some time or other. In this mood one loses for the moment his enthusiasm and zeal in working for God and Heaven. The really tepid man, however, is one who has allowed this mood to become a habit. As a result, he now has no desire for prayer, and he no longer fears and fights temptations as he should. One who does not arouse himself against tepidity, loses many actual graces and opportunities to do good. Without perceiving it, he is slipping closer and closer to serious sin by failing to recognize the occasion of sin.

PRAY:

Lord, protect me against this disease. How will I end up if I start so easily to grow tepid? Will I look for ease and rest on earth, as though I had already arrived in the heavenly country? I still have to fight against the enemies of my soul, and I cannot afford to act as though I were secure against serious sin. In prayer, work, and penance let me

142   The Way of Purification

serve You. I shall seek to know Your Will ever more clearly so that I may serve You, not in my own way, but in the way which You desire. *Amen.*

CHAPTER 59

Remedies for Tepidity

CHRIST:

MY CHILD, it is a sad sight for Me to see men living disorderly lives. I made them for eternal glory. Little do they realize how harmful it is to neglect their daily duties, or to perform them carelessly. Pay attention to your purpose in life, and keep before your mind the image of your crucified King. Consider My earthly life, and blush if you are not doing your best to imitate Me.

2. Your loyalty and progress in serving Me ought to improve each day. Nowadays it is considered a great thing if one can just hold on to some of his original enthusiasm. A person is considered great if he merely avoids evil, or if he can be patient enough to endure life's daily burdens. Greatness lies not merely in avoiding evil, but especially in doing good.

3. It grieves Me to see how half-hearted and negligent so many people are. How quickly they lose their devotion and grow tired of the higher life, because of laziness and spiritual tepidity. May your desire to progress in virtue grow greater each day. Study the holy examples of My saints and learn to appreciate their continual loyalty to Me.

THINK:

If I thought more often of death than of a long life, I would be far more eager to advance in virtue. Occasional thinking about the reality of hell and Purgatory will help me to bear the labors, sorrows, and hardships of daily life. No longer would I love flattery and praise, nor would I be so lazy and half-hearted in serving Christ, my King. I ought to think often about His life and make it the model of my own daily life.

PRAY:

My Saviour, each hour of the day is an important part of my life. Whether I am at work, or play, or rest, I can do these things in a holy way or in a sinful way. Each hour brings its chances for patience, kindness, unselfishness, and other virtues. If I am half-hearted, I will not make the effort needed for acting as God desires. I can cure this disease by spiritual guidance, variety in prayer, meditations on Your life and sufferings, and frequent use of the Sacraments. My Jesus, give me the grace to do whatever I need to avoid tepidity in my daily life. *Amen.*

CHAPTER 60

Evil Thoughts

CHRIST:

MY CHILD, do not be troubled if you are visited by evil tendencies or strange imaginings. Keep your resolutions firm and your intention clear before Me. You are not suffering from illusions, even though at one moment you are full of spiritual desires and joy, and then shortly afterwards you are back in your foolish ways. Some of your defects are to be borne patiently for My sake. I will not hold them against you. In fact, they bring you great merit as long as you are truly displeased with them and refuse to consent to them.

2. I permit the devil to wander over the earth. He is continually trying to kill your desire for Me. He tries in many different ways to draw you away from every holy exercise. He can hurt you only if you follow his suggestions. In his attempts to draw you away from Me, he studies you to see where you are weakest.

3. Satan suggests evil thoughts to cause weariness or despair in you. He would like to draw you away from all prayer, holy reading, or any good work. He dreads seeing anyone make a humble confession. If he could he would stop you from receiving Me in Holy Communion. And yet, in spite of his frantic and constant efforts against you, he is helpless if you decide to stand by Me, with faith, hope and love.

4. Despise the enemy, and fear him not. Fix your attention on your daily occupations. Follow My words in your daily life. Seek grace and inspiration by prayer and meditation. Think often of My life. Honor My saints. Recall and detest your sins. Watch over your desires, thoughts, and intentions. Make your resolutions, renew

them often, and do your best to follow them. Trust in My wisdom and love for the rest.

THINK:

I need not think that I am less loyal to our Lord when I have lost that feeling of devotion which I desire to have toward God and His saints. Holy feelings are a favor which God grants for a moment. They are a short foretaste of Heaven. They are not meant to be a permanent gift in this life. Therefore, I must not depend on them. My true virtues and merit are best known when those feelings are not present. In everyday, hum-drum activities how well do I fulfill my duties? What kind of resistance do I offer to my unreasoning tendencies and desires within me? How devotedly do I try to please God in all things? The devil has not a chance against me if I am really doing my best.

PRAY:

Dear Father of Light, when my mind is overclouded with confusion or anxieties, grant me the light of Your grace, so that I may fix my eyes on Your truth and walk safely toward Heaven. In Your Church I will seek Your guidance as You desire me to do. All the powers of hell are helpless against me, if I will only be wise enough to seek Your truth and use the strength of Your holy Sacraments. *Amen*.

CHAPTER 61

Fear

CHRIST:

MY CHILD, in many a trial and trouble, I come to you and ask you to believe in Me. Put your confidence in Me, and prove that you mean it, by refusing to worry. If your trials were not good for you, I would remove them at once.

2. Do not be frightened. Why worry about coming events? Take care of today's problems, and leave tomorrow in My hands. Many of tomorrow's troubles are only in your imagination. How do you know that you will live another day? Did you ever stop to think of the numberless things which can prevent the trouble which you fear? Lastly, remember that nothing can happen without My consent. Place yourself in My care and fear nothing.

3. The devil can easily make men think wrongly when they live on their feelings. He appeals to their likes and dislikes, and so corrupts their ideas of right and wrong. He gradually guides them as he pleases. His slaves walk blindly along the road to Hell, controlled by their feelings and drugged by their imagination.

4. You will never make this mistake if you are guided by reason and faith. Listen to My voice coming to you through My Church. Follow My words. Keep your eyes on Me. Do not let the world blind you to My presence and My love. Fear not—I am near you. With Me you are walking toward eternal life. Walk bravely on and follow My Will in all things. My peace will be with you.

THINK:

Imagination and feelings rule the lives of many. As a result they fear and avoid a number of things. They do not think with their intelligence, but with their feelings. They exaggerate the unpleasant so much, that they cannot bear to face it. They are slaves of their fears. I must let my intelligence and God's grace bring light and freedom into my daily life. I'll listen often to His words as He speaks to Me through His Church and through grace. By doing this, I will be free of many fears.

PRAY:

Lord, what have I to fear? You know all things and foresee everything which is to happen to me. Nothing can happen without Your consent. You will never consent to anything which is really bad for me. Knowing all this, can I have anything other than peace in my daily life? Let me not offend You by a lack of confidence. I trust in You. I will do my best to remedy whatever difficulties arise, but whatever be the results of my efforts, I will accept them as Your holy Will. In Your all-wise and loving Will I will find my peace. *Amen.*

CHAPTER 62

Despair

CHRIST:

MY CHILD, when temptations persist and keep returning, do not despair. In all real needs I am always near and ready to help you. I will give you My grace and whatever else is necessary for you to keep out of sin.

2. Do not fear or worry. Keep your courage high, and be prepared to go on fighting your temptations. You are not lost because you are tempted often. Your human inclinations do not always follow reason, and so they provide many a temptation to sin.

3. Your first step toward safety lies in realizing your weakness. Secondly, do not become discouraged by temptations. Simply keep on doing your best to turn your mind and will toward other objects. No temptation can make you sin.

4. How often it happens that someone is making his greatest progress at the very time when he thinks that he is slipping. I look at your intention and your effort. By these I judge your loyalty to Me.

5. Go on trying for My sake. Do not consider yourself a failure simply because you feel like one. Be brave and follow Me. I have overcome the world. With My help you shall win the daily battle for Heaven.

THINK:

The tendency to give up is in all men. To overcome it, God gives us the virtue of hope. Why despair? All is not lost just because I feel that it is so. God wants me to hope in His mercy and to trust in His love. Temptations may come and go; they may even linger for hours and days, but it is my will which decides what I really want and what I am in the eyes of God.

PRAY:

My God, I want to obey Your law and follow Your Will in all things. Though my feelings may reach out for what is bad, help me to do what is right and good. Give me a glimpse of Your wisdom, so that I may see more clearly what harm and evil is in all sin. If I should fail in a moment of weakness, let me not despair. I hope in Your mercy. I trust in Your goodness and love. Never will I think that my sins are greater than Your mercy. No matter how bad I have been, Your goodness is great enough to forgive me. Give me the wisdom and strength to hate all sin in the future. I shall not despair nor will I be discouraged by my mistakes. Help me to fight an honest daily battle against all sin. *Amen.*

CHAPTER 63

Vain Hopes

CHRIST:

MY CHILD, some men depend too much on human help or earthly remedies. They forget that every earthly thing is in My hands, and that without Me nothing is of any help. Worldly men trust mainly in their own talents and possessions, or in the power and help of their friends.

2. Money, health, reputation, friends, admiration, superiority over others, these things seem like treasures to worldly men. Yet, these things are not really as valuable as they seem.

3. I am the treasure which brings peace and everlasting joy. When you have Me, you have the one treasure which cannot be taken from you. Hold on to Me by faith and loyalty. Do not depend too much on human beings or earthly helps. Your greatest hope should always be in Me.

4. My love for you will help you and save you where human friends fail and earthly things are of no assistance.

THINK:

The man who lives only for what this life can offer him, is due to face great disappointment and bitter self-reproach. The things he depends on are short-lived. When his earthly life is over, he will see what a fool he is. Jesus alone can give the unbounded love and joy which the human heart craves, but the worldly man will find that he has lost Jesus.

PRAY:

My Jesus, in You I place all my hopes and desires. To You I offer all my sorrows, trials, and disappointments. Let me never treasure what can take me away from You, nor desire anything which can keep me from doing Your holy Will. No friend nor any created thing can take Your place in my life. Stay with Me and teach me how to live my life in union with You. Enlighten me, strengthen me, and correct me, so that I may seek You first and love You above all else. *Amen.*

CHAPTER 64

Worldly Prosperity

CHRIST:

MY CHILD, at times you feel that your earthly life would be much easier if you did not have to follow My law. Worldly people seem to enjoy themselves so much, without bothering about Me. Do not be deceived by appearances. Their life is not as desirable as it may seem.

2. True, they follow after pleasure and forget themselves for the present. In everyone's life, however, there arrive moments when his thoughts turn to himself. One is bound to reflect sooner or later on the shortness of earthly satisfactions. The man who has forgotten Me, will look back and see all his pleasures and joys at an end. Never again will he look forward to happiness.

3. Even while enjoying this world's good things, the worldly man has his share of worries, bitterness, and fear. He knows the meaning of disappointment and failure.

4. As smoke disappears quickly in mid-air, so too will earth's joys vanish. Often

enough earthly pleasures cease pleasing even before they have been lost. What was supposed to bring happiness, too often brings sorrow and disappointment. Many a prominent man of the world ended his days in bitterness.

5. How sad to see young people looking forward to joys and satisfactions which older worldlings have already found too brief and disappointing. Blindly and foolishly, youth runs after the pleasures of earth, forgetting about the only lasting joy—Heaven. Falsely they reason: Why think now about Heaven or hell when death is still so far off?

THINK:

What fools we humans are! We think straight on so many things but when it comes to thinking about eternity, our thinking slows down or stops altogether. To get a clear idea of the shortness of earthly pleasures and joys, I need only to look on the happiness of last year, or even last week. It seemed so all-important then, but it is now faded and gone. Will I ever have so much esteem for that kind of prosperity and happiness that I would sin for them? Would I risk the never-ending and perfect happiness of Heaven for such brief and incomplete happiness? Only a fool would hesitate at such a choice.

PRAY:

My loving God, You want to give me the very best, the all-satisfying happiness of Heaven. You do not forbid me the enjoyments of earthly life, so long as I use them intelligently and rightly. What You forbid is my foolish love for what is wrong and unworthy of my human dignity. Grant me a love for your wisdom, and let me follow Your Will in all things. You alone can give me the perfect, unimaginable happiness which will fill my soul with eternal joy. You ask me to prepare myself for it by a life of goodness and wisdom on earth. I hope in Your help. I now begin again, dear Lord. *Amen.*

CHAPTER 65

Desire for Human Appreciation

CHRIST:

MY CHILD, some people are anxious to make a good impression and to be

esteemed. Others have a strong desire for
many friends. Though these things are
good, to seek them too intently is dangerous.
Such a desire can make a man more eager to
please men than to please Me.

2. Though you owe every man a reasonable consideration and respect, you owe
Me far more. When people expect you to do
something foolish or downright sinful, rise
above all human consideration and remain
loyal to Me. In your daily life, treasure My
love and friendship above all else. If you are
wise, you will avoid anyone who draws you
away from Me.

3. Sometimes you do your neighbor more
good by not letting him know you too well.
Familiarity may show him faults and defects which he had not suspected of you.
Because of this he may lose the inspiration
which your words and example had previously given to him. You need have no fear of
being a hypocrite, as long as you are really
trying to become as good as others think you
are. Too often people will judge you more by
your failures and weaknesses than by your
efforts and ideals.

4. It is foolish to fix your heart on human favor and approval. What others think of you will often depend on what they themselves are, or on how they feel at the time. Human favor is not always based on truth. For My sake give due consideration to every man, but do not seek human admiration and appreciation.

5. Sometimes it is best to avoid human attention and to seek Me in solitude. The praises and admiration of men can turn your head to thoughts of pride, vanity, and foolish self-satisfaction. Some think you better than you really are, and others think you worse. I know what you really are and what you are trying to be.

THINK:

One who is eager to be understood and appreciated by men is a weak man. In this life God alone esteems me as I deserve. His judgment of me will be known and accepted by all men on the last day. The secret of true greatness is to follow God's Will in all things. I need not care for a single instant what any man may think or say. Nothing on earth is more foolish and empty than the unkind thoughts and rash judgments of human beings.

PRAY:

My God, human judgments depend on so many changing circumstances! I can never hope to please You, and still please everyone else in this life. Let me never needlessly offend any human being. Yet, when it is a matter of doing what is right, let me not fear human opinions. Your judgments will stand before all men and angels at the Last Judgment. I want Your approval of my life, because Your word is Truth. *Amen.*

CHAPTER 66

Foolish Pride

CHRIST:

MY CHILD, whatever good things you possess, do not think too highly of yourself. Let Me be your greatest treasure, and let everything else take second place.

2. Whether you be rich, or powerful, or popular, or attractive, remember the plain truth about yourself, and you will not become a victim of foolish pride.

3. Whatever good is in you, it belongs to Me. The things of which men so often boast, are Mine. They consider themselves better than their neighbor because of some talent, ability, or circumstance which I placed at their disposal. I could just as easily have given these things to those who are at present less gifted.

4. Do as much good as you can in your daily life, but beware of becoming proud of your deeds. Without Me you can do nothing. If you consider yourself better than others, you are certainly a fool. I can make anybody and everybody else your superior if I so choose.

THINK:

If God has numbered the very hairs of my head, how can I think highly of myself? I am completely dependent on Him for my next breath. This knowledge should make me fear all pride and self-satisfaction. I can never be impressed deeply enough by the fact of my nothingness. Of myself and without God's gifts, I am nothing. This fact is the basis of all true humility. Can I ever consider myself better than any human on earth? How do I feel when others look down on me? So too, do others feel when I show a sense of superiority. Even if I do not show it, God sees my pride and hates it, because pride is based on a false self-esteem.

PRAY:

My God, lover of Truth, only You are great by Your very nature! All other greatness, virtue, and goodness are Your gifts to us. Have mercy on this proud heart of mine. Please impress me with the truth of my nothingness. Then will I, at last, become kind, considerate, and charitable to those around me. Grant me Your grace, dear Lord, and I will never again, in thought or action, raise myself above anyone else. In gratitude for Your many gifts, I will try to spread Your goodness by being good to others. Kill the pride within me, even if you have to humble me before others. Only spare me the terrible humiliation of having the whole world see my ugly pride at the Last Judgment. *Amen.*

CHAPTER 67

Self-Deception

CHRIST:

MY CHILD, you have no idea how easy it is for men to deceive themselves in this earthly life. Many think that they are living a good life simply because they are performing a few external works. They go to church once or twice a week, say some prayers daily, and commit no public crimes.

2. Yet, I am displeased with them. In their everyday life, they live as though they depended not on Me, but on themselves alone. In a crowd they are not particularly noticeable for their patience, or kindness, or sympathy, or unselfishness.

3. Many are too interested in following their daily occupations and interests to bother how I want them to follow these things. They do not deny My wisdom in theory. They simply disregard it in practice. They act as though I did not quite understand their daily problems. Actually it is they who do not understand their daily problems. If they followed My words,

many of their difficulties would cease being problems.

4. Some people are afraid to apply My words to their everyday life. They are afraid of losing some worldly advantage or earthly enjoyment. These are the people who want to get to Heaven with the least possible inconvenience to themselves. They work, sweat, and suffer, and sacrifice for their earthly interests. Their only check is their fear of hell, not their love for Me.

5. Some people worry their way through life. They do not realize how very interested I am in their daily life, how very dear they are to Me. They act as though I were not interested in their daily needs and difficulties. Too seldom do they think of My nearness, power, wisdom, and love as they go about their daily business.

6. True, a number of these people are being blindly and foolishly selfish with Me. Still, this is not the case with all of them. The real reason why many give Me a partial loyalty and do only part of what I command, is that they do not see how My words are to be applied in their daily life. They read:

"Thou shalt not kill," and then in the same Scriptures they read how I sent My chosen people to make war on their enemies. They find mysteries and apparent contradictions in the Bible, and so, in their confusion, they make up a religion of their own.

7. For this reason did I establish My Church. I gave My Apostles and their followers the power to preach My Truth to all, and I promised to be with them until the end of time. With My help, My Church will interpret My words and commandments. I did not intend that men should have good will and still go on in doubt, guess-work, confusion and fear.

THINK:

There is no reason for self-deception in my following of Christ. I can learn His Will through His Church. If my strength fails me, I can double and triple it over and over again through the Sacraments. My daily life proves how true are my faith in Jesus and my love for Him. Am I one of those whose lives prove them atheists or selfish followers with weak faith, feeble confidence, and cool love?

PRAY:

Jesus, my King and Lord, how much more must You do to prove to me Your wisdom, power, and love? I want my daily life to prove that I believe in You, trust in You, and love You above all else. Help me to learn more about Your religion, so that I may appreciate it better. I hope to make better use of Your holy Sacraments, so that You may give me the strength to do what my natural strength can never accomplish. You want me to give You an intelligent service and loyalty. I want the same thing. I hope to begin today to follow You to Heaven. *Amen.*

CHAPTER 68

The Virtue of Self-Distrust

CHRIST:

MY CHILD, as long as you are on earth, you cannot be certain of your true worth. Only after death will you know everything about yourself. Each day you will learn more about yourself, even things which you do not now suspect.

2. Every man is something of a mystery to himself. In every human heart there is plenty of room for self-deception. The intention which you claim, may not be the real reason which moves you. Deep within you there may be other reasons, selfish, worldly reasons. Because of this truth I want you to develop a healthy self-distrust and a supernatural trust in My help. No matter how holy you may feel, never trust yourself too far. Refuse to rely on yourself alone. Without Me you are nothing, and without My help, you can do nothing worthy of Heaven.

3. Your first reaction to this truth might be to worry about your salvation. I have no desire to alarm you, nor do I wish to make you an abnormal self-centered person. I simply want you to live according to the truth. I did not die on the cross that you might be lost, but that you might gain Heaven. You must do your part in this plan. Make a sincere intention to obey My commandments in your daily life. Prove your sincerity by an honest daily effort. In any doubt consult My Church for direction. After you have done

all this, place all your hope and confidence in My love and mercy.

4. My saints were truly wise in their suspicion of self. Realizing that eternity awaited them in Heaven or hell, they were determined to take no chances with self-deception. They overcame it by a holy self-contempt and self-distrust. They did this in an intelligent way. They fixed their eye on My boundless perfection, the passing nature of earthly life, and the folly of losing Heaven's eternal joy and glory. This vision convinced them that I deserved the best from them, and that their best was all too little for Me. They made doubly sure of their unselfishness with Me by avoiding many things which self-desired and by embracing many things which self-disliked.

5. Even while practicing all this self-denial, they continued to pray that no self-deception might remain in their souls. They made frequent acts of hope, that their good works, penances, and prayers might be acceptable to Me. Without worry, fear, or foolish distress, they admitted My infinite greatness, confessed their weakness and littleness,

and appealed to My mercy and love to help them gain eternal life.

THINK:

How true! So often when I thought I was doing something for God, I became angry, spiteful, or uncharitable toward those who interfered with my plans! The fact that I lost my self-control was proof that I was not working for God at all! My worst enemy is within me—this blind, puny, selfish self! Only when I act for God alone, will my action be at its best. I must pray daily with humility and with hope that I may overcome this contemptible self within me. It deserves contempt because it opposes God's wisdom and goodness. I should treat this self as though it were a child which needs to be trained. Then I should proceed to train it daily by acts of unselfishness and self-denial.

PRAY:

My God, the wisest men of all times are Your saints. You were the object of all their desires. Everything else was secondary. I too desire to place You first in my life. In order to do this I shall have to control this blind, self-seeking self within me. You want what is good for me, not just a temporary good, but what is best for me forever. In following self, I shall lose You. O let me make efforts to be sure that self shall never control me. I want to practice more prayer, unselfishness, and self-denial in my daily activities. I shall seek greater strength in Your Sacraments. Let me treat this foolish self within me with the contempt it deserves. This will be much easier if I keep my eyes on Your wonderful goodness and love. *Amen.*

CHAPTER 69

Interior Honesty

CHRIST:

MY CHILD, when I give you heavenly light and strength do not become proud and self-satisfied. Remember how weak and miserable you are when you are without these gifts. One who is over-confident when matters are going well, often goes to the other extreme of discouragement, sadness, or fear when temptations and difficulties come.

2. Be convinced of your complete dependence on Me. Without Me you are nothing. A deep appreciation of this truth will help

you to control your thoughts and desires. It will keep you strong in time of temptation, so that you will not fall so easily into sin.

3. Fight like a good soldier. If you should fall through weakness, pray for greater help and rise with more determination than before. Beware of self-satisfaction and pride. These two evils lead men into error and sometimes make them incurably blind to their faults and failures. Learn your lesson from the downfall of those who foolishly trusted to their own ability. Let it be a warning to keep you always humble.

THINK:

God has a definite plan for me, a plan which is mainly concerned with my eternal salvation. At times He gives me an interior joy, peace, and eagerness to do more good. At other times He takes away these interior gifts, and I feel dejected, dull, perhaps even sad and discouraged. A level-headed person tries to live a balanced life, without giving in to his moods and feelings. When God sends him spiritual light and joy, he tries to enjoy these gifts with self-control, remembering that shortly he will experience spiritual trials which will take away this present enjoyment. So too, in time of trial, he reminds himself of the joy which he had previously and will have again in due time. Such a person avoids extreme changeableness and the undependability of those who act on their feelings and moods. He is reliable both with God and with his fellow-men, because he seeks to keep control of himself, whether he feels himself raised up in joy or submerged in spiritual darkness and sadness.

PRAY:

My God and Creator, the truth is that I am completely dependent on You for all things. Without You I am nothing and can do nothing. If I admit this dependence on You by my daily life, I shall become truly great. Make me honest enough to live according to this truth. I hope to strive harder to please You in my daily occupations and activities. I will refuse to become proud when I enjoy Your gifts, nor will I become discouraged when You take Your gifts away from me. You have reasons for the way You treat me. I hope to keep my mind on Your boundless wisdom and love, whatever happens today.

Whether I enjoy peace or suffer trials, I want my loyalty to Your holy Will to remain unchanged and unwavering. *Amen*.

CHAPTER 70

Temptation to Presumption

CHRIST:

MY CHILD, the devil tempts you to the sin of presumption in two ways. He does it either by suggesting that My mercy will easily spare you from the punishment due to your sins, or by convincing you that you are strong enough to face any temptation. He is the father of lies and the arch-deceiver. My mercy is above all My works, but it does not destroy My justice.

2. Though I suffered and died to obtain pardon for your sins, you must also do your part in the work of salvation. Have faith in Me; obey My Church; do penance for your sins; and avoid the near occasions of sin. Only if you do your part, will you receive My mercy. Once you are called by the Angel of death, the time for mercy will be over. Then you will meet only justice.

3. As for relying too much on your own strength, remember your complete dependence on Me for each breath, each heartbeat, each second of life. Whoever thinks himself independent and strong, is a fool. He who loves danger shall perish in it. If you presume too much on your strength, you will find yourself weaker than you ever expected.

4. When I give you interior light and heavenly strength, do not be too ready to make them known to others. Remember your unworthiness, and you will make better use of My gifts. You will use them gratefully, humbly and carefully.

THINK:

Presumption is a fool's dream. Man is nothing if God abandons him. One who is convinced of his complete dependence on God, is safe from the sin of presumption and from many other sins. He works and does his best, trusting in God for the necessary strength. When he succeeds in anything, he gives thanks to God. If he fails, he offers God his intentions and his efforts. I should look to God in all things. By being truthful and honest with myself, I will avoid the sin of presumption. God will grant me light and strength to walk daily toward eternal life.

PRAY:

My God and my All, bestow on me the wisdom and honesty to admit my nothingness. Let me do this not merely with words, but especially by my daily actions. Let me not pretend to be bigger than I really am. I will never again try to do what is above my strength. As far as possible I hope to avoid all occasions of serious sin. Those who presume on their own strength and wisdom, are in danger of falling away from You. I desire only that I may daily do my best for Your sake. *Amen.*

CHAPTER 71

Folly of Over-Confidence

CHRIST:

MY CHILD, beware of over-confidence. It can hurt you badly. Never be satisfied with yourself, but try to become better each day.

2. The only man who is safe from serious sin, is the one who fears it. You are very weak. The lightest temptation would conquer you, were it not for My grace.

3. Do not take chances; avoid every occasion of sin, whether it be a person, a place, or a thing.

4. The saints, with all their virtues and penances, did not trust themselves at all. How can you take chances, with all your faults and weaknesses? He that loves danger shall perish in it. If you want to gamble with your soul, remember that you yourself are the stake. You will be lost forever in hell if you die in mortal sin.

5. The only security from hell is a life of continual effort against your faults and weaknesses. Pray often for strength and avoid all near occasions of sin.

THINK:

The security of sinners arises from presumption, pride, and spiritual blindness. Eternity is never-ending. The very possibility of losing Heaven is a terrifying thought. That is why the saints refused to take chances with temptations and sin.

The reward which God will give to his loyal followers is too grand for any description. So too, the eternal state of the lost souls is more terrible than I can even imagine. I cannot afford to take chances in my daily life. I may hope in God's mercy and help, but never should I presume on His goodness. God is kind in every way, but He cannot tolerate presumption. He will not take me to Heaven unless I have done my part to gain this glorious privilege. After I die, His infinite justice will treat me as I deserve.

PRAY:

My loving Father, God of Truth, let me see how truly wonderful Your plan of salvation is. To every man You give many opportunities to rise above this visible earthly life, with its limitations and passing satisfactions. All of us are given the grace to develop a supernatural life of virtue. Each one has the opportunity to share Your divine wisdom by following Your Will. Your grace gives us a heavenly strength to rise above the forces and attractions of this world. Whatever I achieve on earth, let me always remember that without you I am nothing. To You be all thanks, praise, and loyal service each hour of the day. *Amen.*

CHAPTER 72

The Danger of Over-Confidence

CHRIST:

MY CHILD, the security which My saints felt was always tempered with a healthy fear of My justice, but the security of worldly men arises from their pride or presumption. Such men have succeeded in deceiving themselves. They would be horrified if they could see the indescribable risk which they are taking.

2. I want you to have a normal, healthy self-confidence, but be sure that it is based on facts. One fact is that without Me you can do nothing. Self-reliance is good only when it comes from a strong confidence in Me.

3. The self-reliance and over-confidence of worldly men comes from a mistaken idea of their own greatness, or from a selfish notion that I will pardon them regardless of their faults. Then again, some feel that

they are strong enough to face any occasion of sin.

4. At times those who were most respected and admired by men, were in great danger because they forgot their human weakness.

5. Temptations are no sin. In fact, they are often a blessing in disguise because they help men to realize how weak they are. Still, to place oneself in temptation is folly. He that loves danger can only blame himself if he perishes in it. No man can afford to take chances in the matter of temptation. You will have enough to do simply fighting off the temptations which come uninvited. Do not trust yourself too far or you will be placing yourself in temptation.

THINK:

Over-confidence is dangerous. It makes me take risks where there is serious danger of sin. God cannot bless foolishness, and over-confidence is foolishness. I will trust in God, but I will not tempt Him to abandon me to my stupidity. I will bravely face the dangers which have to be faced in my daily life. When, however, I am able to avoid occasions of sin, I will not hesitate to do so.

PRAY:

My Jesus, can I reasonably expect Your help if I do not bother to avoid occasions of sin? Why do I think that I can take chances? The man who takes risks in this matter is being presumptuous. He expects You to give him extra graces against the danger which he brings on himself. I must do Your Will, not mine. Lord, I shall never fail to have confidence in Your assistance, but I refuse to place myself unnecessarily in any danger of sin. That is the wisdom which You desire of me. Let me avoid, as far as possible, all persons and things which draw me closer to sin. I hope that I may never offend You by over-confidence in my own ability or in presuming on Your extra help. *Amen.*

CHAPTER 73

The Dangers of Knowledge

CHRIST:

MY CHILD, knowledge is often the cause of pride and vanity. Some people consider themselves better than others because of their knowledge. They do not realize that knowledge is worth nothing unless it makes one a better man in his daily life.

2. Knowledge can bring many useless distractions. Many things will make no difference in your life whether you know them or not.

3. Some are so distracted by the pursuit of knowledge that they no longer consider their faults and defects. If they were as diligent in rooting out vices and acquiring virtues as they are eager for knowledge, the world would be a better place.

4. Some prefer to be honored rather than be humble, and they are lost in their own self- centered imaginings. They are ruined through vain learning and unprofitable knowledge because they forget Me.

5. The self-wise are rarely able to take orders. They value others only by their knowledge or lack of it, as though man were made up only of intellect.

THINK:

Knowledge is half the man. Action is the other half. The more I learn the more will I see that I am ignorant of many things. True education humbles a man by showing him the grandeur of God's creation, and his own littleness. The most learned men are deeply aware that they know little. If ever I think that education makes me better than my neighbor, then I have missed the spirit of true education. True education should show me more and more of God's place in the world and the glorious meaning of everyday life. Every bit of knowledge can help me in some way, but I must prefer to learn best whatever will enrich my life most, God's teachings through His Church. Unless my learning leads me on to a better life, it is a waste of precious time. A virtuous life makes me dear to God. Education is intended to help me live such a life.

PRAY:

My Jesus, what will it profit me to talk and dispute about great things, if I am not doing great things? My greatest achievement before Your heavenly Father is to advance each day a little closer to Your holiness and goodness. On the Day of Judgment, I shall not be asked how much I have learned, but rather how much I have done. True, I must first learn what is to be done, but let me not think more of learning than of doing. I want to understand ever better what You desire of me. Then, with Your help, I wish to go forth and do it. *Amen*.

CHAPTER 74

Knowledge Without Virtue

CHRIST:

MY CHILD, the desire for knowledge is natural and normal, but it is not good unless this knowledge helps you to become a better man. A simple workingman who follows My words is far better than a learned professor who does not care about My commandments.

2. Your daily life is a journey toward eternity. The knowledge which helps you to gain Heaven, is the first and most important knowledge for you. The more you learn of Me and My doctrine, the better for you.

3. All other knowledge is to be esteemed according to how it helps you to live a holier and more useful life. There are many things which are unimportant in your particular walk of life.

4. If some men were more diligent in rooting out their faults and correcting their defects, they would be much better off than they now are, with their learned discussions about many things.

5. It is better to be great than merely to be considered great. You will be great if you learn My words and act on them in your daily life. If you merely talk about a holy life, you may impress men, but I know you for what you are—a failure forever.

THINK:

Some people value education for itself. They see in it man's greatest achievement. They are mistaken. Knowledge is of no value unless it makes me a better man. It should broaden my view of life, bring me a deeper understanding of people and things, and make me better prepared to receive God's graces. If education makes me more self-centered and proud, if it makes me despise others, it is bad for me. True education should help me live a virtuous life by helping me appreciate God's wonderful creation.

PRAY:

Holy Spirit, my God, inspire me with a love for good and with a healthy knowledge. Show me how to live what I learn, as far as that is possible in my daily life. It is better to live your words than to preach them eloquently or teach them beautifully. The man who can quote line after line of Holy Scripture, is not as great in Your eyes as the one who puts those lines into daily practice. Show me ever more clearly how completely I belong to You. Let no other knowledge ever obscure this first and highest knowledge. *Amen.*

CHAPTER 75

Shifting Moods and Feelings

CHRIST:

MY CHILD, do not become discouraged because your interior dispositions change so easily. At one moment you are filled with a burning desire to serve Me, and a short while later you feel alone and uninterested. Do not be surprised nor saddened by this instability within you. By this process your soul is purified of selfishness in serving Me. In spite of your changing moods and feelings, you can still prove your loyalty to Me. Simply refuse to abandon the intentions and resolutions which you made previously. Even My saints experienced such changes, but they were determined to please Me regardless of feelings or moods.

2. Your feeling of devotion is a gift from Me for the present moment. After you make a good resolution, I may take away this feeling so that you may prove your sincerity or discover your insincerity. It is easy to make high resolves and great promises. Everybody does this in moments of devout sentiments or emotions. Too often, however, good resolutions vanish with one's changing feelings or moods.

3. I want you to live an intelligent life. I give you grace to understand what is better and to desire it. Then I offer you strength and opportunity to follow what is intelligent. If you still go after the better thing when your good feelings have vanished, you prove yourself truly noble, unselfish with Me, and worthy of My friendship and glory in Heaven.

THINK:

No man is ready to see God face to face in Heaven until he has proved himself ready. He must be purified of blind self-interest. As gold is purified in the burning crucible, so too, is it with me. I cannot be sure of my own sincerity until it has been purified by the various occurrences of daily life. By the way in which I take my successes and failures, my moments of satisfaction and my moments of want, I will see what I really am, or need to be. When my will accepts and chooses what God's holy Will sends, only then will I be as great as I was meant to be. To arrive at this, I must conquer my changing moods and feelings by intelligent activity.

PRAY:

In light or darkness, sorrow or joy, let me turn to You, my God, and let me prove that I really am what You want me to be. My words of gratitude, loyalty, and love must shine out in action. Talk is cheap until it is backed up by the gold of action. My moods will change, and my feelings will vary throughout the day, but my will desires to follow Your holy Will in each task and occupation. Grant me strength to prove my real worth by action. *Amen*.

CHAPTER 76

Spiritual Consolation and Desolation

CHRIST:

MY CHILD, when I give you spiritual consolation, accept it gratefully. Remember always that it is a free gift, not due to any merits of yours. Dismiss all self-satisfaction and pride from your heart. I am the source of all that you enjoy. This realization will give you a healthy humility when I grant you some special favor. Beware of vanity. Abandon all foolish ideas of your own value and abilities. Remember, this hour of consolation will pass away, and a time of trial will follow.

2. When consolation is taken from you, do not become sluggish and disinterested in your usual tasks and occupations. Keep up your prayers and good works. Humbly accept My Will and patiently go on with your daily activities. The grace of consolation and enthusiasm will return in due time.

3. These interior changes from consolation to desolation, from joy to sadness, from light to darkness, are not an unusual experience. All of My faithful followers have passed through them. By their steadiness of purpose they proved that they really loved Me more than they loved My gifts.

4. Keep your eyes on Me, whether you are in joy or sadness, whether matters are moving along smoothly or roughly. Whether your heart is filled with doubts or with joyful confidence in Me, see that you follow My words in your daily occupations. Then will your daily life be a steady progress toward the home of peace and eternal happiness.

THINK:

God gives every man the chance to know and improve his character. Many a person did not know his limitations and faults until he met successes and failures. That is why each one has his "ups and downs," moments of satisfaction and moments of trial. The true man of God tries to live a life based on intelligent principles. He does not act on emotion or impulse unless the action makes sense.

PRAY:

Lord, in sorrow or joy, success or failure, I want to live my life intelligently according to Your law. The sorrows and joys of earth are all too short. Hence they should not rule my actions in any sinful way. I am living for Heaven's eternal happiness. Let me not lose that because of any passing hardship or good thing on earth. Lead me through whatever joys or sorrows You want. Only grant me the favor of finally arriving at the perfect life of Heaven. *Amen.*

CHAPTER 77

Progress in Time of Desolation

CHRIST:

MY CHILD, progress in the spiritual life does not consist in having a great deal of interior joy and consolation. It consists in being humble, patient, and free from self-pity when things go wrong. Faithfully go on with your affairs, and do not become careless in your prayers and good works when you no longer find pleasure in them. Continue doing your best in your daily duties in spite of any disinterest, anxiety, or even disgust.

2. Some people grow impatient and careless in serving Me when things do not go as they desire. It is not always in a man's power to choose what he wants in his earthly life. In spite of all your plans and precautions, you can not avoid all disappointments. Even the mistakes and sins of others, which make your life harder, are permitted for a good reason.

3. I have a plan for you, by which you may become truly great. I send you what is best for you. If you follow My Will, you will have My peace on earth and My joy in Heaven. If you rebel, you will hurt yourself and probably some of the people in your life. I owe you nothing. You owe Me absolutely everything. Whether you receive much or little, you are always in debt to Me for all things.

THINK:

Many people judge their closeness to God by their feelings. If they feel devout, they believe they are pleasing Him, and if they feel dejected and gloomy, they think that He has abandoned them. These standards are false and deceitful. I may be proving my best love for God when I least feel like pleasing Him. As long as I fulfill what He expects of me, I do love Him, no matter how I feel. Jesus Himself said: "If you love Me, you will keep My commandments." There is the test of true goodness and holiness. As long as I am following His holy Will, I am following God's wonderful plan for my salvation and the salvation of those with whom I deal. At times feelings may help me to serve God with more enthusiasm, but it is my will that really shows how much I am worth in His eyes. In time of desolation, I should cling to my resolutions and go on with my religious practices as I did when I enjoyed doing these things. That is the way of intelligent love, the way in which God wants to be loved.

PRAY:

Dear Lord, make me the kind of follower You desire me to be—an intelligent follower. No feelings nor moods should determine how I am to serve You this day, I ought to do my best to see Your holy Will and to follow it, without letting my feelings rule my intelligence or control my will. No matter how I may feel about what I must suffer, I know this: You are always watching over me, always helping me walk toward Heaven. Even the evil which You permit in my life, has its higher purpose. You will some day be praised for many things which men now question. With eyes fixed on You, let me go on fulfilling Your holy Will each day. You are my true and perfect Joy, my eternal Glory, my never-fading Crown. *Amen.*

CHAPTER 78

God's Words to the Desolate

CHRIST:

MY CHILD, believe in Me. Put your trust in My love and mercy. Many a time, when you think that I am far from you, I am very close to you. When you feel as though everything is going wrong, then it is that you can give the best proof of your faith and your loyalty to Me.

2. You are not a failure just because things turn out differently from what you desired. Do not judge things by your disappointment or dislike. Keep discouragement

out of your heart, no matter how hopeless matters may appear. Do your best and accept the results as My Will.

3. I am your Maker and your loving God. Your most hidden thoughts are clearly seen by Me. Your eternal salvation is My main interest. When you feel disinterested and disgusted with your daily activities, remember that I have good reasons for letting you feel so.

4. If I have taken anything away from you, you cannot rightfully complain. You cannot claim anything as your own, not even yourself. All things are Mine. Without Me you are actually nothing. Even when I seem to deal harshly with you, I deserve praise and obedience, because My actions proceed from eternal wisdom, and infinite love.

5. What I do to you is done because I love you far more than you love yourself or anyone else. When I send you any trouble or affliction, do not complain or become sad. Peace and contentment will come to you as soon as it is for your best interests.

THINK:

In all things God loves me and thinks of my true happiness. Because I am short-sighted and self-centered, I complain when things go wrong. God could prevent many a disagreeable experience of mine. He doesn't do so for very good reasons. As I grow older and wiser, I shall see how much I over-estimated the passing successes or comforts of earthly life.

PRAY:

Dear Lord, if I knew how very wise You are, and how much You love me, I would soon learn to be content with Your holy Will. In my selfishness, I desired a heaven on earth as well as after death. Now I want to accept Your Will in all things. Whether You send me consolation or desolation, let me serve You as You deserve. I shall try my best to improve myself in daily life. After I have done my best, I shall accept the results as Your holy Will. *Amen.*

PART FOUR
Conquering Bad Habits

BAD HABITS are evil inclinations acquired through repeated bad acts. Unless we overcome these habits, they will gradually become our masters. They come between Our Lord and us, and they can cripple our good will. In order to be true followers of Christ, we must refuse to be the slaves of our bad habits. In Him alone will we find true peace and joy.

How are we to deal with bad habits? A Kempis tells us: Habit is overcome by habit (*Bk. 1, c. 21*). By working to form good habits, we will slowly replace bad ones. God's help will not be wanting.

Just how sincere we are when we say that we love Christ, is seen in our daily effort for perfection. God will not judge us by our failures, but rather, by our efforts. He wants us to try, and to keep trying, to become the kind of person He wants us to be. Over-confidence shows our pride and presumption. Discouragement in time of failure, shows selfishness. Only a humble, determined, and persevering effort can prove genuine love for Christ.

This part deals only with the outstanding habits which keep men from a full generosity with God. By overcoming these, a person quickly advances along the road to true holiness. Above all, we must remember that God's help is most effective with those who keep on trying, no matter how often they seem to fail.

CHAPTER 79

Generosity with God

CHRIST:

MY CHILD, do your best to follow My words in your daily life. Do not depend on human sympathy or admiration to go on living a good life. You know what is right. Do it regardless of the pleasure or pain which it gives you. Let your faith and charity be your strength.

2. If I gave you heavenly consolation for every good deed which you perform, your

life would hardly be a proof of greatness. It would be very easy and very appealing to anyone, even the most selfish. I want you to be a man of truth—one who lives what is right and follows what is true. See what I rightfully deserve, and try to give Me the pure unselfish loyalty which you owe Me. Forget yourself, follow My Will, and you will achieve true greatness—the greatness of a good and holy life.

3. Anybody can be cheerful and devoted when I give him My heavenly consolation. It is a genuine pleasure to serve Me when you enjoy My gifts of interior joy and consolation. Your real virtue and your true generosity with Me, are seen when I take away these holy feelings and inspirations. Do you still want to please Me when you do not feel like doing so? Are your faith and love strong enough to keep you close to Me when your selfish desires want to go elsewhere?

THINK:

The true love of God is not a mere sentiment. It is an intelligent conviction that I owe Him everything. It is a firm persuasion that He deserves the very best service which I can offer. With this realization God offers me the strength to do what is right and good, even when my feelings, moods, and desires, would prefer to act differently. Generosity with God means loving His Will more than my own imperfect inclinations and desires.

PRAY:

My God and my All, I offer You my best and deepest love. You are truly my All. Without You I would have nothing, and would be nothing. From You came all the good things in my life. Your generosity toward me has no limits. May I never refuse to be generous with You. I wish to embrace Your Will in all things, regardless of the selfish likes and dislikes within me. May Your Will be ever accomplished in my life. *Amen.*

CHAPTER 80

Anger

CHRIST:

MY CHILD, anybody can get along with those who are quiet and mild-tempered. It is no great accomplishment to associate with those whom you like, or with those who see things your way. True greatness is proven by getting along with people who are difficult and contrary, or with those who are thoughtless and selfish.

2. Some live at peace with themselves and with those around them. Some on the other hand, have no peace within themselves, and they seem determined to ruin the peace of others.

3. You will find peace only if you are willing to bear patiently what you cannot remedy. He who knows how to suffer patiently for My sake, will receive My gift of peace. He is master of himself, a friend of Mine and an heir of Heaven.

4. If troubles come to you, do not let them disturb you. Look to Me, and at least give Me the loyalty of being patient with My Will. If human efforts fail to bring a solution to your troubles, it means that I want you to bear this trial. I want this for good reasons, which you may not understand just now.

5. Above all, avoid anger when matters go against your wishes. Let no word of resentment fall from your lips. Give a good

example of faith and confidence in Me. Let your patience shine before men.

6. Do not force others to share your troubles by making them feel your impatience, anger or self-pity. Follow My words in these matters, and your present trouble will bring you a joy greater than you can imagine.

THINK:

Our Lord speaks of meekness and humility as two of His special lessons to me. Meekness is the virtue of gentleness with others, especially with those who arouse me to anger. Jesus wants me to take this as a personal lesson from Him. Anger and impatience are often signs of a deep pride or selfishness. I am aroused when matters do not go as I wish. The occasions for a just anger are rare enough. Most of the time I become angry because I lack understanding, or sympathy, or patience, or a willingness to suffer any more than I must. How would Our Lord take those same situations? There is my Model!

PRAY:

Jesus, meek and humble of heart, make my heart like Yours. Make this petition one of my frequent prayers. You want me to be like You. I seem to think that life would be unbearable if I practiced meekness with certain people. Let me understand that meekness is not weakness, but strength— the strength of virtue. You want me to practice meekness? I am willing to try it for Your sake. Show me how to do it. Let me no longer give in to my pride and my selfish desires by the sin of anger. When things are not going my way, let me act as You would act if You were in my place. Make me more and more like You. O Jesus, meek and humble of heart, make my heart like Yours. *Amen.*

CHAPTER 81

Impatience

CHRIST:

MY CHILD, be patient with the defects and weaknesses of others. They have to put up with your defects. If you fail so often in making yourself what you desire to be, how can you expect to change others in a short time? You want to see others correct their faults, yet you are not fighting half enough against your own.

2. You are strict in correcting others, but you are not as strict in the correction of yourself. The lazy and easy-going ways of others irritate you, still, you resent it if anyone tries to interfere with your own self-indulgence. You want others to keep the rules, but you are aroused to anger against anyone who mentions the rules to you.

3. How seldom you judge your neighbor with the same love and understanding with which you judge yourself. You are often disturbed by others because their faults and defects interfere with the routine of your life. You think that you are being zealous for what is right, but if you look honestly into your heart, you will often see self-love at the bottom of your impatience and anger.

THINK:

At times I delude myself into thinking that I am virtuous in matters where I am actually displeasing God! One sure proof that I love God is a patient love of others. The more I try to help others and to be patient with their faults, defects, and shortcomings, the more will I prove myself unselfish and generous with God. God wants me to consider Him as my neighbor. Jesus said that I do to Him what I do to others. Does my daily treatment of others show love of God or love of self? Just as I tend to favor myself in most matters, so too should I learn to favor my neighbor for God's sake. I find it easy to excuse myself. Let me try to excuse the mistakes of others.

PRAY:

My Jesus, I can never be wrong when I love my neighbor and try to think well of him in spite of his faults. True, at times I may have to be stern for his good. Yet, even then, let me act with love in my heart. Your follower must have no hatred or impatience, but only a sincere desire for the welfare of others. Let me never again displease You by any deliberate intolerance or harshness toward those around me. Make me one tenth as patient with their mistakes as You are with mine, and I will never again hurt anyone with my impatience. Remind me often of my own faults, limitations, and defects, so that I may include myself when I pray for sinners. I hope to prove my gratitude and love for You by my patience with others. *Amen.*

CHAPTER 82

Fault-Finding

CHRIST:

MY CHILD, learn the lesson which I taught over and over again by My life and words on earth. I alone am great. All earthly greatness is but an image of My un-created greatness. Man is the work of My almighty hand. Of himself man is nothing. If, however, he follows My words in his earthly life, he will share My happiness and glory in Heaven.

2. How can you think so much of yourself, when you were made from nothing? Why do you think highly of yourself? You have so many faults and defects. Be humble and live as one who admits his limitations. Do not let your actions show pride and vanity.

3. How can you find fault with others, you who are so full of faults yourself? Without My help, you would easily fall into the same mistakes which you criticize.

4. Unless it is your duty to correct others, think more of your own faults than of other people's faults. Work and fight against your own defects, and you will be too busy to be annoyed by your neighbor's defects.

5. What is the best knowledge? To know Me, to look for My holy Will, and to reflect often on how you may eliminate your faults and defects. Act on this knowledge and you will be walking on the road to eternal life.

THINK:

No matter what talents I have, I must never forget that they belong to God. Moreover, in spite of my talents and virtues, I also have faults and defects. Once I am honestly convinced of my limitations and shortcomings, I will find it easier to think well of my neighbor. If my self-love blinds me to the truth about myself, it is not true self-love. It hurts me, and makes life a little harder for those around me.

PRAY:

My Jesus, give me such a love of truth that I will never be blinded by the self-love of pride and vanity. Let my self-love be the healthy self-love of Your saints. They wanted nothing but the best for themselves. They found the best in Your holy truth. They respected themselves for what they were, and they never pretended to be bigger than they really were. Their love for others came from their realization that all men are made to God's image and are loved by Him. Give me such a love for the truth that I will follow it at all times, regardless of my likes or dislikes, prejudices or preferences. Only an honest and unselfish daily life can prove that I really love You, my King and Saviour. *Amen.*

CHAPTER 83

Rash Judgments

CHRIST:

MY CHILD, mind your own business, and do not set yourself up as the judge of those around you. There is a good deal that you do not know about your neighbor. It is not easy to judge others as they deserve. Be wise and leave all judgment to Me.

2. It is far more profitable for you to look to yourself and judge yourself. You can do a great deal about correcting your own faults.

As for the faults of others, the best you can do is to give good example, offer a bit of advice where it will help, and say a sincere prayer for the persons involved.

3. Your concern over your neighbor's faults, does not always arise from a virtue in you. Some people annoy you because you are not minding your own business, or because you have not yet learned patience and understanding.

4. People are not always at fault when they get on your nerves. The real fault is often in you. I suffered many things in silence for your sake. How often do you suffer in silence for Me?

5. Get to work and correct your own faults. You will then be too busy to be annoyed by the faults of others.

THINK:

How much peace of soul I could enjoy if only could learn to mind my own business. Judging others is such a waste of precious time. I am so often wrong when I think ill of others. If I dislike someone, I feel inclined to judge him more harshly than others. If God were my main interest, I would never think ill of anyone, even those who really offend me. How often I am aroused against someone because, knowingly or unknowingly, he has opposed my pride or selfishness in some way. I should not expect everyone to see things my way. Every man is different and each one has his own tastes and experiences. So often God excuses those whom I condemn.

PRAY:

My Lord, I long for a ray of heavenly wisdom, so that I may not be unreasonable in my judgments and opinions about others. You treat each person as an individual. You do not ask me to be like others in my ways. You only want me to take the talents and circumstances in my life, and to make the most of them. You ask us to imitate You as far as we are able, according to the intelligence and grace which each one has. Let me not judge rashly those who do not do things my way. I want to follow Your holy Will in all things. Though I observe the mistakes and faults of others, I will try to refrain from any harsh judgments. If I cannot say something kind of another, I will keep silent. *Amen.*

CHAPTER 84

Uncharitable Criticism

CHRIST:

M Y CHILD, do not believe everything which you hear about others. Men often judge their fellow-men with prejudice. Their judgments frequently depend on their temperaments, tastes, moods, ambitions, and self-love. You will usually be right if you refuse to judge another by the criticisms which you hear about him. Many a man is condemned when he is absent and cannot defend himself.

2. People feel superior when they criticize others. They are apt to exaggerate the faults of their neighbor. If you show interest in their criticisms, they may be encouraged to continue their uncharitable talk. Show disapproval of all back-biting, at least by your silence. Try to change the subject as tactfully as possible.

3. Everyone makes mistakes. The human critic may know how to do something better than this man or that man. He may not, however, know the motives or intentions

of the one he criticizes. He has no right to reveal another's hidden faults except to protect the innocent, or to help the guilty person himself.

4. Remember, too, that you may well be the object of the speaker's criticism when you are absent. Speak now of the criticized one as you would want others to speak of you when you are criticized.

THINK:

One of the worst faults of human nature is that of condemning others. That is why Jesus taught His doctrine of charity. As I judge others, so will I be judged by God. If I condemn others, I too will be condemned. A true follower of Christ is more ready to think well of others than to think evil.

PRAY:

My Jesus, King of my heart, give me some of Your kindness, so that I may always think well of my neighbor. I do not know everything about him. Perhaps he cannot help doing what I disapprove. There may be a hundred excusing causes for what he does. Let me leave all judgment in Your hands and try to overlook what others do. Teach me to mind my own business and to pray for those who seem to need it. Never will I forget Your great Mercy to me, a sinner. As You forgive me, so may I always forgive those who offend me. Never will I reveal the hidden faults of another, except where I am obliged to protect those who are innocent or for the public good. *Amen.*

CHAPTER 85

The Folly of Worldliness

CHRIST:

MY CHILD, beware of the spirit of worldliness It blinds one to the truth and makes him think more of this earthly life than of the world to come. It so deceives a man that he is more ready to work for death than for life. He becomes more interested in appearing great than in actually being great by living a good life.

2. If worldly men took time to think of their earthly life, they would quickly realize how foolish they are for loving it too much. In this world there is so much opposition, pain, sorrow, disappointment, and disillusionment. Rarely are earthly ambitions

fully satisfied. The worldly man often finds bitterness where he had expected sweetness. In the things and people on whom he relied, he sees so many limitations and short-comings. Sooner or later, he will have to admit that the happiness, peace, and satisfaction for which he hoped, are not of this world.

3. Do not let appearances fool you. The worldly man is doomed to disappointment, but My followers will never be disappointed as long as they are devoted to My Will. My promises are not empty words, nor will they deceive those who trust in Me. What I have promised, I will give. What I have said, I will do, if only you will continue to be loyal to the end.

THINK:

The man who follows his feelings and refuses to think, keeps chasing after permanent happiness and peace, where he can never find them. He goes on hoping that after the present failures and disappointment, he will find at last what he has not found thus far. Little does he dream that only in the friendship and love of God can he find what he desires.

PRAY:

My God, all-loving and all-wise, may I find bitterness in any person or thing which holds me back from You. Take away from me whatever leads me into sin. Grant that I may never be enslaved by my feelings, but rather give me an interior vision which will detect sin in all its disguises. Bestow on me courage to resist evil, patience to go on doing what is right, and endurance to continue doing my best. I long for the interior joy of Your friendship and company. Instead of foolish earthly attachments, I want a strong love for Your wise and holy Will in all things. *Amen.*

CHAPTER 86

Needless Curiosity

CHRIST:

MY CHILD, uncontrolled curiosity draws your attention away from your duties and brings needless distractions. It can waste a good deal of time and energy which you might use to greater good. It leads to pointless visiting and useless conversations. It fills the mind with so many empty distractions, which prevent you from freely receiving the holy thoughts and good desires which I send you throughout the day.

2. You would have great peace if you were less curious about things which do not concern you. One who is too interested in the sayings and doings of others, becomes forgetful of the glorious ideal which I present to him—the ideal of pleasing Me in all things and thereby gaining eternal life.

3. Many things occur during the day which do not help you become a better person. What does it matter whether this one has a new garment or that one has failed in some personal project? Think of what concerns you, and of any good which you can do to others. Keep your heavenly goal before your mind, as far as your daily occupations will permit. Avoid idle words and useless activities.

THINK:

A curious nature, intelligently controlled, has often led men to make great discoveries.

Yet, unless curiosity is controlled, it can hurt me forever. My highest interest must be to follow God's law, and so to enter into eternal life. The less I burden my mind with unnecessary interests, the more will I understand and appreciate my supernatural purpose on earth. Too many worldly interests make me forget or disregard my heavenly goal. Many sins of omission and carelessness spring from uncontrolled curiosity.

PRAY:

Jesus, my King, Your enemies are whoever and whatever draws me farther from You and closer to sin. Therefore uncontrolled curiosity is Your enemy. If I am loyal to You, I will fight this enemy of Yours. In so doing, I will also be fighting for my own eternal happiness. Lord, give me light to recognize this enemy and to oppose it in my daily life. *Amen.*

CHAPTER 87

Curiosity of the Eyes

CHRIST:

MY CHILD, many a sinful thought and desire was brought into your soul by your curiosity to see things. This fault draws you toward the dangerous attractions of the world. The memory stores up pictures of what is seen, and in a sense makes these pictures a part of you.

2. By a reasonable control of your eyes, you will find it easier to keep in touch with Me throughout the day. External temptations will not reach your imagination so easily. There will be fewer sinful thoughts and desires to disturb your peace of soul. Many a temptation comes because of your failure to control your eyes.

3. This lack of control is not always due to carelessness or laziness. Sometimes you look at an object to get at least a partial enjoyment of what is forbidden. This is simply another compromise in which you try to serve two masters—your unreasoning natural desires and Me.

4. Sometimes you will tire of My company because you are not enjoying what I command. At such times you will seek to escape from yourself by a freer use of your eyes. I do not begrudge a reasonable need to freshen your spirit with a change of scenery, a new outlook, or new ideas. I merely warn you against too free and easy a use of your eyes.

5. Often what you really need is to renew your good intentions and your motives for serving Me. What is the good of continually seeing new sights? They distract you from your supernatural goal. Desire only enough change to improve the quality of your good works and prayers.

6. Worldly people continually run away from themselves by distracting themselves and feeding their curiosity. A man of God seeks to keep before him the glorious purpose of his daily life—to gain Heaven. He controls his curiosity because it decreases his self-control and disturbs his contact with Me.

THINK:

There is nothing new under the sun. By controlling my eyes I will not be missing much. By looking into my own heart I can see the emotions, tendencies, and desires which move all humans. If I saw everything which is happening at this moment, how much would I learn to improve my life? It is far better to live with God, attend to my affairs and not be too concerned with anything else. Let men of the world bother about passing trivialities, if they so desire. I was born for higher things, things which earn an unending glory and eternal happiness.

PRAY:

My Jesus, in You I have the most interesting, most attractive, wisest, and best of friends. How can I turn from You to pay unnecessary attention to poor limited humans like myself? I sometimes tire of You because I do not know You well enough. If I took the time to contemplate Your life on earth, I would know You and appreciate You much better than I do. I would then find it easier to keep my eyes away from unimportant human events. Help me, my Jesus, to concentrate on You in my daily life, as far as my obligations will allow. *Amen*.

CHAPTER 88

Curiosity about People

CHRIST:

MY CHILD, if you will only leave others alone, they will usually leave you alone. Do not bother about other people's affairs. Look to your own business. Be sure that you are doing all that you should. Are you doing your best to please Me? If so, you are the kind of person you should be, whether or not your neighbor approves of you.

2. It is a human weakness to be curious about the doings of others. You cannot be one hundred percent loyal to Me if you have not overcome this weakness. What does it matter to you what others are doing, unless it is your duty to know? Where it is no concern of yours, go about your own business for My sake. You will not have to answer for the doings of others. You will only have to account for your own thoughts, words, deeds, and omissions.

3. I know each individual. No action, word, thought, or desire is hidden from Me. Your deepest wish and your most hidden intention are clearly seen and perfectly understood by Me. Leave everything in My hands. Make your intention each morning. Try to renew it during the day. Then go about your affairs in peace.

4. Do not pay too much attention to what others do or say unless it is your duty to do so. The unkind thoughts and unjust doings of a man will stand against him on the last day. Then will the truth shine forth, and everyone will be seen and known for what he really is.

THINK:

Minding one's own business is actually a positive good. If others need my help in any way, I ought to try to give what aid I can. As for thinking too much about their personal lives, it is a mistake. By my prayers, good example, and good will, I can offer my best assistance. Certainly I need never talk about the faults of others unless it be to someone who is concerned in the matter. Even then, if no good will come of my efforts, why make them? I have to live my life, and others must live theirs. After I have done what little I can to help them, I should enjoy peace in my own heart.

PRAY:

Dear Lord, my life is a gift from You. It is a matter which concerns You and me. True, I owe love and help to relatives, friends, and fellow-men, as far as I am able. Yet, in many things my life is something which does not concern others. Nor need I be overconcerned about others. Let me never be a victim of idle curiosity. Prevent me from talking about my neighbor, and grant that I may be slow to believe the evil that is said of him. *Amen.*

CHAPTER 89

Curiosity about One's Salvation

CHRIST:

MY CHILD, a certain person was once anxious and worried about his salvation. He threw himself down before the altar and moaned: "Oh, if only I were sure that I will be saved!" At that very moment I placed the answer in his heart. "If you knew this, what would you do? Go forth and do all the good which you would then do, and you will have no reason for fear now."

He saw at once that I had answered his question. He went out joyfully and led a good and useful life. He no longer worried about his salvation, but left his future in My hands. He was interested in one thing alone: "How does God want me to act in what I am now doing?" He who previously was selfishly afraid, was now generously brave for Me. You do the same, and you will live forever. What you will be after death, depends on what you are trying to be in this earthly life.

THINK:

If I do my best each day, I shall be living for Heaven. As long as I am trying to learn what God expects of me, and am doing my best to follow His Will, I need not fear hell.

PRAY:

Lord, I hope to please You in all that I think, do, or say. On You I depend for the grace to do this. As for my salvation, I leave it entirely in Your loving hands. If I do my best for Your sake, I know that You will not forget me. *Amen*.

CHAPTER 90

Love of Novelty and Variety

CHRIST:

MY CHILD, curiosity is a good thing as long as it is controlled by reason and grace. In many things, curiosity does more harm than good. Some people have such a desire to be considered learned and intelligent that they try to answer all difficulties and solve all problems.

2. No man knows all the answers. In fact, there are times when it is better not to know the answer. Just go along, doing your daily tasks and fulfilling your obligations. Learn whatever may help you to live a more useful and more virtuous life. Such knowledge will help you find My peace.

3. At times curiosity can interfere with your best interests. In dealing with My teachings, take them with simplicity and humility, instead of trying to understand the why and wherefore of every statement. At times it is necessary to accept My teachings

simply because they are Mine. Some truths are too deep for your limited human intelligence. If you could have learned them by yourself, I would not have come down to reveal them to you. You must accept them with faith, humility, and simplicity. Am I not the Author of all truth?

4. Control your curiosity. It is better to ignore some things as though they did not exist. You will sometimes find it best to be deaf, dumb, and blind for My sake. You are not ready yet to learn the full truth. For the present fill your mind and heart with those thoughts and desires which will help you gain eternal life. Direct your interest toward things which will make you more honest and content in your daily duties.

5. Remember, the eye is not satisfied with seeing, nor is the ear satisfied with hearing. There is more to your daily life than what you see and hear. You are surrounded by an invisible world, the world of spiritual reality. It will go on existing after this earthly world has passed away.

6. Try to learn as much as you can about the truths which I have revealed. Beware,

however, of proud curiosity, which presumes to understand all things or seeks to impress others with knowledge.

THINK:

Curiosity can lead to greater knowledge, but it can also be harmful. In relation to God's words, man's first concern must be to believe them because God inspired them. If one is more interested in studying God's words than in living them, then his curiosity is not a good thing. As long as one is doing his best to obey Christ's Church, he can safely study God's holy revelation in order to understand it better.

PRAY:

Holy Ghost, divine Inspirer of human hearts, grant me the grace to study Your words humbly and to obey them unselfishly. Let me understand ever more deeply how I may apply Your Wisdom in my daily life. The more faithfully I follow Your holy Will, the more safely and profitably will I be able to understand what You have revealed to the world through Holy Scripture and Christ's Church. *Amen.*

CHAPTER 91

Vain Reliance on Human Help

CHRIST:

MY CHILD, do not put too much trust in human friendships and human remedies. Things human can bring only a limited help in your daily needs. If you depend on them too much, you are doomed to bitter disappointments. Above all the persons and things that satisfy your needs each day, put your main trust in Me.

2. People who are for you today, may be against you tomorrow. Those who please you now, may displease you later on. The things that satisfy you at present, may dissatisfy you in the future. Do not be so foolish as to rely too much on these changeful creatures.

3. I alone know and want what is truly best for you at all times. Only I am unchanging and all-satisfying. Rely first on Me and My holy Will. Depend on everything else only as far as I permit.

4. Too few have the trust that I demand. Many lack the confidence which I desire of

them. If you will put your daily life entirely in My hands, I shall do what is best for you.

5. Heaven's perfect life is the only lasting good for you. Live your earthly life according to My law, and I shall not fail you in your really important needs.

THINK:

May I never depend too much on human beings. They can help me only up to a point. People are human like me. There is a limit to their wisdom, their understanding, and their love. Only in God will I find perfect Understanding, all-satisfying Love, and infinite Wisdom. If I can make God the First One in my daily life, there will be a great change in my outlook, my goodness, and in everything around me. No longer will people have power to rob me of my interior peace. I will not need human company as much as before. I will enjoy a new freedom from the human distractions which at present worry or frighten me.

PRAY:

In all my needs, dear Jesus, let me not depend only on human help. You must be the center of my existence. All joy, all love, all ambition, all success—everything that I have ever known and loved—all of these things are tiny images of the grand, all-satisfying Glory that You are. When I finally see You face to face in Heaven, my God, I will then realize how very incomplete is the joy and happiness of this earthly life. Let me live for You and walk toward Heaven each moment of my life. I want to walk among men with eyes fixed on You. Grant that I may never again depend too much on any human being. *Amen*.

CHAPTER 92

Detractors and Human Opinions

CHRIST:

MY CHILD, do not care too much about who likes you and who does not. Why waste time worrying about who is for you and who is against you? Just do your best to please Me, and I will be on your side. I will stand by you as long as you hate sin and avoid it in your daily life. When I am with you, what does it matter who else is against you?

2. Never be disturbed when others say things that hurt. If you thought more often

of your sins, you might even agree with some of their remarks.

3. Speak often with Me, and men will impress you less than they do now. The more you advance in prayer, the less will you be tempted to talk against others. What they say or do against you, will seem so trivial when you have learned to join Me through prayer and recollection.

4. I know what you really are. What men say about you, will not change what you are nor what I think of you.

5. Just do your best for My sake, and do not worry what anyone may think or say of you. Do not fear the judgments of those around you. Live for Me by trying to please Me in your daily life. Then will you enjoy My peace.

THINK:

In God alone will I find true peace and glory. I must not desire to please men, nor fear to displease them, when there is question of doing what is right. Only God's judgment is important. All men will agree with God's opinion of me at the Last Judgment.

PRAY:

My God, how foolish it is to be concerned about human opinions and judgments! Only You are the Fountain of Truth. As long as I am pleasing You, I need never worry about what humans think. I will do my best to live a holy life, trying to be kind, considerate, helpful, unselfish, and obedient to Your commandments. Never again will I do anything simply to gain human favor. May I never seek the approval and admiration of men! All for You, my Jesus! *Amen*.

CHAPTER 93

Human Friendship

CHRIST:

MY CHILD, how many friends stand by you when you need them? As soon as a sacrifice is required, so many of these so-called friends are busy with other matters.

2. No matter how dear any human may be to you, you still live your daily life pretty much alone. In the middle of the night, or in moments of fatigue, or at times when others are absorbed in their own interests, you get

a momentary awareness of being alone, of being unnoticed or forgotten by others.

3. Do not overestimate earthly friendship. Sooner or later you must leave your friends, or they must leave you. If you depend too much on any human companion, you will have to bear a painful separation later.

4. Human friendship needs My blessing. Try to help your friends come nearer to Me by your good example. Look forward to the purification arid continuation of your earthly friendships in Heaven. With My blessing, earthly friendships can be a lasting thing. In Heaven they will bring a new kind of joy to you and your friends.

THINK:

All true friendship must be based on virtue and loyalty to Christ. Unless I am helping my friends in some way to live a better life, I am not a true friend. So, too, people who are not helping me become a better person, are not real friends of mine, but useless acquaintances. Anyone who brings me closer to sin by his words or ways, is an enemy in spite of any good intentions which he may profess.

PRAY:

My Jesus, Divine Friend of my life, I long to live a truthful life, a life which is not ruled by blind feelings or unthinking emotions. My earthly friends are human like me, with faults, limitations, and shortcomings. Never should any human being come between You and me. In You I have the perfect Friend. All others must take second place. None of them understands me as perfectly as You do. None of them loves me as fully as You. Who can see and help my real needs as well as You? I want to appreciate You for the wonderful Friend You are. In You alone will I find the perfection of friendship. Let me never prefer any other friend to You. *Amen.*

CHAPTER 94

The Friendship of God's Saints

CHRIST:

MY CHILD, if you want the sincerest friendship, you will find it in My saints. My Church has declared them saints because they were heroically loyal to Me during their life on earth. They are

My favorites because they made Me their Favorite. They chose to love Me more than their own life. They served Me with all the unselfishness and generosity at their command. They gave Me the best service in their power, and they denied Me nothing. Whether I sent them labor, hardship, failures, disappointments, or sickness, they accepted all from My hand with complete willingness.

2. Even after the saints have left this world, they are still interested in seeing Me glorified by men. Their greatest desire for you is that you may some day join them in the perfect life and joy of Heaven. You honor Me when you honor My friends. You will also be acting wisely if you request them to join you in asking for My help. What you may not deserve by yourself alone, you may receive when the saints intercede for you. They are far more deserving of My favors than their selfish fellowmen.

3. Honor My saints not only for the help which they can obtain for you, but also because they are the greatest heroes of all mankind. The greater the cause for which

a man lives, the greater the man. The saints lived for My glory, for the praise of My goodness and the following of My truth. Theirs was the highest, most noble, and least selfish of all causes.

4. They labored for Me alone, and loved Me more than any personal advantage or profit. As far as they could, they tried to do their work, hidden from the eyes of their fellowmen. They were working for Me, and they desired no human recognition. They realized that I deserved the best that was in them. In their noble generosity, they could not offer Me less.

THINK:

In God's saints I will find sincere friends and strong helpers before God. Their prayers and friendship will bring me many extra helps from God's hand, helps which they earned by their glorious generosity with God. In their love for God I can see a wonderful example of continual self-giving to Him Who deserves all that I can offer.

PRAY:

My God, I hope to cultivate a better friendship, with Your saints. They have a genuine interest in my welfare, and they sincerely desire to help me.

O holy saints of God, I honor you for the greatness which you achieved by your grand love for God. Help me in my daily needs, but especially in loving God's holy Will in all things. *Amen.*

CHAPTER 95

Devotion to Mary

CHRIST:

MY CHILD, when My mother received the praises of her cousin Elizabeth, she immediately directed those praises to God, the Source of all good. Amid this admirable outburst of humility, the Holy Spirit inspired her to prophesy her future place in the hearts of My loyal followers. Under divine influence she declared: "Henceforth all generations shall call me blessed!" In honoring My mother, you join the countless multitudes who have sung her praises through the centuries.

2. At the very dawn of creation her greatness was foretold. Satan was told that his head would be crushed by the heel of a

woman. Under God, My Immaculate Mother is the most feared enemy of hell.

3. Her greatest praise was expressed even before she became My mother. The Angel Gabriel was instructed to address her as "full of grace," a title reserved for her alone. The better you understand this holy title, the greater will be your admiration for My mother.

4. To be "full of grace" one must have an all-consuming love for God, a self-dedication so complete that all forms of self-interest are subdued by the pure desire to please God at every moment. Even before she became My Virgin-Mother, she had already achieved this exalted virtue. She was already "full of grace."

5. Her response to the angel's message was a perfect summary of her entire life: "Behold the handmaid of the Lord; be it done to me according to thy word!" She lived with the highest purpose possible to man or angel—to devote herself unreservedly to God's holy Will. Many have formed this high resolve, but only My mother has fulfilled it to perfection. Only she is "full of grace."

6. Not only does My mother deserve your admiration and praise, but she also deserves your purest love. In becoming My mother, she also became yours in a very true sense. As your earthly parents cooperated with God in giving you your earthly life, so too did My mother cooperate with God in bringing supernatural life to your soul.

7. She knows and loves you as a true mother, indeed, as the most perfect of all mothers. Her prayers for your needs are frequent and powerful. As she obtained help for the bridal couple of Cana without their knowledge, so does she often obtain help for you in many needs of which you are unaware. As I could not refuse her request in Cana, so too can I not refuse her prayers in Heaven. Her glorious merits bring you many a favor of which you are unworthy. Be a loyal child of your heavenly mother, and your salvation is assured.

THINK:

Mary's highest merit was her self-dedication to God. When Jesus heard a woman praising His mother for having such a wonderful Son, He pointed to His mother's greatest glory: "Blessed are they that hear the word of God and keep it." She who was "full of grace" lived these words to perfection. Therefore she deserves my highest praise. And yet, she deserves something more. As my heavenly mother she has given me her love and attention since my first moment of life. Can I refuse to love her in return? My love will be proved by my obedience to the only command of hers which Holy Scripture records: "Do whatever He (Jesus) tells you." If I am loyal to this command, Heaven is surely mine.

PRAY:

O Virgin-Mother of Jesus, I cannot ask you to be my mother, since you are already that. I will, however, ask you to help me become a grateful and loving child of yours. My devotion to you is not half so generous as your devotion to me. I shall never tire of singing your praises. Your pure love for me has often gone unnoticed and unrepaid. I desire now to make reparation for such deep ingratitude. You are indeed the perfect mother. You have given me the advice and the example which will lead me to the eternal success of Heaven. Moreover, you can obtain for me the light and strength to walk along your holy way. Help me abandon my daily faults and follow you at last along the way to God. *Amen.*

PART FIVE

Self-Conquest Through Mortification

MORTIFICATION means "putting to death." The person who wants to live more for God, must live less for his blind natural appetites and unreasoning desires. He will look to God's holy Will and follow it ever better each day. His likes and dislikes, his feelings and moods will react whenever he tries to do what is unpleasant or difficult, but he seeks to follow his intelligence regardless of feelings and moods.

Thus, the mortified man succeeds in dying to self so that he may live more perfectly to God. He overcomes his natural self in order to follow God's holy Will more perfectly. He kills his faults and defects in order to let greater virtues live within his soul.

A final note must be added if we are to conduct ourselves intelligently in this holy practice of mortification. It is this. Human desires and emotions are natural to man.

That means that they cannot be destroyed. They are made more perfect insofar as one succeeds in controlling and directing them by the grace of God. Thus, "dying to self" means the right use of human emotions and desires. They are to be followed insofar as they help us to fulfill God's holy Will, and they are to be controlled insofar as they hinder us from doing so.

CHAPTER 96

Intelligent Love

CHRIST:

MY CHILD, the more you study My law, the more you will see that what I command is the only intelligent thing to do. I am simply asking that you value persons and things according to their true worth. You offend Me only when you have placed the wrong value on the people and things in your daily life.

2. You would not want counterfeit money in place of real money. Neither should you be satisfied with false values in anything else. If you learn this holy honesty, you will never prefer any human being to Me.

3. When you sin for the sake of any creature, you are putting more value into it than it deserves. You are choosing a passing satisfaction in preference to the lasting joy which I want you to have.

4. If you value things as they deserve, your first interest will be My Will in all things. At present you often deceive yourself. You think that you are acting out of charity, but you are really acting for selfish reasons.

THINK:

An honest life is the only life which will bring no regrets. God desires to help me live such a life. He wants me to esteem people and things for what they are. Such a standard will help me to avoid many mistakes. It will teach me the true meaning of charity and goodness. My affections will be broadened and purified. I will stop judging people and things with prejudice. Selfish motives will become weaker and rarer within me. I shall begin to be the person I have always wanted or pretended to be. I will be a man of truth, an honest man, a man of God.

PRAY:

My God, give me the grace to love people and things according to their merits and worth. Do not let my heart control my head. Let my intelligence guide the emotions within me, and let my will control my unreasoning desires. Grant that I may love what is good and do what is right, even when I feel like acting differently. I will not take it too hard when earthly friends fail me. You, the Best and Greatest of friends, are always with me. As long as I have Your love, and am on the road to Heaven, I have solid reasons for peace and joy. *Amen.*

CHAPTER 97

Man's Interior Enemies

CHRIST:

MY CHILD, nothing gives you more trouble than your unthinking self. Until you have acquired control of your animal desires, your proud ambitions, and your foolish envy of others, you cannot enjoy My heavenly peace.

2. If your heart is not at rest, it is because you are still controlled by this blind self

within you. Your heart is not set on Me, but on the comforts, enjoyments, achievements, or security of this life. Because you are so self-centered and full of worldly desires, you are tempted to sin.

3. Whatever is not from Me and leads not to Me, is bad for you. Some of the saints often asked themselves the question: "How does this help me for eternal life?" That is a very valuable question. If you live by it, there will be less waste of time and more good work in your daily life.

4. Your feelings and desires are good only as long as you keep them under control. Once they become your masters, they will turn your life into a slavery. You will have no peace within yourself, and you will even destroy the peace of those around you. You will become jealous, envious, ambitious, and difficult to live with. You will often omit what you ought to do, and do things which you should not do. You will become too interested in the doings of others, and not interested enough in what you should be doing.

5. You can make a better world by following Me. Begin with yourself. Learn My truth and let it govern your passions, your every desire, all your fears, and each word and deed in your daily life.

THINK:

The man who has not learned to mortify himself, has within himself the enemies of peace and goodness. He is easily aroused against those who thwart or oppose his selfish desires. He sees the obligations of others, but he remains blind to his own. He blames little things in others, while he excuses bigger faults in himself.

PRAY:

My Jesus, You conquered the world of passion and selfishness. By Your life of mortification, prayer, work, and loyalty to the Father's Will, You merited for me all the necessary graces to overcome self in my daily activities. I wish to begin a mortified life. I want to practice self-control as often as I can, even when there is no question of sin. By my mortification, I hope to obtain greater graces to fight future temptations. If I am ready to suffer for You now, I will be prepared to fight for You then. I hope in You for the strength to begin. You deserve this of me. Let me forget self and think only of Your all-perfect goodness. *Amen.*

CHAPTER 98

Attachments

CHRIST:

MY CHILD, as you go through life, your heart tends to attach itself to many things. If these attachments become too strong, they will make you their slave. You will eventually sin because of them. True, your natural likes and dislikes are not decided by an act of the will. You can, however, control them with the help of prayer, mortification, and My Sacraments.

2. Purify your love for all earthly things, by using them wisely according to My law. Only with a pure love such as this can you escape the slavery of earthly attachments. You will never again be too troubled at the possibility of losing something, be it a friend or a cherished possession. Nor is this a form of misguided selfishness. You are

simply choosing first things first—God before creatures.

3. Refuse to be a slave of anything on earth. Love Me and My Will more than all else. You are still disturbed and displeased when matters go against your wishes and desires. You still fail to understand the passing nature of earthly things.

4. Let no human being nor earthly satisfaction mean so much to you that you would sin for them. If you love anything that much, your love is misguided and foolish. You are preferring a reflection of God to God Himself.

5. If you want true joy and real greatness, be attached to Me above every person and thing in your earthly life. Let your desires and love be guided by My wisdom, and they will never lead you into folly.

THINK:

My true welfare lies not in possessing or enjoying many things on earth, but rather in using what I have wisely and sinlessly, with the intention of pleasing God. Riches, honor, praise, admiration, power and superiority over others, or whatever else may attract me on earth, all of these things must one day pass away. Why be too interested in what I am sure to lose? Unless I use them as God desires, I will use them the wrong way, and they will draw me away from Him. The more I come to know God, the more will I desire to lessen my attachments on earth. I will try to be more aware of Him throughout the day. My real needs are few. True, human nature objects to being deprived of what it likes. Still, I ought to get rid of whatever does not really improve my life.

PRAY:

My God, You are the perfect Good. Whatever attracts me in any human person or in anything, is but a tiny reflection of Your infinite perfection. How can I be so foolish as to prefer a reflection to the reality? Yet, that is what I do when I displease You by sin. Help me to face this truth. From now on I desire to live for You by a proper use of things in my daily life. Whatever leads me into sin must go. Let me love and choose only what will help me please You. You know what is best. Show me Your Will and give me strength to follow it. *Amen.*

CHAPTER 99

Conflicting Emotions

CHRIST:

MY CHILD, when you have received the grace to think My way, you will never again fall into sadness. One can be sad only when he is deprived of something which he desires very much. Most human sadness is born of worldly attachments.

2. If you want Me above all else, you will not be sad at being deprived of anything on earth. The more you come to realize what I am, the more you will want Me above every created thing. Only sin can make My followers sad. Yet even then, they soon turn to Me and abandon their sadness.

3. The sadness of the worldly man comes from his self-love. He is sad because he does not have what he wishes. He is often moved to anger at those who hinder him from getting what he wants. He becomes jealous of what he loves, and envies those who have what he desires.

4. Follow Me and live in peace. Do not be troubled if something is said against you. It

is not the first time, nor will it be the last. In fact, more is said behind your back than what you hear. Do not lose any sleep over the judgments of men. Do your best for Me, and seek My approval. If you are pleasing Me, you have good reason to be glad.

5. Do not become over-anxious or worried about anything. I do not expect the impossible from you. Why should you demand of yourself more than I demand? Pride makes you desire perfection as quickly as possible. The humble man seeks perfection according to his strength. He does his best and renews his efforts when he has failed. He does not deceive himself. He really tries his best. When, however, he fails, he is neither surprised nor excited. He is genuinely sorry, looks for guidance, and begins again.

THINK:

Sadness, fears, and worries will always rob me of peace until I have learned to embrace God's Will in all things. When I have done this, I will no longer be troubled, whether I live here or there, whether I work with this person or that one. I will see God's hand guiding me through the trials of daily life, teaching me patience, love, and sorrow for my sins. I need only do my best. That is enough for God. It ought to be enough for me, too.

PRAY:

My Jesus, a true follower of Yours knows how to keep his eyes fixed on You in spite of conflicting emotions. You love me. I know that You are ever near to help me live this daily life of mine. All that You ask is that I keep trying and be content with the results which You send me. The final goal is Heaven's eternal glory. If I believe all this, have I any true reason for worries, fears, or sadness? How can I be swayed by my shifting emotions when I am living for the grandest success of all? Help me to remember my goal as I go along in my daily activities. I do not want to sin for anything on earth. You deserve my very best. Lead me along and help me hate all sin. *Amen.*

CHAPTER 100

Self-Conquest

CHRIST:

M Y CHILD, you will never face a greater battle than the battle against your unreasoning feelings and desires. These are your passions. They are your most stubborn and most dangerous enemies. This blind and lower self within you is so close to you that it is almost invisible to you. It tries to make you think and feel its way instead of My way. Treat this lower self as an enemy. Acts of mortification will help you to advance in self-control. I will strengthen your efforts with My grace.

2. The fight for self-control is harder than bodily or mental labors. Your lower self is more determined in pursuing what it wants than your will is, in seeking Me. Self will start with a mild desire and gradually develop a strong habit. You must fight what is bad from the very first time it appears in your life. If you cannot overcome evil when it is small and weak, how will you ever conquer it after it has become a strong habit?

3. True peace of soul is found not in surrendering, but in controlling your desires and appetites. Control means using things according to My laws of reason and revelation. Self-control requires determination and even violence to self in opposing what is wrong. Do this and you will prove true loyalty to Me.

THINK:

My daily life is really a battle, with opposing forces arising both inside and outside of me. My most dangerous enemies in this battle, are the enemies within the gates, the blind, unreasoning desires deep within me. They are never quite dead, never completely satisfied. The real "I" is seen in what my will chooses to follow: either the law of intelligence and faith, or the law of pride and blind feelings. Prayer, Sacraments, and mortification are the weapons which will overcome the enemy. The battle will become much harder if I allow any bad habit to grow strong. Relying on God's grace and following the directions of His Church I will conquer sin and advance in virtue each day.

PRAY:

My King and Saviour, You overcame temptation and sin to give me a holy example and to bring me grace to follow Your example. Make me a loyal follower of Yours in this daily battle against my proud and selfish human nature. I hope in Your assistance, and I will begin this day to practice mortification wherever possible. I shall keep trying to live an intelligent life, a life of obedience to Your all-wise Will. Let me subdue the dangerous enemy within me by frequent mortification. *Amen.*

CHAPTER 101

Examples of Self-Conquest

CHRIST:

MY CHILD, read the lives of My saints, and you will learn a great deal about life's daily battle. Why were they so loyal to Me? Because they had grasped the secret of all success in this fight for Heaven. They saw the infinite goodness and lovableness of God, and the passing nature of all earthly joys and satisfaction.

2. Their main interest was to follow My Will in everything and to mortify every contrary feeling and desire within them. When they noticed a fault, they started fighting it at once by doing the opposite of that inclination. They overcame their faults by positive action. If they were guilty of pride, they looked for a chance to be humiliated, and they thanked Me for sending these opportunities to them.

3. You must become that interested in your perfection. At present you hardly conquer a single fault in many years. You fear the discomfort and inconvenience of the fight against self. The slightest unpleasant experience puts you on the defensive for your rights and for the things you like.

4. I am ready to help you the moment you make up your mind to begin in earnest the fight for Heaven.

THINK:

Yes, I am still in favor of my blind, unreasoning desires. When will I imitate the saints by an honest daily effort to get rid of my faults? How I shall wish, at the Last Judgment, that I had done so! On that day

I shall rejoice if I have honestly tried to follow Christ, my King. How quickly the pains of the battle will be forgotten when I receive the congratulations of all God's Blessed! How grateful I shall be to God as I look at the misery and woe of those on the left side, those who lived only for self!

PRAY:

My Jesus, You showed Your divine power to the Apostles by commanding the winds and the waves. Command the tempests of selfishness within me, and let me become, at last, empty of this false and hurtful self-love. True love seeks what is good. Let me have true love for myself, that is, let me seek what is really good for me and for others. My true good lies in Your holy Will, because You know what is best for me. Free me from my passions and my unreasonable desires. Purify my soul and make me brave enough to suffer anything rather than sin again. *Amen.*

CHAPTER 102

Mistaken Self-Love

CHRIST:

MY CHILD, here is the secret of all perfection—forget self-interest and follow My Will in all things. You want what you consider good for you, but you are often wrong in your calculations. I want what is really best for you, and I am never mistaken. If you want to be the kind of person I want you to be, learn My truth and do My Will. Then leave the rest to Me.

2. Every human fault arises from a mistaken self-love. Men overcome their faults only as far as they really abandon their selfishness and follow Me. Some make a half-hearted effort, and some make a ninety percent effort, but only a few make a full effort with no reservations.

3. If you gave all of your goods to the poor, without giving your heart to Me, you have done nothing as far as eternal life is concerned. Even great penance means nothing unless you are determined to fight against your faults. There is no substitute for

true virtue. The basis of true virtue lies in this—that you accept and prefer My Will in all things.

4. You are not so wise as you think. You do not always know what is truly best for you. No man is richer, no one is happier than he who loves My Will in all things. Empty your heart of every other desire, and place your daily life in My hands. Work, and pray, and do all that is right and good for you. When things do not go as you desire, do what you can to remedy them. After you have done all that common sense demands, accept the results as My Will.

THINK:

Here is the key to God's peace, and yet I hesitate to use it. Can God be mistaken? Can He be wrong? Why do I not find His peace within me? It is simply because I have not yet succeeded in placing my life in His hands. I am not quite sure that He will do what I would like. Yet I know that He loves me more than I love myself. He wants what is surely good for me, not merely some deceptive good thing. Do I want to look out for myself, even if it means committing a sin here and there? Sin hurts me far more than I realize.

PRAY:

My Jesus, show me how to begin at last a life of obedience and loyalty to Your Will. Let me forget self and become more unselfish with those around me. Wherever I can, I hope to do things for others. Sin must be hated for what it is self-deception and stupidity. How can I ever do what is wrong, knowing that it hurts me and offends You? I will try, with Your help, to live my daily life as a true and loyal follower of Yours. What You forbid is forbidden because it is bad for me. How can I ever insist on sinning again? You have proven Your love for me in a thousand ways. I hope to prove my love for You by trying to act as You want me to act in my daily life. *Amen.*

CHAPTER 103

Fear of Suffering

CHRIST:

MY CHILD, as long as you are afraid to suffer, you will not possess My peace.

This fear will make it too difficult for you to follow My Will. In many things you will sin and do what is bad for you.

2. Be loyal to Me if you want My peace on earth and happiness unending in Heaven. Be loyal to My Will, whether I send what you like or what you dislike. For My sake live your daily life bravely, even when it involves hardship and suffering.

3. Many pursue an imaginary happiness. When they get what they want, they soon find out that it does not bring them the joy which they had expected. They gradually tire of it and the search for happiness is on again.

4. Do not blame the place where you are, nor the people around you if you do not have peace of soul. If you went elsewhere and met new people, you would still be the same you, with the same old faults and defects. You might become a changed man, but you would not necessarily be a better man. As soon as the old situations arose, you would still have to fight the battle from which you ran away. Being better means overcoming your faults, not putting them

to sleep by avoiding disagreeable circumstances. The change which you must make is a change within yourself. Begin today with the help of My grace. Make a continual effort to mortify self-love.

THINK:

Until I have overcome my faults, I can never be sure when they will flare up again and make me offend God. I must try to face situations in which I can practice the virtues opposed to my faults. If I am an impatient person, I should look for opportunities to practice patience. So too with other faults. Only action will prove what faults I have and which virtues I need. The man who is afraid of inconvenience or suffering, will never advance in virtue. He lacks the courage to face the unpleasant situation which can strengthen his virtue. True, I am not to look for occasions of sin, but I can find many an ordinary condition of my daily life which can act as a normal test of virtue.

PRAY:

My Jesus, only practice will perfect my soul. Only action can show me how far I have developed the graces which You have sent me. Do not let me go on avoiding the unpleasant situations which are a necessary part of my life. Let me face them and deal with them as You want me to. Where I should be unselfish, or humble, or patient, or trusting in You, let me practice these virtues. I refuse to go on living with my faults. I wish to begin at last to attack them by practicing the opposite virtues. As opportunities arise, let me recognize them and use them for Your sake. *Amen.*

CHAPTER 104

The Gift of Grace

CHRIST:

MY CHILD, when I give you actual graces, your mind receives holy thoughts, your will has good desires, and you feel drawn toward Me. Such graces are special gifts of Mine. They help you to rise above earthly attractions and worldly satisfactions.

2. Never oppose My actual graces, but follow them and use them faithfully. You will then prove your loyalty to Me, and you will merit still greater graces. By prayer, sacraments, self-denial, and self-conquest your

spiritual life will grow. Little by little a marvelous change will come over your thinking, your desires, and your actions. You will be living a holier life, a life more like Mine.

3. In baptism I gave you sanctifying grace, by which the Holy Trinity became your Guest. My divine life was placed within you to make you worthy of Heaven. No matter what wonderful things a man may do, unless My sanctifying grace is in him, his accomplishments are merely human, and their glory will one day fade away. No arts, no strength, no beauty, no genius, no eloquence—nothing on earth, be it ever so admirable, is worthy of Heaven until it has been elevated and purified by sanctifying grace.

4. Natural gifts and talents are possessed by both good and bad people. Sanctifying grace, however, is possessed only by the good, and it makes them worthy of Heaven. So great a gift is this grace that neither the power of miracles, the gift of prophecy, nor any other gift or talent can compare with it. This grace changes a man and makes him more like Me. Without it man remains

bound to earth and controlled by his human nature.

THINK:

The grace of God! Next to God Himself, this is my most precious possession! With His actual graces God speaks to me, draws me on toward my true, eternal greatness, and gives me strength to do supernatural, God-like deeds. In the unbaptized adult and in the soul which has sinned seriously, it takes one or more actual graces to bring Sanctifying Grace to the soul. With Sanctifying Grace one becomes a temple of God, with the Blessed Trinity dwelling within the soul. This privilege makes the unworthy sinner worthy of Heaven, makes the weak strong, and bestows on the person a dignity which no earthly power or position can give. The more I make use of actual graces, the more do I increase the Sanctifying Grace within me. This makes me a closer friend of God, stronger against temptations, and deserving of a still higher place in Heaven.

PRAY:

My loving Creator and Father, I am unable to do anything worthy of Heaven unless

Your grace enlightens, strengthens, and assists me in my thoughts, desires, words, and actions. Only with Your help can I do what You desire of me. Without Your grace I am helpless against the slightest temptations. May I never neglect the actual graces which You send me throughout the day. I hope to turn my back on whatever threatens to deprive me of Sanctifying Grace. As long as this Grace is with me, You Yourself are my constant companion. With You I wish to walk safely each hour of the day toward Heaven's eternal happiness. *Amen.*

CHAPTER 105

Nature Versus Grace

CHRIST:

MY CHILD, I want you to become a spiritual man, that is, one who is wise enough to recognize the various forms of self-deception and the many graces which come your way each day. There is in your nature a deep selfishness which does not always seek what is really good for you. It often wants what merely seems good. Listen to Me and learn the difference between the mistaken desires of nature and the truly good desires which I send by My grace.

2. Nature is selfish. It will try to enjoy everything on earth and still gain Heaven. Even where sin is involved, nature attempts to make excuses, for self and looks for reasons to favor self. Grace simply looks for My Will, turning away from all occasions of sin and self-deception.

3. Nature hates all restraint. It wants to follow its own likes, its own desires, and its own will. Grace is interested in self-control, self-conquest, and obedience to authority. It seeks to please Me in everything and in every way. It looks for opportunities to suffer something more for My sake.

4. Nature is interested in self. It works for its own interests. In whatever it does, it looks to its own advantage and profit. Grace follows My interests. It tries to help as many people as possible, and leaves all self-interest in My hands.

5. Nature loves honor and respect. Grace accepts all honor and respect in My name and offers them to Me, knowing that without Me, man is nothing.

6. Nature is afraid of shame, contempt, or insults. Grace does not mind such things because it cannot forget how much shame, contempt, and insults I embraced for the sins of men.

7. Nature loves bodily ease and comfort. Grace loves to keep busy so that it may present a fuller life to Me.

THINK:

Seeing these differences between nature and grace, I ought to become more eager to do things for God and to forget this selfish nature of mine.

PRAY:

O Holy Ghost, Giver of grace and Sanctifier of all men, I wish that I could give You the unselfish devotion and loyalty which You deserve. You are my God. So often throughout the day, You send me good thoughts and holy desires. How long will I go on paying so little attention to Your holy inspirations? Grant that I may become wise in the ways of nature and grace. Let me become what I should have been long before now. I want now to follow what You desire of me. When You show me sin in my daily life, let me hate it and avoid it. When You tell me how I am to live, let me not be a coward who puts things off. My God, lead me on toward Heaven's glorious life each hour of the day. *Amen.*

CHAPTER 106

Grace Versus Nature

CHRIST:

M Y CHILD, nature reaches out for things which are attractive, or curiosities. It is repelled by what is ordinary and inexpensive. Grace refuses to be drawn too strongly to anything on earth. It deliberately chooses ordinary things, and even unattractive things, so that it may not become too distracted from Me in daily life.

2. Nature easily rejoices at gaining and winning things, but frets at any loss. Grace is not so easily troubled if it loses some worldly advantage, nor is it so disturbed when it must give up an earthly gain.

3. Nature is irritated at unkind and harsh words, but grace knows how to keep an even temper in the face of cruel and mean persons.

4. Nature prefers to receive rather than to give. It likes to have little privileges. Grace is more ready to give than to receive. It tries to avoid privileges, and even prefers to have less than others, so as to be more like Me, the King of sacrifice.

THINK:

All of this is actually happening in my life. At times, I am too blind to realize what is going on within me and around me. I do not always want to do what God desires of me. At every step the battle goes on, the battle of blind selfishness versus the grace of God in my soul, the fight of evil against goodness. Only when I am asleep is this warfare quiet.

PRAY:

My God, how important even little things seem when I hear You interpret them in the light of eternity. So often what I consider a small matter, is really big because it is a choice between my will and Yours. Nothing is little, nothing is unimportant, nothing is insignificant in my daily life. What I think, do, or say, shows what I want and what I am trying to be. Make me more aware of Your presence in my life. If I see You more clearly, I will be more willing to forget self and to follow Your holy Will. Grant me grace to be more for You and less for this blind and unreasoning self within me. *Amen.*

CHAPTER 107

Nature and Grace

CHRIST:

MY CHILD, nature wants to have plenty of what it likes. It is not satisfied with only just enough. Grace seeks only what it needs to live a good life.

2. Nature wants many friends and companions. It prefers those who have power, and flatters those who can give favors. Grace loves all people. It even wishes the welfare of enemies. It honors all men according to their position. It favors most those who are truly in need of help. It honors goodness more than goods. It respects virtue more than talent.

3. Nature easily complains of its wants and troubles. Grace is silent before people. It presents its needs first to Me.

4. Nature judges each thing according to how it helps self in this earthly life. Grace values each thing according to how it helps man to follow My Will.

5. Nature holds on to its own opinions. It will fight and dispute against anyone who seems to challenge its imagined greatness. Grace offers its opinions simply, discusses without resentment, and leaves to Me those who disagree.

6. Nature is curious to know the secrets of others. Grace prefers to know what My words are and to avoid needless distractions.

THINK:

How repulsive my nature can be when it is not controlled! It can make life miserable for me and for the people around me. Grace draws people toward God. It spreads love and happiness wherever it reigns. When grace becomes the ruling force in my daily life, I shall have the wonderful peace of Christ. My peace will spread to those around me, and their life will be better because they have known me.

PRAY:

Holy Ghost, God of peace and joy, I lay my life at Your feet. Do with me whatever You wish. Empty this heart of selfishness and fill it with grace. Shine out in me so that those around me may feel Your holy presence in their life. Let them become better because they have known me. All this You will do if only I can learn at last Your glorious lesson of grace. Help me to let Your divine Will rule my life every moment of the day. Not my feelings, not my earthly self-love but Your holy wisdom and grace must lead me along. Lead on, my God. I hope to act as You wish in all things today. *Amen.*

CHAPTER 108

The Control of One's Desires

CHRIST:

MY CHILD, the moment you desire anything too much, you lose My gift of peace. The proud and the covetous are never at peace. The poor in spirit, the humble man, enjoys a heavenly peace of soul.

2. To set your life in order, you must begin from within. Begin with your desires.

Allow yourself to want only what I want you to have. Do not desire what is not for you. Why desire things which will tie your heart too much to this earth?

3. Surrender yourself to My Will, and you will gain a victory over all earthly things. Examine your desires. Even when they seem good and holy, they can hurt you by demanding too much attention, and so preventing you from fulfilling your duties and obligations.

4. I want you to have the freedom of My true followers. Love My wisdom and choose My Will, and you will never be downcast if your plans or your friends fail you. So long as you have done your honest best, believe firmly that am pleased with you. This above all must you desire—to please Me in all things.

THINK:

My true perfection is based on God's word and His grace. With His help, I can gain a self-control far beyond anything dreamed by worldly men. This control is needed even in things which are good and holy in themselves. I must look first to my duties and obligations. Any holiness which makes me neglect these, is not from God. Over-eagerness brings anxiety, fear, and nervousness. It makes me less able to do my duties. It diminishes my recollection and interior peace, and makes me more subject to impatience, anger and rash judgments. Uncontrolled desires and intentions can make me fall into sin. They can make me imprudent, so that I may try to help others too much. Others may resent my help, and because of me, refuse to do what is right.

PRAY:

My Jesus, let me do Your work for Your sake, and not for my own pride and self-satisfaction. As long as I want what You want, I will act prudently and safely. Let me not try to rush what must be done slowly. If I fret at my failures, I am working for myself and not for You. Your Will is to be done, not mine. I hope to attempt all the good within my reach, but I will not be over-anxious about the results. If I lose my presence of mind and my peace of soul, it is because I am thinking more of Your work than of Your Will. I need only do my best.

The rest depends on the people around me and Your grace. Let me never think that I am bigger than You. I now put all things into Your hands. *Amen.*

CHAPTER 109

Controlling One's Own Opinion

CHRIST:

MY CHILD, everybody likes to follow his own way of thinking. Every man prefers to associate with those who agree with his ideas. Yet, it is so foolish for you to think too highly of your own opinion.

2. Nobody knows all the answers. The man who is always talking does not advance much in knowledge. A good listener will always learn more than the one who talks too much.

3. It is not always necessary to point out the mistakes of others. Even when you know better, you need not always express your opinion. In fact, many discussions are unnecessary and unimportant. So often, too, opinions depend on people's likes and dislikes. Why argue when it is not an important matter?

4. To those who know how to control their tongues for My sake, I grant the grace of interior peace.

5. Do not love your own opinions too much. Be humble enough to seek advice when you need it. Do not try to be independent of all other opinions. Different opinions may bring you a broader understanding of yourself as well as of others.

THINK:

At times I must hold my tongue for the sake of peace. Many unimportant things are said and done in daily life. It is my pride that makes me want to correct people at the slightest opportunity. Corrections are unnecessary in many things. I should not place too much confidence in my own sentiments and opinions. In small, unimportant matters I do no harm by keeping silent and listening to opinions which do not agree with mine. It takes a deep humility and a delicate charity to act in this way.

PRAY:

O Jesus, King of truth, help me to preserve peace and harmony among those around me. Teach me to work and labor for what is right. Let me never listen in silence to what is contrary to Your teachings, or hurtful to my neighbor or my own soul. Yet, show me how to be considerate of other people's feelings and opinions as far as it can be done without compromising Your truth. Grant me the humility to follow advice when necessary. Let me love Your truth more than my own opinions. *Amen.*

CHAPTER 110

Love of Solitude

CHRIST:

MY CHILD, let Me show you the great value of prayerful solitude. When you converse with men, you often come away with useless distractions, false ideas, and unwanted desires. When you communicate with Me, your understanding of life is deepened and your outlook is broadened. Human conversation usually ties your thoughts to this earthly life, but talking with Me raises your thoughts above the narrow limits of your mortal existence. Human conversation often brings an exaggerated esteem for the passing glories of earth. Heavenly conversation brings a clearer vision of the eternal glory which awaits you.

2. Come aside and rest a while in My company. Do this as often as you can during the day. Learn to appreciate My friendship in solitude. This will make it easier for you to keep a holy intention in your activities, a clear conscience, and peace of mind. Love to pray and labor unseen by humans, and you will discover many little ways of pleasing Me more. My light falls on prayerful hearts like seed falling on rich soil.

3. It is easier to control your thoughts and desires by staying at home than by going out too often. Frequent visiting and going out bring too many distractions. You cannot safely appear in public until you have developed a love for solitude.

4. In prayerful solitude you will receive a deep appreciation of your heavenly goal in life. A man of prayer speaks when speech is useful to himself or his neighbor. He will not waste his energy and squander his thoughts in idle conversation.

THINK:

What a marvelous interior knowledge and power will be mine when I have learned to enjoy holy reading and meditation on the things of God! I will share His thoughts and follow His all-wise Will. In prayerful solitude I can find the light and strength to live a holy and truly successful life on earth.

PRAY:

My ever-present God, I hope to turn to You at different times throughout the day to tell You whatever is in my thoughts. Grant that I may gradually become more and more conscious of Your nearness to me, and of Your loving interest in whatever concerns me. Let me turn to You as easily as I turn to my human friends. I need this grace in order to live a truly virtuous life. Help me, Lord, to develop a livelier prayer-life in my daily activities. *Amen.*

CHAPTER 111

The Virtue of Silence

CHRIST:

MY CHILD, there are times when you ought to keep to yourself and avoid conversation. There is no profit in unkind talk, rash talk, or indecent talk. What is the good of wasting time with idle disputes or with boasting?

2. True, there are times when light conversation brings needed relief and necessary recreation, but talk which does not help the speaker or the listener to live a better life, is a shameful waste of precious time, time which will never return.

3. Think before you speak, and you will never regret your words. The spoken word cannot be recalled. It is not always possible to undo the harm caused by thoughtless talk.

4. Many saints have avoided the company of men whenever possible in order to enjoy a closer union with Me. One of them once remarked: "As often as I have gone among men, I returned less a man." Isn't this true of you when you talk too long? It is easier to keep silence altogether than to stop talking when you should.

5. In silence I shall speak to you with less interruptions. My words will come in the form of ideas, desires, intentions, and

resolutions which arise within your soul. You will hear My voice with less distraction. Love silence and learn to use it well. Then will you draw closer to Me, as I am close to you.

THINK:

Silence is truly a virtue when practiced for God. In developing a love for silence, I will learn a deeper wisdom, a broader outlook on everyday life, and a brighter vision of God's nearness and love. In human conversations, I will listen more and talk less, I will learn more and make fewer mistakes. People will respect my judgments more because I will think before speaking. Each time I open my mouth, I will do so for a definite purpose, a good purpose. God's wisdom will take the place of my human folly, and my words will help those who hear me.

PRAY:

Dear Holy Spirit, my God, teach me to talk well and wisely. Let me avoid useless conversations. Help me to speak often for You. Grant that my words may never hurt men of good will. May my words always bring consolation to those in sorrow, guidance to those who are confused, light to the ignorant, hope to those who despair, comfort to those who are troubled, and good advice to those in need. Take my lips and make them Yours. Take possession of my mind and make it an instrument of Your goodness and a channel of Your truth. I hope to become a man of silence, that is, one who prefers to talk to God rather than to men. In my human conversations, may I always bring You closer to them and them closer to You. *Amen.*

BOOK TWO

The Way of Imitation

BOOK TWO

The Way of Imitation

THIS IS THE SECOND STAGE in one's spiritual development. In abandoning his serious faults and his predominant venial sins, the spiritual beginner has laid a solid foundation of many virtues. In a sense, however, his spiritual growth thus far has been a negative sort of thing; that is, he has advanced in the various virtues by resisting the faults to which they were opposed.

Christ's follower is now invited to rise to a higher degree of union with God. He is to do this by imitating the example which Christ set in His earthly life. Jesus said, "He that sees Me, sees the Father also." Therefore, the more Christ-like one becomes in his daily life, the more God-like will he be.

This second level of the supernatural life is known as the illuminative way, the way of enlightenment. By drawing closer to Christ in friendship, man comes to understand God more clearly and appreciate Him more fully. Jesus said, "I am the Way, the Truth, and the Life . . . Learn of Me . . ." Christ's follower must now take his eyes away from himself for longer periods, so that he may concentrate more and more upon his King and Model. He no longer practices the various virtues of daily life to oppose his faults, but to show Christ a greater love and loyalty.

PART ONE

Following Jesus in Daily Life
A. Learning of Christ

CHAPTER 1

Knowledge and Wisdom

CHRIST:

MY CHILD, those who follow Me, do not walk in darkness. With Me there is neither guesswork nor error. I have given you an example in My daily life. In order that you might not misunderstand My example and My words, I founded My Church to explain them. To keep you from the torture of doubts and from all foolish extremes, I promised to preserve My Church from error in her religious and moral teachings.

2. Follow Me, and you will be walking the path to eternal life. Do not let your emotions confuse your thinking. Control your foolish pride and let Me guide you through My Church. She will speak your language and will prevent you from misunderstanding My teachings. By a frequent use of My sacraments you will gain a deeper appreciation of My Truth.

3. Many are deaf to My voice. They say that they follow Me without any human stepping-stone. These people are deceiving themselves. They are simply too proud to submit themselves to the human guides whom I set over them. Their religion consists only of what they understand. or like, or find convenient.

4. I do not want self-made men among My followers. Mere human judgments are too feeble to follow My teachings without error, and mere human strength is too weak to obey My commandments without the supernatural help of My grace. Sincerity is no substitute for truth and right. True, I want you to follow your conscience in your daily life, but without My Church you will not always be sure that your conscience is correct.

5. Come, follow Me in your daily life. I am the Way, the Truth, and the Life. In Me you will find the most important knowledge of life, and the only sure way to eternal happiness. Learn My Truth and follow My example in your daily life, and your reward will be greater than words can ever express. Meditate often upon My earthly life. As

far as you know how, imitate Me in your daily activities. With Me you will have peace and a daily progress toward Heaven's eternal joy.

THINK:

Christ wants no guesswork, but a sure course of action. The King of Truth wants His followers to possess the truth. He speaks to me through the Scriptures, the Christian tradition, my prayers, and the circumstances of daily life. I can learn the true interpretation of these things from His Church. It is not always easy to be sure what God desires of me. Even my good intentions may lead me astray into ridiculous extremes. Only Christ's Church can guide me with certainty. When She speaks, Christ speaks. He promised to be with Her all days until the end of the world. A true follower of Christ will look to His Church for the knowledge and wisdom of Christ.

PRAY:

My Jesus, I thank You for leaving me Your Church. I see so many sects which claim to have Your blessing and support. Yet, they contradict one another in many doctrines. You have granted me the favor of knowing Your one, true, apostolic Church. She still stands today, after centuries of opposition and persecution. The many attempts of Satan to destroy Her have failed, as You promised they would. Empires have risen and fallen, but Your Church goes on telling the world Your holy teachings and commandments. You still speak through Her, offering truth and wisdom to all men. Let me always follow Her guidance in all matters of faith and morals. *Amen.*

CHAPTER 2

The Divine Teacher

CHRIST:

MY CHILD, My grace is richer, deeper, grander, and more glorious than any other possession or achievement on earth. It shows you what is better and more profitable for your eternal success. It strengthens you against all earthly attractions and makes you the true master of your own life.

2. My grace brings you a yearning for Heaven and freedom from many earthly fears. All graces are gifts from Me. Actual

grace enlightens your mind to see some truth more clearly and appreciate it more deeply; then it gives your will an inclination toward the good which you see; and finally it offers you strength to follow that good, if you so desire. Every actual grace contains these three elements.

3. I speak to different persons in different ways, according to their background, abilities, and efforts. I do not always use words when I speak within your soul. Often My message is received and understood in an instant. In your reading, reflecting, and prayer, I often speak to you. I help you to understand more clearly what you read in books or hear in sermons. The grandest sermon would be just so many words if I did not bless it with My grace. It is I who enable the listeners to understand it, desire it, and live it.

4. My grace cannot help you unless you accept it and make use of it. Read, reflect, and pray, so that you may better understand what I want you to know. Make frequent use of My sacraments to gain strength for life's daily activities. Through My Church

and your own interior life I will guide you each day toward eternal life.

THINK:

Jesus is ready to help me at every step. He wants me to become more and more like Him in my daily activities. His Church, His sacraments, and His grace are always ready to assist me. With the help of these, I am to do my part each day. I must see what virtues I need most, consider how Jesus would practice these virtues in my place, and then make a determined effort to imitate Him. He expects a continued effort in spite of repeated failures and constant difficulties.

PRAY:

O Jesus, My King and Teacher, grant me the wisdom to listen to Your voice and to follow Your holy example. You said that we must strive to be perfect as our heavenly Father is perfect. You also told us that whoever sees You, sees the heavenly Father also. There is no greater achievement on earth than to imitate Your divine goodness in my daily life. Lord, I have many faults and numberless weaknesses. Yet, at Your command I shall try to become daily a little more like You. This is what You desire of me. Grant me the strength to begin at last. Let me make an honest effort throughout the day. I promise that I will refuse to be discouraged by my failures. I am determined to begin over again no matter how often I may fall down in my resolutions. You deserve such loyalty and unselfish devotion. Help me, my Jesus. *Amen.*

CHAPTER 3

Christ's Lessons

CHRIST:

M Y CHILD, learn to listen to My voice, and you will make great progress in a short time. One who listens to Me learns much more rapidly than one who relies only on his natural talents. My lessons bring wisdom, peace, and spiritual strength.

2. My faithful pupils learn to value earthly things for what they are really worth. They understand how quickly worldly honors fade. They know how short-lived earthly prosperity is, and how perfect and undying are the joys of Heaven. They realize how

puny and weak human love is when compared to the love of the infinite God.

3. My lessons are suited to each individual. Whether they use books, or prayer, or sacraments, or personal guidance of a spiritual director, I reach their soul through these different means, giving them light to understand and strength for action.

4. What I say to each person depends on his spiritual level. Some people never get beyond the most ordinary knowledge because they have made no efforts to rise any higher. To those who try to come closer to Me, I bring greater understanding of some particular truth. To those who make frequent efforts to give Me their best attention, I grant a wonderful interior vision, a deep insight into the beauty and grandeur of My holy Truth.

5. Beware, however, of all foolish extremes. These are never inspired by My grace. They arise from spiritual pride, spiritual gluttony, or some desire for self-satisfaction. Never forget this: whatever interferes with your daily duties and obligations, is against My Will.

THINK:

I must become a spiritual listener, turning my mind to God occasionally during the day. Whether I use books or my own efforts, Jesus will reach me and give me His thoughts. He will help me to know His desires and to see His Will Where any doubt or question arises, as to whether my inspiration is truly from God, I should consult a priest. Jesus longs to tell me many things about life's deeper meaning and Heaven's wonderful joys. I cannot hear His voice unless I learn to pause and listen for it.

PRAY:

Lord, make me eager to hear Your voice and to follow Your holy words in my daily life. My pride and foolish self-seeking make me so deaf to You that too often I hear only the voices of this world. One distraction after another fills my thoughts. Give me grace to hear Your loving voice within my soul. Grant me a great, unselfish generosity to give You more of my time and attention. You desire only my true and lasting welfare. Make me an active listener; that is, one who honestly tries to follow what You tell him.

I shall avoid all self-deception and foolish extremes by consulting my confessor in all doubts or difficulties. Never will I follow my inspirations if they interfere with my daily obligations. Speak to me Lord; Your servant is listening. *Amen*.

CHAPTER 4

True Perfection

CHRIST:

MY CHILD, when I send you spiritual desires and interior consolation, do not consider yourself holier than you were before. Spiritual progress does not consist of these gifts alone. They are not proof of higher virtue.

2. True spiritual progress and all solid virtue consist of self-surrender to Me. Seek to know ever better what I think of your daily life. Try to understand more clearly what I desire of you. Do not think that you know enough, or that you are doing well enough in your daily life. As long as I deserve better than what you are, you must not be self-satisfied.

3. Your effort must be to gain more and more of My thoughts, My desires and My outlook on life. You must also try to guide and control your daily life as I desire. Do this with complete devotion to My Will. With equal peace of soul give thanks for whatever I send you, be it visible success or failure, prosperity or adversity.

4. My loyal disciples follow Me in humility and in selfless obedience. Their patience keeps them from discouragement and their charity preserves them from disgust. They advance in perfection each day, pleasing Me more and more in their way of thinking, speaking, and acting. Come, follow Me along the path of true perfection.

THINK:

Many people do not know the true meaning of Christian perfection. They think it merely means going to church, saying a certain number of prayers, and avoiding all serious sins. One who does this much is holy because he is in the state of grace, and consequently has God dwelling in his soul. Such a person, however, may be very imperfect, being careless about his lesser faults and defects. Others think that Christian perfection consists of extraordinary spiritual manifestations like visions or extreme penances. These things, however, may not necessarily come from God, but from a sick mind, or one's own self-love, or even from the devil.

Christian perfection begins with the state of grace, but it aims further. One who seeks this perfection, strives to live more fully for God by a greater imitation of Christ's earthly example. He seeks to dedicate himself as completely to the Will of the heavenly Father as Jesus did. Hence he tries to think, speak, and act more like Jesus each day. The greater his success in "putting on" Christ, the greater his degree of Christian perfection.

PRAY:

My Jesus, model of all true perfection, You said that I must be perfect as Your heavenly Father is perfect. You also said that he who sees You sees also the Father. Therefore, by being more like You in my daily life, I shall become more like our heavenly Father. As I go along throughout my daily activities, make me more conscious of Your holy example. Show me how I may imitate You in each event of daily life. To dispose myself for these wonderful graces, I shall try to read, meditate, and reflect how I may become more like You. Give me strength to remain loyal to You when my selfish human nature clamors for its own satisfactions. I desire to give You this greater loyalty because You deserve it. You have done so much for my sake. Help me do more for You. *Amen.*

CHAPTER 5

A Sustained Effort

CHRIST:

MY CHILD, do not be afraid nor discouraged at hearing my instructions about the way to perfection. Pray for a burning desire to follow Me along this way. Make a daily effort to do so. Many people refuse even to consider such an effort. Others make a half hearted attempt, but they turn away at the first sign of difficulty. My loyal followers try again and again, in spite of repeated failures. By their refusal to quit, they go far in the work of self-perfection.

2. Make your resolution to follow My example in your daily life. Then do your best to fulfill the resolution. Do not judge your progress by your feelings, nor by visible signs. Just purify your intention, concentrate on the virtue you need or desire, and strive to eliminate all natural self-seeking. How few are those who are really all for Me, those who try to please Me in all things simply because I deserve it.

3. True, this perfection is not reached in a day. However, it will never be reached if you never start trying. It is not easy to live entirely for Me, continually trying to control and direct your feelings and selfish desires for My sake. I shall stand by you to guide and strengthen you. Still, you will have to do your part. Make every effort to guide your thinking throughout the day, so that you may not lose sight of Me in your various activities. From time to time test your pure intention by contradicting your natural desires.

THINK:

It is not enough to make good resolutions. I must also make plans, practical plans about keeping the resolutions. Having done this, and having begged God's blessing, I should get busy with the virtue or fault in question. Failures need not discourage me. Rather, they should strengthen my determination to see this matter through. My loyalty to Jesus will show itself in my refusal to abandon this glorious effort for Christian perfection. As far as Jesus is concerned, if I am willing to try, and to continue to try in spite of failures, He will be content with me. Sincerity and honest effort are the surest signs of unselfishness with God.

PRAY:

Dearest Lord, this work of self-purification is not the work of a day, nor is it easy. I long to make whatever daily effort is necessary. I yearn for the day when my thoughts will turn easily, almost naturally, to the higher things in life. I desire to see the eternal importance of the temporal matters which occupy me today. This will come with my spiritual growth. I must do what reading, reflecting, and praying I can, in order to gain the graces necessary for this degree of union with You. As I continue to practice mortification and self control, I shall come closer and closer to this spiritual state. *Amen.*

CHAPTER 6

Dispositions of a True Follower of Christ

CHRIST:

MY CHILD, if you want to be a true follower of Mine, gain control over your blind selfishness. Many never enjoy My friendship and love because they never really try to reach Me. They pay too much attention to their unreasoning natural desires and blind human appetites.

2. Your unreasoning nature wants more than what is necessary. In order to become the master of your life, rid yourself of all unnecessary desires. Learn to live with less, and you will have more time for Me.

3. The more you surrender to your human desires, the more you will be distracted from Me. The secret of union with Me lies in separating yourself from as much as possible in this life.

4. Turn your back on whatever threatens to come between you and Me. Indeed, be

ready to abandon any person or thing which
does not in some way help you become a better man. Your earthly life is so very short.
Do not waste any of it.

5. If only you will make the effort, I shall
help you to rise above earthly distractions.
My grace will give you a keen appreciation
of My greatness, goodness, and love. It will
also fill your heart with a higher love and
a heavenly peace. You will learn to prefer
My Will to your own, and the world will no
longer seem so all-important to you.

THINK:

This brief lesson contains the secret of
great perfection and peace. If I do not have
Christ's peace, it is because I have not dared
to follow His teaching. I ought to let His
words guide me in my daily activities. My
moods, feelings, and desires will be good for
me only if I control them and direct them as
Jesus commands. Why do I waste precious
time with things that are unnecessary,
things which fail to improve my daily life?
As I rise higher in perfection, I will see the
foolishness of many things which now have
power to sway and attract me.

PRAY:

My Jesus, light of the world, be the light of my soul, so that I may never again go astray in the darkness of worldly desires and blind self-deception. Let me be brave enough to abandon any person or thing which leads me away from You in my daily life. I want to look to Your Will before following my natural desires. You know what is good for me. I want to follow Your wisdom in everything I do throughout the day. I beg You for strength to follow Your Will when it leads me toward what I dislike or fear. O Jesus, be my light and my strength. *Amen.*

CHAPTER 7

Christ's Call to Action

CHRIST:

MY CHILD, do not be too impressed by the beautiful language or witty sayings of men. My standard is not one of words, but of action. My teachings are meant to influence your will. If you live them in your daily life, you prove your love for Me. Only action will satisfy this heart of Mine. The most beautiful words are not half so beautiful to

Me as the life of one who follows My teachings in his daily activities.

2. Never read or learn anything for the sake of appearing wise. Do it but only to improve your daily life. Some people study in order to impress others. Their knowledge is vanity because it does not make them better in action. As a good tree is known by its good fruit, so too is a good man known by the goodness of his thoughts, words, and deeds.

3. Though I am pleased with good desires, I am convinced only by action. How hard do you try to follow your good desires? That is how much you really care for Me. Never forget My words, "If you love Me, you will keep My commandments. Not he who says, 'Lord, Lord!' will enter the Kingdom of Heaven, but rather he who does the Will of My Father, he will enter the Kingdom of Heaven."

4. Learn of Me, and you will have the best knowledge. Follow that knowledge in your daily life, and you will be living a wonderful life. You will be admired and praised by the

angels and saints of Heaven, and by Me, the King of Heaven.

5. Many things are unimportant. They bring you only a distracted mind and they prevent you from following Me more perfectly in your daily life. Put these things out of your life, so that you may give Me a fuller loyalty and a more perfect love.

THINK:

Words are meant to point out truth, and desires help me reach out for it, but action is the most convincing proof that I really love God's Truth. I need to be more simple in my following of Christ. What He says I should honestly try to do. His Church will protect me against any imprudence, extremes, and errors. In following Christ I must seek neither attention nor excitement, but a simple loyalty of action. Only in this way can I avoid self-deception and false self-interest in its many disguises.

PRAY:

My God and Saviour, until I seek You above all else in daily life, I deserve only pity and contempt; pity for my folly, and contempt for my stubborn wrong-doing.

Never can I find greater good for myself than in Your holy Will. Nowhere shall I discover a more devoted loyalty to me than the loyalty of Your Sacred Heart. Make me less a man of words and more a man of action. I can never again deceive myself in Your service if I make action my standard of loyalty. You Yourself will guide me through Your holy Church and strengthen me through Your sacraments. I hope to turn this daily life of mine into one great act of love for You. *Amen.*

CHAPTER 8

Standards of Christ

CHRIST:

MY CHILD, there is a great difference between a man who learns by natural talent alone, and one who learns with the help of My grace. The knowledge which comes through grace is far higher, richer, and nobler for your daily life than any other knowledge.

2. My knowledge brings a holy joy and a new energy to the soul. He who possesses it

sees much more in life than what appears on the surface.

3. Worldly wisdom is foolish in comparison with the knowledge which I give. I teach the freedom of self-control and the joy of spiritual perfection.

4. The world is often fascinated by the deeds of selfish and proud men, but the virtues of daily life do not always interest the worldly-minded. Worldly people envy one who is rich, strong, attractive, clever, a good writer, a good singer, a fine workman, etc. They would be wiser if they admired and imitated the patient man, the prayerful man, the unselfish one, the considerate person; in short, those who seek to imitate Me in their daily life.

5. Worldly people judge greatness by external appearances, but I judge first and foremost what is within a man—his desires and his efforts.

THINK:

Christ teaches me the greatest knowledge in all the universe—the knowledge of God's love and man's true greatness. Christ's peace will be mine when I have received His knowledge and have begun to live it in my daily life. People will no longer have power over my interior dispositions because I will really belong to God. He will be my guiding light. My standards for respecting people will be His standards. My eyes will be so fixed on Him that I shall become less and less influenced by self-interest or human judgments.

PRAY:

O Jesus, You are the Truth of God! Amid the darkness of confused thinking and conflicting ideas, Your light of Truth shines bright. Let my judgments never be influenced by the people who disagree with Your standards. Though the world may laugh me to scorn, I will fear no human judgments, as long as I loyally follow Your standards in my daily life. Too often have I been guilty of selfishness, pride, and vanity in my own thoughts and judgments. I looked at external appearances, visible results, and human recognition. You look at the faith, love, and unselfish intentions in our actions. These are the virtues which make my actions holy and make me like You. I hope to follow these standards from now on. *Amen.*

PART ONE

B. *The Means for Advancing in Christ's School*

CHAPTER 9

Spiritual Reading

CHRIST:

MY CHILD, reading and reflecting are a great help to your spiritual progress. My doctrine is explained in many books, written under the supervision and guidance of My Church. Some of these books are written simply, and some are very profound and learned. Choose those which will help you most toward a greater understanding and appreciation of My Truth. Do not read to impress others, but rather to be impressed yourself. Read so that you may learn My way of thinking and of doing things.

2. Read the Holy Scripture, but be sure that it is a version approved by My Church. I inspired the human authors of these holy writings, but I did not inspire the men who later translated these works. My Church

has the power to detect errors and inaccuracies wherever My Truth is involved.

3. I promised to stand by My Church to the end of time. I said that the gates of hell would never conquer Her, and that those who believe in Her would be saved. I never said that Scripture alone was to guide anyone toward eternal life. In fact, through My Apostle Peter I warned everyone that the Scriptures are not always easy to understand; nor do all men find salvation in them. You can see the proof of this in the numberless opinions and beliefs which separate so many sects from one another. If I agreed with all of them, I would be contradicting Myself many times.

4. Follow the light which I left behind Me—My Church. Those who hear Her, hear Me. Learn the truth which I have left in Her care. My truth will be a light to you in time of doubt and worry. It will give you a wonderful mirror of life, to help you detect where sin may be lurking and where greater virtue lies.

THINK:

Reading brings me many thoughts. It helps me to understand better what I already believe. It keeps my outlook on life fresh and unconfused. It also keeps my enthusiasm alive. One who does not read, is like a man who tries to live on the smallest possible amount of food and sunshine. His spiritual life will eventually shrivel up and become anemic. It may even die when a strong temptation comes along. I can read safely only when I follow the guidance of Christ's Church. He has given Her power and authority to direct me in all matters of faith and morals. I want to read, reflect, and pray a little each day so that I may follow Our Lord more intelligently in my daily activities.

PRAY:

My Saviour, let me never become mechanical in my religious practices. You gave me so much when You gave me Your Church. Through Her I can make my daily life ever richer. Give me the wisdom to read and reflect often upon Your wonderful teachings. Grant me a deep interest in Your holy truth, and a supernatural joy in learning more about life's most important treasures. I desire to share Your outlook and viewpoint in the daily events of my earthly life. I hope to understand You better by a more frequent reading of spiritual books. *Amen.*

CHAPTER 10

A Prayerful Disposition

CHRIST:

MY CHILD, many would like to live a more prayerful daily life. They desire the peace which comes from a closer union with Me. Still, they will not do what it takes to reach this heavenly peace.

2. Let Me tell you how to achieve this. Limit your activities to a few useful projects, and abandon all useless interests. To do this you will have to control some of your present desires. When you have limited your interests, you will have more time to turn your attention to Me.

3. Then shall I teach you the wisdom of the saints and bestow on you the joy of the angels. You will gradually become more conscious of My nearness, and you will learn to

speak and act differently in your daily life. The trials and troubles of earthly life will frighten you less and less.

4. This deliberate separation from all useless interests is necessary for you if you are to come closer to Me. Such interests are like chains around your mind. They tie down your attention and prevent you from turning easily to Me throughout the day.

5. Too few know how to give Me their full attention for any length of time. Too many people are continually absorbed in unnecessary distractions. Happy are the eyes which see Me often throughout the day. Happy the ears which hear My voice above the distractions of their daily activities.

THINK:

I really need to tear myself away from all needless activities and unnecessary distractions in order to come closer to God in my daily life. God gives great graces to one who earnestly strives to improve his daily contact with Heaven. That man will see more in this earthly life than those who live mainly for this world's good things. As long as my mind and desires are controlled by earthly interests, I shall find it difficult to reach God. I must take definite measures to prefer God's company to human company. The struggle will become easier as I come to know God better.

PRAY:

Lord, let Your holy grace fall on this sinful heart of mine, so that I may love most what is most lovable, know best what is most important, and desire first what is most valuable. Let me fear and hate whatever draws me away from You. I do not want to judge things as they appear, but as they really help me to please You more. Teach me to pray. Help me to love Your company and to seek it as often as possible. Make me aware of Your presence throughout the day. *Amen.*

CHAPTER 11

True Devotion to Christ

CHRIST:

M Y CHILD, some people have Me on their lips, but not in their hearts. Some express their devotion to Me with prayer books; some do it with holy pictures; and some do it with holy images or external signs. Now all of these things are good, but they are no proof of true devotion to Me. They are only a means to help men practice devotion. These holy objects are useless if they do not influence your daily thoughts, words, and actions.

2. True devotion to Me is not a mere feeling, nor is it a passing emotion. It is an act of respect and loyalty to Me. Genuine devotion consists of a personal attachment of your will to Mine. It is a sincere intention to please Me in all things, a disregard of self in doing whatever I desire of you. It draws you close to Me, not only in your thoughts and desires, but also in your daily actions.

3. As you prove such devotion, I shall grant you still greater graces. Your mind will rise more easily to heavenly thoughts. Your heart will strive more constantly after greater virtues. You will advance daily in true perfection, thinking, speaking, and acting more like Me.

4. My loyal followers gradually learn to get along with less and less of this world's

good things. They feel an urge to devote more time to good works and to prayer. They find that time spent with Me is all too short, and they yearn for a more perfect union with Me.

THINK:

Though I may use books, pictures, and religious articles, I must never think that these automatically make me holier. They are external helps to holiness. They can help me come closer to God by reminding me of His presence and by arousing in me a greater desire to please Him. If, however, these external objects do not affect my daily activities, I may as well not have them. Wearing a crucifix will not save a man who refuses to be patient with his daily trials. So too my devotions at home can never take the place of Sunday Mass. The standard of true devotion was set by Jesus Himself: "If you love Me, you will keep My commandments." How am I living the commandments of Christ? That is the sure gauge of my devotion to Him. Will I be foolish enough to think that I please God simply because I say a certain number of prayers daily, or use certain religious articles, or even go to church daily? Doing these things is only half of my spiritual life. The other half consists in showing goodness and unselfishness in my dealings with people. One half without the other is incomplete, and therefore unsatisfactory to God.

PRAY:

My Jesus, I want my daily life to be a fulfillment of all that you teach me through books, prayers, and other religious objects. I desire to live what You tell me through the Church, through the sacraments, and through my own interior life. My kindness, patience, generosity, and unselfishness in my daily life will prove that I use religious articles because I love You, and not for selfish or superstitious reasons. I want to use these articles to improve my daily loyalty to Your holy Will. I will also use them to obtain Your blessings on my daily occupations. Finally I will use them as a badge of loyalty to You, so that I may remind others of You. Let me never separate my interior life from my external dealings with people. *Amen.*

CHAPTER 12

Distractions in Daily Life

CHRIST:

MY CHILD, so often you kneel before Me only in body. In spirit you are somewhere else. Many times you begin to think of Me or speak to Me, and then find yourself thinking of other persons or things.

2. You say that these distractions come to you in spite of your good will. Let Me show you how to deal with distractions, so that you may learn at last the secret of My loyal followers. Only action is the proof of sincerity. How sincerely do you desire to turn your attention to Me throughout the day?

3. Distractions are thoughts, imaginations, feelings, and desires which hold your attention longer than they deserve. At a time when you might direct your attention to Me or to some profitable activity, you often find yourself fighting to keep control of your thoughts. These distractions are due to the various experiences which you have in your daily life. By diminishing these

experiences, you will also lessen the number of your distractions.

4. True, you are obliged to give your attention to a number of people and attend to various duties and needs throughout the day. Yet, you need not give your attention to these people and things any more than is necessary. You could eliminate many a distraction without neglecting the necessary obligations of your daily life.

5. If you really want to become more aware of My nearness to you throughout the day, you must do your part to gain so great a favor. Begin at once to examine what comes between you and Me. See how many things you can eliminate in your daily life without neglecting your duties and obligations. Unless you make a determined effort to concentrate your attention on Me, you will always be the victim of distractions.

THINK:

Holy desires are worthless unless they are put into action. The saints tried so hard to keep their attention on God. They deliberately avoided all unnecessary distractions. They learned how to fix their minds on holy things throughout the day. They knew how to enjoy God's company. True, I must give my attention to my duties and obligations. So often, however, I give my attention to what is unnecessary. Is it any wonder that I find prayer hard or strange? I want to begin today to avoid unnecessary distractions, so that I may think more often of God and speak to Him more frequently throughout the day.

PRAY:

Dear Holy Spirit, my God, please come to my assistance in this daily journey toward eternity. Let me see earthly pleasures according to their true value, without expecting too much from them. Forgive me when my mind wanders in prayer, and grant me interior strength to avoid unnecessary distractions. Show me how to recollect my thoughts and control my senses, and let me forget worldly things when I am united with You in prayer. Whatever leads me away from You is worthless and dangerous. You are my greatest treasure. In all my activities I desire to be aware of Your nearness, so that I may live my earthly life in union with You. *Amen*.

CHAPTER 13

Striving for Devotion

CHRIST:

SON, the grace of devotion is not just a holy feeling, nor is it a religious mood. It is an intelligent attachment of your will to Me and to whatever I command or desire of you.

2. This is a very great grace. I will grant it to you if you will make a sincere effort to turn your back on whatever hinders your spiritual progress. You must empty your heart of all useless interests in order to make room for Me.

3. Often it is such a small matter that prevents one from obtaining this grace. Misguided self-interest cuts many people off from this glorious gift.

4. I desire you to have this grace. It will make you loyal to Me in all things. If you do not have it yet, it is because you have not yet prepared your soul for it. Pray for it and labor for it. Gain control of your feelings

and unreasoning desires by acts of self-denial and self-sacrifice. Above all, begin a determined battle against the outstanding faults in your daily life.

5. With this grace of true devotion, you will find many things easy which now seem difficult and impossible. You will never again lose sight of My power, wisdom, and love, and you will consider it a privilege to follow My Will.

THINK:

If I make a firm and persevering effort to abandon my foolish love for unnecessary distractions, God will give me the gift of devotion. From then on, I will have a steady loyalty to Christ. I will no longer depend on feelings or moods, but will follow God's Will intelligently and faithfully even when I do not feel like doing so.

PRAY:

My loyal and loving Saviour, you lived an earthly life of devotion to Your Father's Will. By self-giving action You made reparation for my many acts of disobedience to His holy commandments. By self-giving action You also proved Your love for me. You

gave me an example of true devotion. Grant
me the grace of true and solid devotion to
You, so that I may prove my love for You by
self-giving. No matter how I may feel, let me
do only what is pleasing to You. I desire not
only to avoid all sin, but also to do many little extra things for Your sake. Make my devotion like Yours—a constant self-offering
which will prove my love beyond all doubt.
Amen.

CHAPTER 14

The Daily Path to Holiness

CHRIST:

MY CHILD, live your daily life in My
presence by trying to be constantly
aware of My nearness to you. The more you
strive to develop this virtue, the more I will
help you to acquire it. With this grace you
will grow in love and kindness toward others. Your faults will become smaller and
less frequent, and your goodness will shine
before the world.

2. This daily labor for virtue requires a
continual effort. You must go on trying, like
a man swimming against the current. To

stop trying, even for a little while, is to lose ground. Without a determined and constant effort there will be no progress.

3. Do not be afraid of work, inconvenience, or suffering. My way to Heaven was the way of prayer, work, and suffering. My love is symbolized by the cross and My pierced heart. Let your love for Me use the same symbols. Live a life of prayer, work, and suffering. As I chose to make personal sacrifices for you in My daily life, so too should you seek daily opportunities to make personal sacrifices for Me.

THINK:

To earn Heaven I must become God-like in my daily life. It seems so impossible. Yet God Himself wants to lead me on toward this goal. A lively consciousness of God's presence will help me to control and direct my likes and dislikes. Gradually there will be less and less unguarded moments, less slips into my old faults. I shall gradually come to see God's Will in every event that comes along. God desires to grant me this wonderful grace. I must prepare myself for it by beginning today to practice acts of faith in God's presence, and acts of self-offering in my daily activities. Too many people make a feeble effort to improve themselves, and then give up because of repeated failures. Others claim they feel too small and unworthy of such a gift from God. Their real reason, however, is not a virtuous one. They are afraid of the effort required or the sacrifice involved. It is God who wants me to aim this high. It is therefore my duty to follow His Will by trying my best over and over again.

PRAY:

My Jesus, help me to become aware of Your nearness to me throughout the day. I do not wish to fail You. You want me to aim at the highest perfection. You said: "Be perfect as your heavenly Father is perfect!" That means I must never feel that I am good enough, no matter how virtuous I may become. I intend to start trying today, trying to be more like You in everything I do. You are my Model because You also said: "He that sees Me, sees the Father also." You are the perfect image of Your heavenly Father. By imitating You, I shall become more

God-like. My efforts will be much easier if I can become constantly aware of Your nearness to me throughout the day. Grant me this wonderful grace, so that I may become what You desire, a true man of God. In this way every moment of my earthly life will be a step toward Heaven's perfect life. *Amen.*

CHAPTER 15

Human Hurts

CHRIST:

MY CHILD, what is man that you should fear his contempt or insults? Today he seems so strong and powerful, and tomorrow he will be laid in his coffin. Fear only sin, and stand by Me. Human words and even injuries are not as terrible as they seem. My martyrs, who now shine forth in heavenly glory, can tell you how true this is.

2. The harsh critics and the persecutor hurt themselves far more than they hurt their victims. They shall not escape My judgment. I will deal with them as they dealt with their fellow man. Do not seek revenge

against them by word or deed. Leave them to Me, without wishing them any harm.

3. If the criticism and fault-finding of others confuse and discourage you, turn to Me and let Me strengthen you with patience. I shall relieve you in your confusion and injury.

4. Remember too that this suffering may well be offered to Me as a reparation for your many sins against Me. This consideration will make you more willing to be despised and forsaken by people. You will then find strength to bear this present trial in peace.

5. At times it is good for you to suffer opposition and to have people think ill of you and slight you, even when you mean well. This is often a valuable means for gaining humility and patience. Then will you call on Me to judge what goes on within you as you realize the unreliability of human judgments and friendships.

THINK:

As long as I live among human beings, I must expect misunderstandings, differences of opinion, criticism, and even bad will. Different people will treat me differently. I tend to treat others as they treat me. If I do this, I shall be making a mistake. Jesus wants me to treat everyone kindly, patiently, and unselfishly, for His sake. He wants me to see not them, but Him. He will say at the last Judgment, "You did it to Me." People may think me a fool for not seeking an eye for an eye and a tooth for a tooth, but Jesus wants me to forgive and pray for those who hurt me. If I find this too hard, I need only think of what He has done to forgive me my sins and draw me toward Heaven.

PRAY:

My loving and all-wise Saviour, You lowered Yourself to the ground to make up for my many sins. You even asked the Father to forgive me as You hung in agony on the cross. Am I greater than You that I should resent the unkind ways of those around me? In making up for my sins, You embraced many of the human trials which I resent in my daily life. Will I refuse to be like You by my impatience with the human faults around me? Besides, I should not forget my sins. I can offer these trials in reparation for the selfishness which I have shown You in my daily sins and imperfections. Grant me the wisdom to see this truth, and give me the love to follow it. I shall fear no man's words or judgments as much as I fear my own pride and selfishness. *Amen.*

CHAPTER 16

A Higher Love

CHRIST:

MY CHILD, the more you desire the glory of Heaven, the less will you care for the good things of this life. The glory and praises of men are all too short. They are imperfect and dissatisfying in one way or another. Your greatest praise and glory on earth will come not from people, but from a good conscience.

2. When you have the grace to live this truth, you will look peacefully on many things which trouble the worldly man. You will see others esteemed and honored, but you will go unnoticed. Others will succeed in their efforts, while you taste failure and disappointment. Others will speak and impress their hearers, whereas your words will make little or no impression. Others will ask

and obtain their request, but you will ask in vain. Others will be trusted with some responsibility, and you will be overlooked as though incapable.

3. True, your human pride will rebel at such treatment. To bear it in silence is no mean accomplishment. Yet, I want you to rise even higher than this. I want you to draw closer to My heart and taste a bit of My power and love. Then will you rise above the desires and ambitions of this earthly life. You will disregard your own conveniences and inconveniences. You will be so eager to do more for Me, that you will take with joy what you once avoided and despised. As you grow in this higher love for Me, you will come to forget all self-consideration. You will eventually love Me so much as to despise self.

THINK:

If the saints are examples of this higher virtue, then it is true that the love of Jesus makes one desire ever more of suffering and contempt. This higher love makes a man look for the cross in daily life and embrace it heartily. The Apostles actually rejoiced when they suffered humiliation and contempt for Jesus' sake. They were happy to embrace what most men fear and avoid. I cannot quite appreciate this great grace now, but I should pray for it. Moreover, in my daily life, I can at least try to be glad when little contradictions, reproaches, failures, and the like come to me.

PRAY:

Dearest Lord, this higher love is possible only if I place You above all other desires. Many do this in their words, but too few actually do it in their daily life. I will not feel hurt at being unnoticed by others, if I want to be noticed only by You. It is because I do not really see You as my highest Treasure that I sin by anger, resentment, envy, and vanity in these human trials of everyday life. I desire to begin at last to do my daily tasks for You alone, and to seek only Your thanks, appreciation, and love. Let humans deal with me as they will. As long as I have Your friendship, my life will be an eternal success. *Amen.*

CHAPTER 17

Recalling the Sufferings of Jesus

CHRIST:

MY CHILD, do you wish to know the secret of My saints? Would you like to understand how they could suffer so many things in peace, and even with joy? They meditated often on My trials and sufferings. By burying themselves in My life, they drew strength for many trials. They placed their hearts within Mine and were filled with a love which could bear all things for My sake.

2. Come to Me and enter into My heart. You will find strength and comfort in your daily trials and sufferings. You will no longer mind being slighted and neglected by people. You will face evil tongues and bad will with a calm and peaceful soul.

3. All this will you do because you know Me and understand My life. I, too, was despised by men in My earthly life. In My hour of greatest need, while My enemies mocked and insulted Me, I was abandoned by My friends. For love of you I consented to

be despised and to suffer an untold agony. Will you, then, dare to complain when you have to bear similar things? I had enemies who said many evil things against Me. Can you, then, grieve because you do not enjoy the friendship and good will of everyone? How can you be a true follower of Mine, if you will not carry My cross? Those who wish to reign with Me, must suffer and fight with Me.

THINK:

This is the secret of the saints. They were so deeply in love with Jesus that they wished to share His life. They wanted to be His friends not merely in His glory, but also in His battles and trials. If I want to be a friend of Jesus, I too must be with Him in suffering and in trials. I must not feel sorry for myself, nor even consider myself. This I can do in my daily life. I need not consider the people who make my life harder. I should see only a glorious opportunity to suffer something for the love of Jesus.

PRAY:

My loving Saviour, I desire to be a true friend of yours as You have been, and are, my truest and best friend. Let me drink Your bitter Chalice as You drank it for my sake. I wish to forget self and leave all consolation in Your hands. For myself I ask only that I may carefully bear whatever trials and sufferings come to me this day. You deserve all that I can bear, and more. Nor will I forget that the sufferings of this life are not worthy to be compared with the glory that is to come. Let me offer you all of my heart. It is little enough! *Amen.*

CHAPTER 18

Man's Daily Cross

CHRIST:

MY CHILD, I had to bear many trials throughout My earthly life. Knowing this, how can you seek rest and pleasure for yourself on earth? Believe Me, it is a great mistake to expect anything else but suffering and hardship in this life! Man's earthly life is full of miseries and crosses. Wherever you turn, you will find a cross.

2. If you carry it willingly, you will find greater strength in the cross, and it will lead you towards Heaven. If you bear it

unwillingly, you only make it a greater burden than it already is; and you still have to bear it. One who runs away from the cross is only running toward another cross, perhaps a heavier one.

3. There is no other road to Heaven except the way of the cross. No man can escape his cross. Even My saints went through their earthly life, burdened by the cross. Not a single hour of My earthly life was free of the cross. I entered into My glory by suffering and dying upon the cross. Do not fear the cross. I shall help you to bear it.

THINK:

As I embrace my daily cross, I shall find Jesus standing on the other side of it, waiting to help me carry it. I shall not have to carry it alone. My daily life is a partnership with Jesus. He walks every step of it with me. As He proved His love for me by embracing His cross, so do I prove my love for Him by embracing my daily trials. True, I may always try to solve my daily problems and remedy my troubles. When, however, my efforts have failed, I should not lose my self-control by impatience, anger, or rebellion against God's Will. Nor need I seek to avoid all of the trials which come my way. At times I can deliberately allow myself to endure things or people who annoy me, at least a bit longer than I would naturally like. The more I grow in genuine love for Jesus, the less will I fear or resent the cross.

PRAY:

Lord Jesus, my crucified King, let me never fail to recognize Your banner—the cross. You said, "If anyone wishes to come after Me, let him deny himself, and take up his cross daily, and follow Me." Your words are clear. If I love the cross, I am a true follower of Yours. If I refuse it by anger, impatience, fault-finding, criticism of superiors, and unkindness, I am no true follower of Yours. Grant me the light to recognize Your cross when people and events annoy and disturb me. Let me consider the situation, try to remedy it if necessary, but at all times face it with Christlike self-control. Each moment of the day, I wish to be aware of Your nearness. When trials come, I wish to handle them as You did in Your earthly life. In union with You I hope to make this life of mine a daily act of love for You. *Amen.*

CHAPTER 19

Desiring the Cross

CHRIST:

MY CHILD, to bear your daily cross, to actually love it, to gain control over your body by punishing it, to avoid honors, to desire insults, to despise yourself and to want others to despise you, to bear all trials and disappointments with peace of soul, to desire no prosperity in this world all of this is not natural to any normal human being. One who has these desires and follows them out, is either abnormal, or he is putting on a show to get admiration or some other human satisfaction, or else he is receiving the higher wisdom of divine grace.

2. Without My grace, such spiritual victories over self are impossible. Your weak human nature could not rise to such heights of supernatural virtue. My grace brings you a strength unknown to the worldly man. With this strength you can gain control over your pride and earthly self-seeking.

3. Be a good and loyal soldier of Mine. Be determined to embrace your cross for love of Me. I warn you now that if you are resolved to prove your love for Me, you can only do it by embracing your daily cross of annoyances, labors, disappointments, opposition, and even different forms of persecution. The higher you rise in true and solid virtue, the more easily will you recognize your crosses and embrace them. In fact, as your love for Me grows, so too will your love for the cross.

4. When I feel that I can trust you with a heavier cross, I will give it to you. Fear not, however, for I will never burden you beyond your strength. With these heavier crosses I will be offering you greater glory and happiness in Heaven.

THINK:

My strength to bear the cross will come from the cross itself. I need only prepare my soul for it by prayer and self-training. I should practice little acts of self-denial in preparation for the unexpected trial which will soon come. Then, as I am faced with the trial, Jesus will help me understand its higher value. He will show me how I can draw closer to Him by embracing this cross with patience and self-forgetfulness. The more selflessly I embrace my daily crosses, the more shall I find in them wisdom, understanding, love, and supernatural strength. I shall see through the emptiness of earthly satisfactions and pretense. My self-sacrifices will bring me a firmer love for Jesus, and I shall gradually find it easier to suffer my daily trials for His sake. In fact, if I generously follow these graces, I may even receive grace to desire a heavier cross for love of Jesus.

PRAY:

My crucified King, I kneel now at the foot of Your cross, and consider the heavenly lesson which You teach from there. In Your suffering I shall learn how I, too, should embrace my daily crosses, in order to make reparation for my sins, become more fit for higher graces, and offer to You a love purified of selfishness and self-consideration. You deserve such devotion from me. True, my human nature shudders at the thought of suffering any insults, criticisms, mockery, failures, disappointments, and pain. With the higher wisdom and strength which I shall gain through my present crosses, I shall prepare myself for still greater ones. You alone can perform this glorious change within me. I hope for it, with the help of Your holy grace. *Amen.*

CHAPTER 20

Benefits of the Cross

CHRIST:

MY CHILD, when you have come to know the full value of the cross, it will no longer be such a puzzle to you, nor will you ever again seek to avoid it. You will then see it as a valuable help for many spiritual gifts right here on earth. You will embrace your daily trials with joy.

2. In the cross you will find a deep interior peace and joy. You will understand why those who hate or fear the cross are to be pitied. The cross will bring you a clear mind which will see the heavenly value of what you are enduring. The cross will help you to think straight. You will look on the cross as a ladder raising you up toward Me.

Your mental and spiritual health will be excellent because you will be free from fear, confusion, and discontent. In the daily cross you will find a fuller life, a deep sense of My nearness to you, and of your daily progress toward Heaven. Temptations cannot shake one who truly loves the cross.

3. If there were anything on earth better than the cross, would I not have chosen it? The cross, more than anything else, will enrich your soul with many virtues on earth, and countless merits in Heaven, The cross will best prepare you for your last and most important examination. No man can be sure of his own true worth until he has learned to recognize and embrace the cross in his daily life. That is why I commanded: "If anyone wishes to come after Me, let him deny himself, take up his cross, and follow Me."

4. Never forget for a moment this truth: Through many trials will you enter into the eternal kingdom of Heaven. Therefore, take up your cross daily and follow Me.

THINK:

I must never forget that Jesus' life on earth was a protest against all blind human pride and selfishness. These are my worst enemies. Therefore, I must embrace my daily cross as a protection against pride and selfishness. Secondly, Jesus embraced His cross as an example of true virtue. He followed His Father's Will in preference to His own human will. Therefore, I must do likewise when my daily life is disagreeable or difficult. Thirdly, He died for me to prove His personal love for me. In embracing my daily cross, I shall prove my personal love for Jesus.

PRAY:

Lord Jesus, since Your way is narrow and despised by the world, grant me the privilege of walking this way unafraid of the hardship and unaffected by the contempt of worldly people. You said that the servant is not greater than his master. Help me live as You did each day. In this way alone shall I reach my true perfection on earth and my eternal happiness in Heaven. I refuse to be attracted by anything else in my daily life. I now accept my daily cross from Your hands. I embrace it with the desire to bear it gladly for the rest of my life. Grant me vision to see You instead of the people involved in my daily trials. Give me strength to go on when my feelings rebel and seek to escape the daily cross. I hope to live this daily life in union with You, my divine Model and King. *Amen.*

PART TWO

Virtues Leading Directly to God

CHAPTER 21

Faith

CHRIST:

MY CHILD, he who believes My words possesses the truth. I have spoken to the world; firstly, through man's conscience, secondly, through the Prophets, thirdly, through My personal life on earth, and finally through My Church.

2. My Church continues My work on earth. Her voice is My voice, and Her authority was given to Her by Me. "He that heareth you, heareth Me," I told My Apostles. They still carry on My work through their legitimate successors. The Scriptures and the Traditions would have been subject to errors and misinterpretations, if I had not left an infallible Church.

3. Do not be surprised if you cannot understand all that I teach. As the intelligence of adults is greater than that of a child, so too is My Divine Intelligence far above that of mortal men.

4. He who believes only what he can understand is limiting himself to a very small portion of the Truth which I revealed. Human reason is weak, and it may be deceived in many things. That is why I told My Church to teach "what I have commanded," promising to preserve Her from error. Had I not made these promises, you would have no way of being sure that you are following My words correctly. Only to My Church did I grant a guarantee from error. "He that heareth you, heareth Me," I told My Apostles. The world today needs that guarantee more than ever. And therefore My promise still stands.

5. I do not demand great intelligence. I ask only for faith in My words and loyalty to My Will. I will not deny My grace to any man who is willing to pray and labor for My gift of faith.

THINK:

God wants faith and a holy life. Whatever I cannot understand, I can safely believe on His word. He cannot deceive me because He is the Fountain of all truth. When I take God's word, I am performing the most intelligent act possible to man. I can learn God's thoughts and holy Will by learning the doctrines and commands which His Son placed in His holy Church. Christ speaks to me through His Church. He teaches me His unerring view of life and offers me His holy peace. In His sacraments He gives me His own heavenly strength to avoid what is wrong and to do what is right.

PRAY:

God of truth, can I ever doubt what You have revealed through Your Divine Son? Jesus has brought me Your message. Moreover, He has preserved that message from error and misunderstanding in the Church which He founded. Through His Church He has promised to speak to me and to guide me on toward eternal life. Let me never tire of learning ever more and more about Your holy truth. Make me eager to use Your holy sacraments as often as possible. Only when I fail to use these heavenly gifts, does the battle for Heaven become too difficult. Let me prove my faith by a continual effort to know You better and serve You more perfectly in my daily life. Grant that

I may make full use of Your wonderful gift to me—the Church. May I never be so foolish as to depend only on my small human knowledge and strength in the daily combat for Heaven. *Amen*.

CHAPTER 22

Gratitude for God's Gifts

CHRIST:

MY CHILD, let gratitude never leave your heart. You have no idea how much you owe to Me. After giving you each moment of life, I offer you mercy when you sin. I send you My grace to arouse you to penance for your sins and to fight against future temptations. All this I do for you because I love you. I desire to raise you up to a heavenly glory, though of yourself you are nothing.

2. Man's greatest ingratitude is his ingratitude to Me, since he owes Me absolutely every thing in his life. No one else can ever deserve the thanks which you owe to Me. Ingratitude can prevent Me from granting you still greater favors.

3. An ungrateful man will never use My gifts as well as he might. Only when you keep your eyes on Me will you make the best use of My gifts. The man who enjoys My gifts without considering the Giver, will sooner or later fall into sin. As soon as he forgets about his complete dependence on Me, he begins to make too much of himself.

4. Be a man of truth. Refuse to live a lie. Be grateful for each gift of Mine. Do not consider yourself worthy of anything. Remember that without Me you are nothing. Be grateful to the Divine Goodness that called you into being.

5. Let your gratitude extend to all things in life, even to the less pleasant and more difficult things which I may send you. I have planned your life with My wisdom and love. All things are meant to help you in one way or another.

THINK:

If I began to count the things which I owe to God, I would never finish counting, because each added moment of life is another gift. The best gratitude which I can offer Him is to use His gifts properly. He has given me intelligence to do this. When my intelligence is uncertain, I can consult His Church. Obedience to His holy Will is my best gratitude. Every sin is an act of ingratitude for the particular gifts which I am misusing at the moment.

PRAY:

My Creator and Father, earthly parents, with their love and care for their children, are but an imperfect image of You, the all-loving Father of all. Each second of our lives is a loving gift of Yours. You watch over us, help us, and keep us in existence each moment of the day and night. Instead of an occasional "Thank You," we ought to shout it with every breath. We can do this best by obeying Your holy Will in all that we do. Grant us the wisdom of gratitude, so that we may one day receive from You the greatest gift of all—the happiness and joy of Heaven. *Amen.*

CHAPTER 23

The Supernatural Virtue of Hope

CHRIST:

MY CHILD, one of the most wonderful virtues in your soul is the virtue of hope. I placed it there as a tiny seed at your baptism. It was to grow and help you through life's trials and difficulties. This is the virtue which makes you desire Me as the Highest Good. It inspires you to look forward to Heaven's unending joys, and confidently expect from Me whatever help is needed to gain eternal life.

2. This virtue calms all fears and worries about your salvation. It helps you look to My power, see My goodness, and rely upon My love. It makes you firm and confident when doubts and difficulties tempt you to turn away from Me in despair. Supernatural hope makes you expect My help in your daily efforts to live a good life.

3. This heavenly gift of hope, however, is incomplete without your sincere daily effort to fulfill My Will in your daily life. He who expects to gain eternal happiness

without doing his part, is guilty of the sin of presumption.

4. Hope makes your prayers more effective. I cannot refuse one who firmly and confidently expects My assistance in his real needs. The man of hope wants only what is really necessary for his final success. Even when he prays for an earthly favor, he wants it only if it will improve him or the person for whom he prays. The perfection of this virtue is a complete self-surrender to My wisdom in all matters.

5. The supernatural virtue of hope gives vision to the mind, strength to the will, courage to the heart, and endurance to the body. It makes one sure of victory because he relies upon Me, the all-knowing, all-powerful, all-loving God. This wonderful virtue brings a sense of security to the soul. Work out your salvation in hope and fear not, for I shall never fail you.

THINK:

St. Paul says that "We are saved by hope." How true! With such a virtue in my soul, how can I be lost? I will turn to God with a firm confidence. I will place my life in His hands by embracing all of His commandments, and by fulfilling His Will, even when it is disagreeable or difficult. God will not be outdone in generosity. He will supply whatever strength is necessary for this. Once I develop this holy virtue of hope within me, I shall know at last what it means to be free of fears and doubts. I shall then possess the peace of God.

PRAY:

O God of love, all powerful and all wise, I turn to You today in hope. I want to be Yours, as You Yourself want me to be. Let me prove my sincerity by doing whatever is necessary to obtain this holy favor. You want to give me the supernatural strength to become ever more perfect in my daily life. You will never deny me whatever is truly necessary for my highest success. I desire to begin at last to live a life of loyalty to Your wonderful plan. If I look toward Heaven in my daily activities, many things Will become easier. Sadness, discouragement, fear, and despair will never torment me. Lord, show me the way. I long to follow Your holy Will, along this road to peace and heavenly glory. True, You may lead me along rough paths at times, but I must not forget that my final destination is well worth the trouble. *Amen.*

CHAPTER 24

Man's Main Hope

CHRIST:

MY CHILD, as long as you are on earth, you will have to make use of food, rest, medicine, recreation, companionship, etc. However, do not make the mistake of considering these natural things as the only remedies of your various needs. Otherwise you will place too much hope in them, and expect more from them than they can give you.

2. Only from Me may you expect perfect, all-satisfying happiness. Be wise and place your greatest hope in Me. I am the Maker and Preserver of all things. Nothing could help you if I did not give it the power to do so. Whether or not you realize it, I am your Highest Good. Without Me there is no lasting good, no enduring happiness.

3. If you hope in Me above all else, you will not be disappointed. I shall not fail you in what is truly best for you. Do not place too much hope in any person or thing on earth. Use whatever you can honestly obtain to improve your earthly life, but do not live as though this life were the only life.

4. I am your Creator and Redeemer. Place your main hope in Me. Follow My Will as perfectly as you can, and when earthly friends and remedies fail you, do not despair. I shall not fail you. Stand by Me, and I will help you reach the all-satisfying success of Heaven.

THINK:

Hope keeps men ever striving in this earthly life. So often they find disappointment and dissatisfaction in things which they had desired so eagerly. Yet with renewed hope they re-direct their efforts toward other objects, still seeking the satisfaction which they have failed to find. Too often men limit their vision. They do not see that nothing can ever give them the slightest degree of satisfaction unless God gives it the power to do so. I should never lose sight of this fact, but I must look to Him with gratitude and with hope in all my needs. God has perfect control over all things at all times, and I receive them as from His hand. My main hope must be God. I can accomplish this by making intelligent use of all that I have and all that comes my way each day. In this way I shall prove that I treasure God more than all earthly goods, and that I hope to be with Him forever in Heaven.

PRAY:

Lord, no matter how unworthy I may feel, I hope to be with You in Heaven some day. I place all of my hope in You, relying on Your goodness, wisdom, and love. Help me to prove this hope by a loyal following of Your holy Will in all that happens to me today. I will deal with all things and events as You desire; that is, without pride, impatience, or any other form of selfishness. I will use whatever I need with the intention of pleasing You rather than pleasing myself alone. In my use of earthly remedies, I will not forget that Your holy Will is still governing every move I make. Never will You abandon those who hope in You. In You I place all of my hopes. Do with me as You see fit, since no one knows and seeks my welfare more than You. *Amen.*

CHAPTER 25

Trust in God

CHRIST:

SON, all men must have some friend in whom they can place their confidence and trust. Without such a friend you cannot live happily. The more that friend means to you, the greater will be the happiness which he brings you.

2. What human friend can ever mean as much to you as I do? Who thinks of you as much as I do? Consider how much I have done for you, and you will easily understand that I am your truest friend.

3. To neglect Me is to neglect Him Whom you need most and Who loves you most. When you trust in humans without considering My place in your life, you are building on sand. All intelligence, strength, and every good thing are My gifts. Without these gifts you are nothing, and your life is a wasted effort.

4. Your human friends can fail you, at least by their inability to help you in all things. Their judgments can be quite mistaken, and they can lead you astray even when they wish to help you. You will find perfect and unfailing friendship only in Me, and in My angels and saints. Let your greatest trust and confidence be in Me at all times.

THINK:

Humans are so often fooled by appearances. Some people are impressed only by visible results. Their praise is worthless because they fail to see the inner goodness of others. Or again they do not realize how brief are the trials and joys of this present life. Am I that shallow or do I try to follow God's way of thinking? Is my trust in Him shaken by the judgments of worldly-minded people? It is never God Who lets me down, but it is I who fail Him. I refuse to trust in Him completely by letting Him govern my daily life as He wishes. As a result I find myself slipping or failing in life's greatest achievement—the daily battle for goodness and holiness.

PRAY:

My God, what greater folly is there than to think that I can manage my daily life without Your guidance and assistance? Yet, on many occasions I do just that. I go about my business without consulting You. You are my surest refuge and my glory, my hope and all-powerful Helper. Without You I am truly nothing, and my life is a wasted effort. Only with Your help can I hope to reach Heaven's eternal success. Let me never again waver in my confidence. No person, no thing, no event, will ever again shake my trust in You. I shall esteem my friends for what they are worth, but never will I think more of them than of You. My loyalty shall be first to Your holy Will and then to all others. *Amen.*

CHAPTER 26

Trust in Divine Providence

CHRIST:

MY CHILD, everything on earth needs My support in order to continue in existence. Not for a single moment can I withdraw My power from anything. If I did, it would vanish into the nothingness from which I created it. I provide for all things from the moment they begin to exist, so that they may accomplish their purpose.

2. I am the Fountain of all good, the Power of all life, the Depth of all knowledge. To trust in Me is your highest wisdom and deepest consolation.

3. The more you see of earthly consolation, the more you will realize how limited, brief, and imperfect it is.

4. When you have learned to place your main hope and confidence in Me alone, you will enjoy the peace of a pure heart. Do not merely talk of Me as your one great hope. Prove your sincerity and virtue by a firm trust in My wisdom and assistance, no matter what happens in your daily life.

5. Prove your complete confidence in Me by setting no conditions and making no reservations. Want what I want for you. Prefer My decisions for you in all things. I will send only what is best for you.

THINK:

God cannot want anything except what is best for me. He made me only for one reason—to give me the all-satisfying happiness which my heart craves. My mistake lies in thinking with a worldly outlook. I do not always realize that the good things of this life are but imperfect reflections of God. They are tiny hints of the good things which God has prepared for those who truly love Him. Hence it is the height of wisdom for me to place my life in His hands and to leave it there. This means that I will do my best each day to live intelligently, seeking what is right and good, and avoiding what is wrong and sinful. I will not be over-anxious to get what is beyond my reach, nor will I foolishly fight against what I cannot avoid. God will see that I get what is truly best for me. As long as I am doing what is humanly possible, I may be sure that God will not let me suffer anything which is not good for me in the long run.

PRAY:

Father of mercies, my loving God, to You I lift up my eyes, and in Your hands I place my life with all its cares, labors, duties, joys, and sorrows. My trust will always be in You above all else. Let me never displease

You by fears, worries, or self pity. You are taking care of Me in all that occurs each day. You love me so much more than I realize. Guide my thoughts, words, and actions this day and every day of my earthly life. I hope to follow Your holy Will as it comes to me in life's daily circumstances and events. Though I must use things to better myself and to solve my problems, I will never rely on them as though they were my only refuge. I want to see You behind everything which I use. I desire to see you leading me on toward eternal glory in all that happens to me this day. *Amen.*

CHAPTER 27

The Virtue of Charity

CHRIST:

MY CHILD, at your baptism I placed the virtue of charity in your soul, expecting you to develop it after you had reached the age of reason. This is the virtue which causes you to love Me above all things for My own sake. It also enables you to love others for My sake.

2. This virtue is your highest perfection. There is no greater achievement in human life than to love Me, the Supreme Good. No natural love can compare with the supernatural love of charity. Charity loves what is best, and it loves for the highest reason. The man of charity loves Me above all else because I am the Highest Good.

3. Charity makes a man more God-like. You read in Scripture that "God is Love." By charity you become like Me, loving all that is right and good.

4. Charity is the perfection of all other love. It reaches out to My perfect goodness and places Me first among its preferences. Even in his love for created things, the man of charity seeks them because they help him come closer to Me in daily life. He no longer accepts any person or thing according to his likes and dislikes, but according to their goodness; that is, according to their ability to draw his thoughts and desires more firmly toward Me. He prefers those persons and things which help me please Me most.

5. Develop this holy virtue in your daily life. Do it firstly by keeping My

commandments, secondly by honoring Me frequently in private prayers and acts of public worship, thirdly by dealing unselfishly with people for My sake.

6. True, you have to protect yourself against the selfishness and bad will of people on earth, but in so doing beware of being bitter, inconsiderate, or unjust toward them. For My sake wish everyone well, and as far as you are able, help those in need. In this way you will prove that you possess genuine charity in your soul.

THINK:

At baptism charity was planted as a seed in my soul. As I reached the age of reason and learned of God's holy gift, I was expected to develop it by a continual effort to use it. My efforts plus God's further graces make the seed of charity grow within me. How have I used this precious gift? Without charity all other virtues lose their supernatural value. This means that I cannot gain Heaven until I have learned to practice charity in my daily life. As I advance in this virtue I become more like God, thinking and acting more and more like Him. I must begin today living as Jesus would live this life of mine. In spite of many failures, I must go on trying.

PRAY:

My God, You desire to make me eternally great. You want me to reflect Your perfection in my daily thoughts, words, and actions. May I begin at long last to be a reflection of Your love in everything I think, say and do. I desire to be patient, kind, thoughtful, helpful, and long-suffering, just as You have been with me, a sinner. In spite of my selfish nature, I want to love You as You deserve. In all things let me never forget Your wisdom and goodness, so that I may always consider and follow what pleases You. My model in all this is Jesus, Your divine Son. He is the model of perfect charity. Let me strive each day to become more like Him and less like myself. *Amen.*

CHAPTER 28

The Effects of Charity in Daily Life

CHRIST:

MY CHILD, when true charity fills your soul, it brings many wonderful effects into your daily life. These effects are due to the fact that charity looks for Me in all things. In his desire for a more perfect union with Me, the charitable man seeks to be more like Me in his daily life.

2. Since love always seeks to express itself in some form of self-sacrifice, the charitable man seeks to offer his attention and help to his fellowmen for My sake. Following My words, "You did it to Me," he seeks to serve Me in the people who need his help.

3. The man of charity is patient in many circumstances which arouse others to anger or disgust. He refuses to become impatient because he is keenly aware of My great patience with him and with all sinners. In his love for Me he prefers to reflect My patience and meekness, rather than anger or revenge. When compelled to defend his rights, he does so without harshness or meanness.

4. His kindness brings confidence and encouragement to those who are afraid or downhearted. Others never hesitate to ask for his assistance because they know that he will not willingly refuse.

5. The charitable man never envies those who have more earthly goods, greater talents, or better success. He is content to possess My love and to accept My Will in all things.

6. In his dealings with others he is considerate and fair, because he is not over-eager for his own gain. His love for Me has freed him from all unreasonable ambition and from the vain desire to appear better than others.

7. One whose heart is filled with true charity refuses to judge others rashly. He prefers to believe good of others rather than evil. When people do him wrong, the charitable man is more pained at the offense to Me than at the harm done to himself.

8. The holy virtue of charity makes one so honest that he can admit the truth, even when it points out his limitations and defects. True charity makes one humble

enough to face all facts, even disagreeable ones.

9. These are some of the effects flowing from genuine charity. When this divine virtue is earnestly developed, it fosters many other virtues needed in daily life. The way of charity is the shortest to God because it is the fastest way to Christian perfection. If you strive to develop this glorious virtue in your daily life, you may rest assured that you are walking toward eternal life each moment of the day.

THINK:

The charitable man is the most perfect reflection of God on earth. When he is near, those around him feel a certain awareness of God's presence. His love for God overflows in his soul and touches the hearts of those around him. Being charitable means being a saint. This is the answer to my dreams of success. I can become an eternal success. By my unselfish charity I can draw closer to God in my earthly life, and I can also bring others closer to Him. I can earn the eternal glory of helping others gain Heaven.

Through charity I can do most for God, most for my fellowmen, and most for myself.

PRAY:

Dear Lord of love, You are continually giving Your assistance to me and to all things created. Every moment of existence is a gift from You. I can rise to my highest glory by imitating You. The more I give of myself for Your sake, the more will I resemble You. My greatest proof of love for You will be this effort to become more God-like, since this is Your greatest desire for me. Grant me the grace to favor You in the future as consistently as I have favored myself in the past. Take the place of self in my thoughts, desires, and actions. I ask only that I may never become so rash as to follow my own will, not even in this holy desire to prove my love for You. The higher I aim, the more obedient must I be to my spiritual director. Otherwise the devil will succeed in drawing me away from You through some foolish extreme. Lord, make me generous enough to try, and humble enough to follow direction in an honest daily effort to give myself entirely to You. *Amen.*

CHAPTER 29

Daily Growth in Charity

CHRIST:

MY CHILD, without the virtue of charity, all other virtues lose their supernatural value. What good will it do you to believe in Me, or to hope in Me, if you do not love Me?

2. This love must be shown in a sincere daily effort to please Me, no matter how disagreeable the task at hand. In fulfilling My Will, you achieve your highest perfection and your greatest good. In all things I lead you toward what is truly best for you.

3. When you consider that I have given you everything that you are and have, you should not find it difficult to love Me. A frequent consideration of My numberless benefits will help you draw closer to Me in gratitude. This gratitude will bring you a desire to please Me more in your daily life. If you follow this desire, you will be proving your love for Me.

4. As you advance in this love of gratitude, I shall grant you still higher graces.

I shall help you understand Me better. As you come to know Me more intimately, you will appreciate more and more My boundless goodness. You will gradually surrender yourself more completely to My Will. You will no longer permit yourself to resent My Will, but you will finally be convinced that I seek only what is good for you. Your love of gratitude will be transformed into a higher love, the love of friendship.

5. In this higher level of perfection, you will rise above yourself. You will no longer sympathize with your unreasoning desires when they seek to disregard My Will. You will control your feelings toward the people in your daily life. Whatever good you do them, you will do it for the best reason—you will do it for Me.

THINK:

If I give God's grace a chance, following its inspirations throughout my daily life, I shall grow in perfection each day. My charity will aim higher and higher, eventually rising above the natural attractions and distractions which now draw me away from God in my daily activities. I shall gradually rise from my present imperfect love of God to a purer love. My good deeds will be done more and more with an appreciation of His boundless goodness. I need only begin this day to offer my activities to God, and to renew my intention from time to time so as to prevent selfish motives from stealing into my soul. In God's own good time, He will raise me up to that perfection which He desires to bestow upon me.

PRAY:

O God of love, Generosity is Your name. Who has ever been as generous with me as You have? Wherever I look, I see Your gifts. Whatever I do, I am using Your gifts. What shall I do for You, Who have done so much for me? Since this will please You above all else, I want to purify my love for You. I shall do my best to make better use of the many graces which You send me each day. I desire to rise from a love of gratitude to a love of friendship. I long for the day when I shall live this earthly life of mine mainly to please You. Whatever my daily obligations may be, I want to do them chiefly for You, my all-deserving God. *Amen*.

CHAPTER 30

Submission to God's Holy Will

CHRIST:

MY CHILD, I know all things because I made all things and keep them in existence. Whatever powers and abilities are in each person or thing, they were put there by Me. Whatever happens is foreseen, planned, and permitted by Me. My plan seeks your welfare, not just the welfare which your limited intelligence can see, but your truest and most lasting welfare.

2. When you feel like questioning My wisdom, remember what you are and who I am. You are the work of My hands. I gave you the intelligence with which you judge matters, and the will with which you make your choices. If you disagree with My decisions, remember that I see all the reasons which you see, and many other reasons which you do not see. All of your thinking is perfectly clear to Me. When I choose differently from you, it is because your choice is not for the best.

3. On every occasion do what you think is best. Whenever necessary ask for My help, but do it with a desire to accept My decision in the matter. End every petition with this perfect ending: "Lord, if this is really good for me, please grant it; but if You decide differently, I want whatever You want." Place your hopes, ambitions, and efforts at My feet. Do your best and leave the rest to Me. I will dispose things for your highest welfare.

4. Never think of talking to your Creator as to an equal. You are the work of My hands, and without Me you are simply nothing. Your very next breath belongs to Me. It is a gift of Mine to you. Speak to Me with the humility of one who acknowledges this truth.

5. I love you. Why are you troubled, as though I did not care about you? Rely on My wisdom and love, and I will bring peace into your heart. Worries and fears will not leave you until you submit yourself to My Will in all things.

THINK:

If I could even imagine my complete dependence on God, I would never find the least fault with His holy Will. He knows and controls all that can possibly happen and all which will actually occur. He needs no advice nor instructions. He wants me to seek good things and strive for whatever improvements seem desirable. He wants me to ask for what I cannot obtain myself. He demands, however, that I do all this intelligently, without preferring my own desires to His wise and holy Will. As long as I have a firm confidence in His love, and a complete submission to His wisdom, I may be sure that He will send only what is best for me.

PRAY:

My Creator, I am truly Your property since You made me and keep me in existence each moment of the day. Yet, You want to deal with me as Your child. You are all-knowing and all-wise. Grant me the wisdom of preferring Your holy Will in all things. Of all the harm which can come to me on this earth, the worst is my own disagreement with Your loving plan for me. I here and now place my daily life at Your feet. Do with me as You see fit. I shall use the intelligence You gave me to better myself as far as possible. When, however, my plans and efforts fail, I shall not rebel or complain against You. I cannot desire my own welfare and advantage as wisely as You do. In Your holy Will I hope to seek my greatest success from now on. *Amen.*

CHAPTER 31

Perfect Self-Surrender

CHRIST:

MY CHILD, few men on earth have peace of soul because few care to let Me manage their lives as I wish. Many put more faith in their own limited abilities than in My infinite wisdom and power.

2. Some resign themselves to My Will, but they make a few exceptions; and in these exceptions they trust themselves more than Me. In these matters they are ready to sin rather than to have their plans changed. Others surrender themselves in all things, but after a while they begin to weaken in some particular matter. They are too impatient to wait for the perfect reward which I have prepared for those who love Me. None of these people will ever know Me intimately

nor will they ever receive the peace of soul which I have promised to my loyal followers. Their loyalty is too imperfect because of a false self-interest.

3. Forget self and you will find someone far greater—Me. Let Me decide what your life shall be each day. No offering of yours can please Me completely until you have given Me the greatest gift of all—your will. Do this by preferring whatever I send you each day. Do your very best, and then accept the results as My Will.

4. In everything that comes to you this day, see My Will. Use your intelligence and your will to live a useful and holy life. When matters displease you, practice My patience. Imitate the virtues of My daily life on earth. Practice My virtues when the occasion arises, and in all things refuse to sin.

THINK:

Since God is all-powerful, He is able to give me whatever I need; being all-wise He knows what is best for me. My mind is so small that I cannot even begin to understand how very much He loves me. I may rest assured that He wants only what is truly best for me. True, there are times when I am puzzled at the things which God permits to happen. This is only another proof of my mental smallness. The most intelligent thing I can do, is to place my life in His hands, to let Him direct my daily life as He will. This I do by my patience, understanding, generosity, and unselfishness in my daily activities. When I must provide for myself, I should do it without too much concern or anxiety, and without disregard for justice and charity.

PRAY:

Dear Lord, I am beginning to understand at last. I shall reach the peak of wisdom on the day when I truly surrender myself to Your wise advice, following Your holy Will in my daily activities. You are present in all that I do, say, and think, in big and small matters, when I am alone and when I am in company. I please You when I do things Your way, and I displease You when I act differently. Dear Jesus, You gave me a holy example. Let me begin at once to be more like You in my thinking, speaking, and acting. True, I shall fail often, but at least I can offer You the loyalty of trying over and over again. In spite of a million failures each day, I hope to prove my sincere desire by beginning again after each failure. *Amen.*

CHAPTER 32

Fervor in God's Service

CHRIST:

M Y CHILD, read the lives of My saints and consider their wonderful fervor in following My Will. Fervor is a prompt and ready will to follow whatever I desire. It is not a matter of feeling or mood, but a loyal attachment to My Will.

2. Can you say that you are living a life that matches the unselfishness of My saints? They were unable to say "no" to Me, no matter what I asked of them.

3. Whether it was sickness, labors, failures, or criticisms, My saints did their best, accepting, and even preferring, whatever I sent them.

4. Imitate their loyalty to My Will, and you will experience their peace of soul. Your labors will seem less difficult because I will give you greater graces.

5. The fervent man is eager to know My Will in the various events of daily life. Though his feelings and moods may change, his will is ever the same—to please Me in all things. Indeed, his greatest satisfaction comes from following My holy Will.

THINK:

The more I learn to think straight, the better will I see the inner simplicity of earthly life. I was put on earth to gain the eternal glory and joy of Heaven. I shall earn this unimaginable happiness in proportion as I reflect the goodness of God in my daily life. He wants me to become daily more like His Son in my thinking, speaking, and acting. The saints learned God's thoughts and Will, and they earnestly tried to live each day as God desired. They knew that God's way was the only intelligent way. They grew in strength through the sacraments, prayer, and an honest daily effort. They learned to do many things which had once seemed too difficult or even impossible.

PRAY:

My God, the reason why I make so many mistakes is that I do not take the time to learn Your holy Will more clearly. Another reason is that I am afraid to try. Still another reason is that when I try, I do not make a full and generous effort. I am bound to fail if I try to improve by my natural effort alone. If I made more frequent use of the sacraments, prayer, solitude, meditation and reading, my success would be assured. But no; I make a good resolution and then expect my old faults to disappear. You want determined action. Lord, time is so short. Please do not let me waste any more of it with halfhearted efforts and incomplete measures. Let me strive to understand what You desire of me, and let me use every help at my disposal to follow Your holy Will in my daily life. *Amen.*

CHAPTER 33

Perseverance in God's Service

CHRIST:

MY CHILD, only he who perseveres to the end will be saved. Good resolutions will not help you unless they are followed right to the end of life.

The Way of Imitation

2. With the help of My grace, be determined to follow My Will in your daily life. Follow it regardless of feelings. Moods and feelings will change with the changing hour of the day, but your will must stand firm in loyalty to Me.

3. Sometimes you will enjoy what I send you, and sometimes you will dislike it. At times you will be eager to obey Me, and at other times you will be sluggish. Yet your will can rise, with the help of My grace, above these changing feelings. Your true worth is proved by a determined effort to follow your good resolutions.

4. The Fathers of the desert learned this heavenly wisdom long ago. Never were they fooled by the devil's temptations nor by the self-deception of their human nature. By prayer, fasting, penance, and work, they overcame the enemies within them and outside them. With eyes fixed on Me, they saw Heaven as their goal, and they made their daily life a journey toward eternal happiness.

5. You too will be tempted to abandon your good resolutions. You will fear for

your health, worry about your friends, be disturbed by human opinions, and become troubled about imagined dangers.

6. Follow My advice. Keep yourself busy with prayer, self-denial, and good works. I will soon send you greater graces and you will find yourself closer to Me than before.

7. For the present walk in faith, hope, and obedient charity. Later you will realize that the trials which troubled you were actually good for you. They helped you to see which virtues you really possess and which are still needed in your daily life.

THINK:

It is after I have made my resolutions that the battle begins. Not only will the devil tempt me more, but I shall also have to take misunderstandings, and even bad will, from neighbors who resent my change for the better. My worst enemy, however, will be my own human nature. It will dislike the harder course of action which I am now following. My imagination, my old habits, my likes and dislikes, these will cooperate in order to make me abandon my resolutions. On such occasions I ought to get busy with some activity which will help me overcome, or at least disregard my lower nature's rebellion. God will send me light and strength in due time if only I will hold on to my resolutions in the present darkness of fears, doubts, and dislikes.

PRAY:

My Jesus, there are no words to describe the grandeur and glory which await those who follow Your holy Will in their daily life. That is why You never tried to tell us what it is like. When we enter into your glorious Heaven, we too will say with St. Paul that no eye on earth has ever seen, no ear has ever heard, nor has anyone in this world even imagined what You have prepared for Your loyal followers. Yes, no matter what suffering we may endure in this life, these sufferings will never be great enough to earn the smallest joy of Heaven. Grant me the wisdom to keep my eyes on that goal, so that I may never become discouraged or cowardly in life's daily battle. *Amen.*

CHAPTER 34

Words of Consolation

CHRIST:

MY CHILD, do not let yourself be crushed by the various activities which you have undertaken for My sake. No labor, no suffering, no penance or prayer should discourage or sadden you. What you do for My sake will help you far beyond your fondest dream.

2. Your earthly hardships and trials are rapidly passing away. The longest life on earth is short. Only eternity is unending. Bear your difficulties, troubles, and sufferings with patience. I will relieve you as soon as it is good for you.

3. Whatever you endure on earth, is a very small price to pay for the Kingdom of Heaven. When you arrive in My heavenly kingdom, you will see how truly My Apostle Paul spoke when he said that the sufferings of this present time are not worthy to be compared with the glory to come.

4. Put yourself in My hands and strive to be as independent as You can of your

human needs and of human consolations. Bring your joys and sorrows to Me. Make Me your best friend and your closest companion. As long as you go through your labors and hardships in My company, you will not find them too hard.

THINK:

Life's daily hardships and difficulties are less a burden when I let Our Lord help me. I will therefore concentrate more on Him and less on my trials. He will teach me to remedy what should be remedied and to bear what I cannot control. He will show me how much He suffered for my sake. He will remind me of the shortness of earthly life and the grandeur of Heaven. He will encourage me and cheer me up in my sadness and discouragement. Unless I remember to walk with Christ in my daily activities, I shall gradually walk away from Him.

PRAY:

My Jesus, it is good for me to suffer some trial from time to time. At such times I find myself realizing how weak I am and how little I can depend on the people and things on which I relied. In such trials teach me to lean on You, to look to Your holy plan for me, and to consider the brevity of all earthly satisfactions. You deserve my loyalty because of what You have already done for me. You deserve much more than I can offer because of what You have prepared for me in Heaven. Let me often consider that the night is quickly forgotten when morning comes. With eyes on You, my risen King of glory, let me go through the darkness of earth as one who looks beyond it.

CHAPTER 35

Becoming a Companion of Jesus

CHRIST:

MY CHILD, turn to Me as often throughout the day as your duties will permit. Learn to turn to Me as others turn to their loved ones and friends. I will give your mind great thoughts, which will raise you above your narrow earthly view. My thoughts will refresh you, console you, make you wise, strengthen you, and give you joy.

2. Prepare your soul for My loving companionship, and I shall draw closer to you with greater graces. I shall raise you up

from your natural human level to My heavenly heights. There you will have a broader view of life, a deeper understanding, and a greater strength for life's daily activities and burdens.

3. Strive to meditate upon My earthly life. Learn to enter into all that I experienced on earth. Every thought, every word, every act of Mine was lived for love of you. You have a place in My earthly life, and My life belongs to you. Therefore, learn to share it now through meditation and reflection.

4. Learn to pierce the barriers of time and space by the use of prayer. The more you strive to step into My earthly life and become a companion of Mine in it, the more actively will I share your earthly life by granting you greater graces.

THINK:

What a wonderful privilege—to be able to step into the earthly life of Jesus and become a closer companion of His! I can share His every thought, word, and action. Ah! But isn't that just a bit of imagination on my part? No. He lived every second of His earthly life for me. Being God, He thought of me personally from all eternity. Surely He did not stop thinking of me while He was working out my salvation. Because of His infinite love for me, His earthly life belongs to me. For my sake He lived each moment of it. I have every right to step into it and share it with Him through mental prayer. I can do this by contemplating what He did, meditating on what He said, and considering what He thought and felt in each event.

PRAY:

My loving Saviour, my heart is overflowing with joy for having discovered a precious secret today! I can step over the barriers of time and space. I can come to You in Your earthly life as You come to me in mine. Today I have found You in a new way. I will not let You go, but I will hold on to You. I desire to do whatever is necessary to become a true companion of Yours. As earthly friendship requires time, attention, and sympathetic understanding, so too will I give you my time, my attention. I will make my best efforts to understand You better by daily meditating upon what You said and did in Your earthly life. I shall read a portion of Your life and mentally live it with You for a while each day. You will grant me the grace to gain the same benefits from this experience as I might have gained had I followed You as one of Your disciples. Lord, grant me the faith and the love which I need to give myself to You in this wonderful method of prayer. *Amen.*

CHAPTER 36

Sharing Christ's Passion

CHRIST:

MY CHILD, as soon as one decides to come closer to Me in his daily life, he encounters many difficulties which previously were either absent or unnoticed.

2. First of all, his human nature will rebel at being restrained. His feelings and unreasoning desires will object to the stricter control which he now uses over them.

3. Secondly, he will find resentment and even opposition from the people around him. Some will suspect his motives when they notice that he is trying to act better than he did before. Others will resent him because

he reminds them of what they themselves ought to be.

4. Lastly, the devil will make use of this internal and external opposition to tempt My follower. He fears the good which My follower will accomplish in holding to his new resolutions.

5. The more you try to give yourself to Me in your daily life, the harder will this life become. I tell this to you so that you may expect these trials and difficulties.

6. No amount of difficulties and trials will frighten you if you learn to draw strength from My sufferings and death. My Passion will teach you a wisdom which will outwit all the deceits of Satan and all worldly opposition. As you meditate on My sufferings I will give you a super natural strength of mind and will. You will overcome all temptations.

7. In My Passion you will see more clearly My love for you. You will see how I bore all those torments for your sake. You will also understand My wisdom more deeply, as you observe the same forces opposing Me as oppose you in your attempt to follow Me more closely.

8. I permitted My feelings to overwhelm Me in My prayer and bloody sweat in the Garden of Olives, and again in My desolation upon the cross. In My Passion I felt the bitter disappointment of losing My people, the ingratitude for so much good done, the envy of the worldly-minded, the misinterpretation of the selfish, the rejection of the proud and ambitious, the abandonment of the cowardly, and numberless other human faults in those from whom I had a right to demand loyalty.

9. Satan made use of everything which could make My last hours unbearable. All of my enemies, both angelic and human, found Me strong against all of their opposition. The very spite which they were working upon Me, was to bring forth all the supernatural graces which would save the world.

10. Have no fear. I shall never permit you to be tempted above your strength. As I overcame the world, so too will you. In My Passion I obtained the graces which you will need to conquer your temptations. Have confidence in Me. I shall not fail you in your needs.

THINK:

By meditating upon the sufferings of Jesus, I shall receive greater knowledge and strength to help me overcome the temptations of daily life. The forces which oppose me today are the same as those which opposed Him in His Passion the forces of evil. These are the forces to which men yield when they sin. In overcoming them, I share not only the sufferings of Christ, but also His victory over sin.

PRAY:

My suffering and crucified King, can I expect an easy life when You lived such a hard one? No. I want to be like You as far as I am able in this earthly life of mine. Let me choose to work, pray, and suffer as much like You as possible. The greatest privilege I can obtain is that of living a life like Yours. You chose and bore every suffering and hardship for My sake. Let me choose to work and suffer for Your sake. I hope to meditate often upon the sufferings which You embraced for me. As I do so, help me grow in the desire to suffer more for You in my daily life. *Amen.*

CHAPTER 37

Interior Transformation

CHRIST:

MY CHILD, as you learn to share my daily life through meditation and prayer, you will become more like Me in your own daily life. Your thinking will slowly be transformed into My way of thinking. My outlook on life will replace yours. So too with your manner of talking and acting. Your old self will gradually vanish and a new self will take its place. All this will you do, with the help of My grace, in order to become a loyal friend of Mine, living in constant union with Me.

2. One of the most wonderful effects of this transformation will be that you will also share My desires, My intentions, My dignity and power. In a true sense your earthly life will be a continuation of Mine. You will have power to petition My heavenly Father in My name, and He will grant your petitions for My sake.

3. Both for yourself and for others you will be able to obtain many extra favors

and graces, which might otherwise not have been granted. Thus your daily life will release to the world a large share of the help and mercy which I merited by My earthly life and sufferings.

4. This is the biggest reason for Satan's opposition to you. He will never tire of tempting you. If he cannot gain your soul, at least he may prevent you from helping others over whom he has more influence. Your life of friendship with Me will weaken many of his temptations against others, for whom you can obtain extra actual graces.

5. Remember this when you feel no desire to do more for Me through prayer, good works, and self control. I have given you the privilege of helping Me in the work of saving the world. Though you are not necessary in this divine task, I have given you the privilege of being useful in it.

6. In this daily battle for the souls of men, you can be a very effective soldier of Mine. Satan never abandons his attempts to make men fall into mortal sin. So, too, you must never allow yourself to grow weary of interceding for souls in danger of sin. Do it by

prayer, self control, self-sacrifice, and by your general intention in whatever you are doing at the moment.

THINK:

There is no other Redeemer of men than Jesus. He alone is necessary. All others are merely useful in helping His work. Jesus did enlist the aid of His apostles and His Church. These were commissioned to go forth and make disciples of the whole world. I have a share in that divine commission, since I am a member of His Church. In a true sense Jesus made me a part of Himself. Through His Church, His sacraments, and His actual graces, He offers me more and more of His thoughts, desires, intentions, outlook, purpose, and power. As Jesus earned light and strength for all men to know God's truth and fight against their temptations, so can I help people gain a larger number of the actual graces which Christ gained for them. As His daily life was the source of all salvation, so can my daily life be a channel of grace for people in need of greater graces. The more I devote myself to the imitation of Christ in my daily life, the more actual graces can I obtain for people throughout the world. This Christ-likeness is my greatest possible achievement on earth.

PRAY:

My Jesus, let me always see the deeper, eternal importance of my daily life. Let my thoughts, desires, and intentions center around You every moment of the day. I can truly make a lasting impression on the world. I can obtain extra actual graces for people in all conditions of life, graces which may make the difference between their eternal salvation and their eternal loss. Lord, though You do not need me nor anyone else, You have granted me the privilege of helping You in this glorious task of helping people gain Heaven. Do not let me fail You in this all-important work. I shall no longer measure my day's work by my visible activities. I hope to keep before my eyes the grand, worldwide mission which You have laid before me—the mission of gaining actual graces for people in need. *Amen.*

PART THREE

Man's Relation With His Neighbor and With Himself

CHAPTER 38

Charity to All

CHRIST:

MY CHILD, let Me fill your heart with charity, so that you may love Me with a full and perfect love. Charity sees Me in all My works. Even when doing things for men, it does them for My sake.

2. Be good to all, but refuse to sin for anyone. There can never be any excuse for doing what is wrong, and displeasing to Me. Still, there are times when you may postpone your religious duties in order to help someone who needs you. In this case you are still pleasing Me. One who is not interested in the needs of his neighbor, is not really interested in Me. Your devotion to Me is proved by action. For My sake help others as much as you are able.

3. In your efforts to help others, beware of falling into impatience when your plans fail. Guard also against an over-eagerness to

change others. If they insist on continuing in their error, pray for them and leave them to Me. You have done your part. I know how to draw good even out of the evil which men do.

4. Whenever you cannot correct a defect in yourself or others, be patient and pray for My assistance. I will not let evil win out in the end. If all men were perfect, you would have little to suffer for My sake.

5. Every man has his faults and each one has his burden. Men ought to bear with one another, help one another, console one another, and warn and instruct one another. Treat others as you want Me to treat you at your judgment.

THINK:

Charity is the virtue which enables me to love God above all others and in all others. I love Him above all others as long as I hate all sin and practice the virtues I need in daily life. I love God in all others firstly, when I try to treat my neighbor with the respect and consideration which is due to him, and secondly, when I make the most of the things which I possess and the opportunities which come my way. In all these persons, things, and opportunities I can prove my love for God by acting toward them as God desires. In all this Jesus is my model.

PRAY:

Lord, I admit that You are all-good. You deserve all that I have and all that I possess. How truly I mean these words will be proved by my attitude toward the people and events in my daily life. Let me treat others with the love which You desire of me. Grant that I may reflect Your wonderful patience in life's daily trials. I want to keep trying in spite of my weakness and faults. If I cannot prove my love by any great improvement, at least I can prove it by a continual effort to improve. I shall never stop trying because this is the least I can do for love of You. *Amen*.

CHAPTER 39

Human Respect

CHRIST:

MY CHILD, human respect is the fear of being criticized or corrected by people.

Live your life in My presence, and do not think too much of what people may think or say. As long as your conscience is clear, the thoughts or words of men can neither add to nor subtract from your true worth. You are not a better man when people praise you, nor are you worse when they find fault with you. You are what you are, and I see you as you really are.

2. Your value in My eyes does not depend upon the judgments of people. I look upon your heart. I see your intentions and your sincere efforts. Men judge you mainly by your external actions. They cannot be sure of your merit or guilt in the deed. Too often they judge you by their own likes and dislikes, or by their own vanity and fixed ideas.

3. In this matter try to imitate My Apostle Paul. He tried to please everyone, becoming all things to all men. Yet he made no account of what people thought of him. He knew only too well that it is impossible to satisfy everyone. He labored hard to improve the lives of men, but he could not prevent the harsh criticisms and judgments of some.

4. Like Paul you too must place your life in My hands and leave all judgments to Me. Defend yourself against unjust criticism by humility and patience. When silence would do more harm than good, pray for a prudent tongue and then defend yourself with the truth.

THINK:

It is consoling to realize that while people see only the action, God sees also the desire, the intention, and the sincerity of my effort. I need only be sure that I am doing my honest best, without self-deception or pride. God will see that truth conquers in the end. Evil tongues and harsh judgments will not hurt me for long if I trust more in God than in myself. I shall not put off any good deed nor perform any wrong one for fear of human criticisms or even mockery.

PRAY:

My heavenly Judge, I leave my life at Your feet. I desire to do my very best for Your honor and glory. I want to seek Your truth and to follow it in my everyday life. I will not bother to defend myself against misinterpretations and misunderstandings, unless I am obliged to avoid scandal or unnecessary offense. As for the rest, I shall leave all judgment in Your hands. Save me from my own conceit and self-seeking. Forgive the evil tongue that ventures to judge me and the foolish heart that dares to condemn. Let me never omit a good deed nor perform what is wrong, through fear of being mocked or hurt by men. You alone are all holy, You alone are my Lord; You alone are Most high! Men are so often wrong in their judgments. I will never again let their opinions turn me away from Your holy Will. *Amen.*

CHAPTER 40

Peace of Soul

CHRIST:

MY CHILD, My saints lived in this world without complaint. They were aware of their own defects, and they offered up their daily trials in reparation for their faults. They developed the virtues of humility and simplicity in order to avoid self-deception. Their greatest fear was that they might deceive themselves into a sense of their own goodness, or even of superiority over others. By living with eyes fixed on Me, they lived in peace.

2. If you want to enjoy My gift of peace, learn to control your selfishness in many things. Do your best but do it for Me. Give Me the best loyalty within you because I deserve it. Do not always expect a reward for the good you do. I have already given you more than you can ever repay Me.

3. If you cannot help others against their faults and defects, the only thing left for you is to mind your own business. Let them go along the way they have chosen. Why lose your peace of soul, or even sin by anger?

4. First keep yourself in peace. Then you can see more clearly how to bring peace to others. A peaceful man has far more influence than a merely learned one. Everyone is impressed by the man who has peace because all feel the attractions of My grace within him. Do not desire anything more nor less than My Will, and My peace will remain with you. Then may you hope to bring this peace to others.

THINK:

All men desire peace, but so few do what it takes to obtain true peace. Some think that they will find it in financial security. Others seek it in continual activity. Others hope to find peace in human friendship, or praise, or admiration. These things are not the source of true peace. A daily life of straight thinking, and unselfish following of God's Will, is the one and only source of true peace. Interior tranquility is God's gift to those who love His truth and obey His Will in their daily life. Resentment against some circumstance or other, robs many people of their peace of soul. I should learn to live with what I cannot control or eliminate in my daily life. God will help me rise above such things if only I will give Him a chance to share my life.

PRAY:

Lord, help me to do what is necessary to obtain the wonderful peace which You have promised to us, the peace which our souls crave. Grant me the grace to seek Your holy Will and to live it in all that happens to me this day. I desire to bring Your peace to those around me. I will try to help them when it is possible, and I will leave them to You when my efforts are useless. Your holy Will will be my first concern in everything that occurs today. Those who seek to live as You desire, fulfill the highest wisdom and attain a heavenly peace even in this earthly life. May I be one of these faithful followers? *Amen.*

CHAPTER 41

Lasting Interior Peace

CHRIST:

MY CHILD, peace I leave to you, My peace I give to you. This is My promise to all My loyal followers. Everybody wants peace of soul, but so few are willing to do what is necessary to obtain it. My Will is the only door to true and lasting peace. This peace is given to those who are gentle and considerate with their neighbor. I do not hesitate to grant it to those who are truly patient, and to the humble.

2. You could possess all of these virtues and you could enjoy My wonderful peace if only you would follow My directions. Prefer

to do the will of others rather than your own will. Always seek the lowest place, and let others be preferred before you. Forget self-interest and follow My instructions. Give all for all, and do not make any exceptions in your offering to Me.

3. Why do you refuse to have complete confidence in Me? I know what is truly best for you. I can send you nothing that is really bad for you. You do not love yourself one fraction as much as I love you. Let me govern your life. Be convinced that I will take good care of you. Only when you have learned to do things My way, only when you seek My Will above all else, only then will you possess the priceless treasure of My peace. Where I reign, there does My peace flourish.

THINK:

Peace is the tranquility which comes from order. Order means that everything is as it should be. When my life is running as it should, I shall have peace. Who knows better than God how my life should be lived? Therefore, if I want peace, I must follow God's holy commands. Why do I lack this peace? It is because somewhere in my life, I am not faithful to God's directions. His directions may seem too difficult, or even impossible, but they are not really so. God will never burden me above my strength, nor will He ever command the impossible. If I lack the strength to follow His wishes, it is because I am not doing what it takes to gain that strength.

PRAY:

Jesus, my King and Saviour, when will I understand that You command only what is best for me? In my blind selfishness I run away from You and from my true and lasting welfare. I want to be free and without frustrations, yet I allow myself to become tied down with earthly interests which are neither necessary, nor good for me. Teach me, impress me with this truth, that when I disagree with You, I am actually my own worst enemy. Convince me beyond all doubt, persuade me, once and for all, that my greatest advantage will come from following Your directions throughout my daily life. Then will I know the wonderful gift of interior peace, which You promised to all

who follow You, the peace which everyone
seeks, but few possess. *Amen.*

CHAPTER 42

Obstacles to Peace of Soul

CHRIST:

MY CHILD, as I have already told you,
where there is order, there will you find
My peace. My peace does not leave you until
some disorder has entered into your soul.
This disorder may be in your thinking or in
your will.

2. Thus, for instance, some people, either
through ignorance or through neglect, fail
to see life's daily events My way. They are
troubled, anxious, ready to do anything for
some need or advantage in their earthly
life. My loyal followers work for their needs,
but they do not forget Me. They consult My
Church when they doubt what is to be done.

3. Never take your eyes away from My
teachings. Otherwise you will easily be deceived. Consider My judgments more than
the judgments of worldly people. Let no
human praise, nor human fault-finding, influence your loyalty to Me.

4. Then again, disorder may arise in your will. You may want some worldly advantage or earthly success, regardless of My Will in the matter. If this is so, you shall be deprived of My peace. You may distract or deceive Yourself for a time, but My grace will continue to disturb your conscience.

5. Be truly wise. Do not have any fixed desires. Place all your hopes, plans, and efforts at My feet. Follow what seems wise and good, but do not make up your mind to have what you desire, no matter what the price. If you follow your unreasoning desires too strongly, you will only find regrets and remorse later on.

THINK:

There is only one way to true and lasting peace. That way is God's Will. The man who lacks interior peace either wants what God does not want him to have, or refuses to take what God wants him to take. One who does his best to embrace God's holy Will, will receive Christ's peace. What about me? Am I trying to embrace God's holy Will in all that happens to me each day? To do this perfectly I must see the full picture of life. I must see God directing, supporting, and permitting whatever occurs, be it good or evil. In allowing evil to happen, God has reasons far beyond my understanding. My highest wisdom lies in embracing the evils which I am not able to remedy, accepting them because God permitted them to happen to me. When I have succeeded in wanting only what God wants me to have, I shall know the wonderful peace of Christ.

PRAY:

All-wise Creator, You know what is best for me. Everything which You permit in my life, is good for me in some way. You do not ask me to understand all of these things, but only to accept them because You permit them. True, You expect me to do my best to correct the wrongs which happen to me; but when I cannot correct them, that is when I am to embrace them for Your sake. In seeking Your holy Will above my own likes and dislikes, I shall find the grace of interior peace. With this peace I shall think more clearly in my daily life. I shall also find it easier to control my unreasoning desires, since I shall more easily see how unreasonable and foolish they are. Lord, help me share Your holy wisdom by following it in my daily life. *Amen.*

CHAPTER 43

Good Judgment in God's Service

CHRIST:

MY CHILD, never be completely idle. Try to have enough interests and activities to keep you reasonably occupied at all times.

2. Beware, however, of overactivity. No matter what you do, be sure to consider the limits of your strength. Different people have different talents, abilities, and strength. You cannot keep up with everyone in everything.

3. Bodily exercises should be practiced with good judgment. They are not to be equally undertaken by all. Each person should match his exercises with his strength and daily occupation. The extreme love of bodily exercises is frequently another form of pride or vanity. Eventually it will injure your health.

4. In every activity, be it physical or mental, you must be your own master. Do not let any interest gain too strong a hold on you. Otherwise it will gradually paralyze your better judgment and make you its slave. You will no longer be able to do what is best for yourself. Your thoughts and desires will be controlled by this strong interest.

5. Always strive to maintain your interior freedom from all things. Only then will you be able to think straight and choose what is right and truly good for you.

6. In your external activity, do not try to appear better, or even different from the ordinary good people around you. In your public actions beware of putting on a show. One who is really better than others tries to be better in My presence and for My sake, and not for the admiration or praise of men.

7. Your first obligation at all times, is to fulfill the ordinary duties of daily life. Do these as perfectly as you can for My sake. After having fulfilled these obligations, you may follow your own personal inclinations away from the eyes of men. Fulfill your public devotions without unnecessary show. If

you want to do extraordinary things for Me, do them privately where I alone will see you and praise you.

THINK:

Again and again I am faced with the fact that my worst enemy is this silly self-love of mine. It is silly because it seeks such flimsy glory and such shallow satisfaction, while it should be striving for the eternal glory and perfect satisfaction of Heaven. Even in seeking to become better and holier, I often have the wrong motives. I seek it for my own glory instead of God's glory. He wants me to better myself, so as to be more like Him in my daily life; but I keep wanting to appear better than those around me. As a result of this blindness, my spiritual life remains weak and unsteady. My improvement must begin from within, in my thinking, my intentions, and my purpose. When I have made God my main goal, I shall begin to show balance and good judgment in my external actions.

PRAY:

All-wise and loving Father, thank You for a very precious lesson today. As long as I think straight, I shall exercise good judgment in my daily life. If You are truly my main goal, if I desire Your Will in all things, I shall avoid many a foolish extreme. I know that You see my efforts and that You are satisfied as long as I am doing my reasonable best. When I strain and go to extremes, I usually do it for some selfish reason. Therefore, help me live a balanced life, at least by avoiding all deliberate show. Let me not desire the admiration or attention of anyone except You. As long as I follow Your holy direction, I shall never become a slave to my work, nor to any other created thing. The greatest sacrifice which You ask of me just now, is loyalty to my daily obligations. Let me not go to any extremes, but let me do my best for Your sake. *Amen.*

CHAPTER 44

God's Wisdom in Daily Life

CHRIST:

M Y CHILD, let Me teach you some of My heavenly wisdom. This gift is more precious than all the gold and wealth on earth. My wisdom is far above that of men.

2. The main reason why men judge so wrongly is that they think too much of this earthly life and not enough of the eternity which awaits them. They defend their earthly judgments with all kinds of worldly reasoning, and therefore they often fall into errors and sins.

3. I do not want you to be deceived by wrong human reasoning. As long as men disagree with My judgments, they are wrong. You may understand the human reasoning better than you understand My judgments, but this merely proves how far My wisdom is above all created intelligence. I gave to man the limited intelligence with which he judges. You insult My infinite intelligence if you prefer the reasoning of men to My word. I see what they see and infinitely more than they see.

4. Worldly men are foolish, not because they value the good things of this world, but because they value these things too much. They are too ready to offend Me for some earthly gain or advantage. They fail to consider the full truth about themselves, and therefore they get false notions about their

own greatness. They fail to see that all true greatness is a gift of Mine.

5. They seek praise and admiration for some passing earthly achievement or talent, when they should be seeking the all-satisfying praise and admiration which I will grant to those who gain Heaven.

6. Your true greatness lies in reflecting My goodness and wisdom in your daily life. You do this by following My wisdom in all things. What men praise in you is worthy of praise only if it pleases Me. Not everything that seems good is truly good. What men call right is not always right. You will never be confused by worldly wisdom as long as you keep your eyes on My work. Look to My Church and you shall possess My truth.

THINK:

This modern age is so filled with conflicting beliefs and philosophies. It is truly confusing. Yet, I can avoid all confusion if only I will let God guide me through His Church. I shall possess God's peace if I refuse to let people confuse me, with their ideas and theories. God made all the good things on earth, yet He warns me against loving them too much. These things are good for me only if they help me to please God and follow His Will. Otherwise I must look on them as harmful for me.

PRAY:

Eternal fountain of all wisdom, my God, I realize now how hard it is to think straight among worldly people. Their false reasoning sounds so logical at times. Yet, how can they be right if You disagree with them? I want to live a life of happiness, but not the false and passing happiness of earth. If I must make a choice between earth and Heaven, then I want to choose the best things first. I will make good use of the things I possess on earth. Never shall I love them so much as to offend You. I will try to think more and more Your way in my daily life. I will learn Your religion better and better. Your word shall be my sure guide to Heaven. I rely upon Your holy grace to give me the heavenly strength which I shall need. *Amen.*

CHAPTER 45

Holy Obedience

CHRIST:

MY CHILD, all legitimate authority comes from Me. My Will is shown to you in every reasonable command of legitimate authority. In obeying those who have authority over you, you obey Me.

2. You cannot decide what you will like or dislike, since your feelings are not always under your control. You can, however, decide to follow what you know is right and good. Obedience to authority is an act of the highest reasoning. If I am the source of all legitimate authority, then you obey Me every time you obey your lawful superiors.

3. Meditate upon this truth. Strive to see Me in those who command you. In so doing, you will find it much easier to take orders. This kind of obedience frees your mind from all sense of inferiority. It also diminishes the human resentment which you may naturally feel. Self-deception and pride are best overcome in a life of holy obedience.

4. Seek to purify your self-offering to My Will by a more perfect obedience in your daily life. In obedience you sacrifice more than your possessions. You sacrifice yourself, your feelings, your time, and your free will. The more you strive to eliminate your natural reasons, the more pure will your self-sacrifice be. Obedience includes the sacrifice of everything else.

5. When you feel inclined to disobey superiors, remember that I, your Saviour, lived a life of obedience to human superiors during My earthly life. How then can you, who are dust and ashes, refuse to follow My example?

6. Never give bad example by disobedience. Your obedience makes it easier for others to obey. Never seek particular privileges except when absolutely necessary. If you try to live without the restraints of obedience, you are simply raising yourself on a pedestal, which is pride or self-indulgence. No man can live without some measure of obedience in his life. Indeed, no one can be a good superior unless he himself knows how to obey. You can command safely and wisely

only if you have learned to obey humbly and promptly.

THINK:

God loves order because order is born of intelligence. Where order is lacking there can only be confusion and destruction. If I want to please God I must put order into my life. Not only am I to obey the direct commands of God, but also His indirect commands; that is, the orders which come to me through my lawful superiors. Only if they command what is sinful, must I refuse obedience. Obedience will always be a blow to my human pride, unless I make it an act of love for God. Jesus shows me how this is done. He became obedient to human superiors to make up for my sins of disobedience and also to give me an example of perfect obedience. Can I refuse to become more like Him? I do refuse every time I disobey those who have authority over me.

PRAY:

My Jesus, obedient Son of the heavenly Father, You obeyed His holy Will even to the point of dying for my sins. How can I ever forget this? Will I consider myself better than You by refusing to obey the commands of my lawful superiors? No matter how much I claim to love You, my claims are only words until I prove them by a life of unquestioning obedience to Your holy Will. You speak to me through Your Church and through all those who have a right to direct and command me. Let me see You in them. I want to obey You in them. Grant me the grace to hear Your voice when duty calls me to my daily occupations and activities. I want only one favor from You, the grace to offer myself to You daily by a life of obedience to my obligations. *Amen.*

CHAPTER 46

The Virtue of Humility

CHRIST:

MY CHILD, humility is a much misunderstood virtue. Many people think it is an unreasoning sense of inferiority, or a lack of self-appreciation. In reality humility is far from this. It is an honest facing of facts, admitting them, and acting according to them. The humble man lives free of all pretense and self-deception. This honesty with facts helps him to think clearly and act fairly in his daily life.

2. When you see others honored, praised, or admired, do not yield to envy or resentment. Let facts rule your life. If they deserve honor and admiration, give it to them. If not, maintain a charitable silence.

3. So too, when you are criticized, blamed, or despised, do not be disturbed. Look at the truth. If you are guilty of an accusation, ask pardon and mend your ways. If you are innocent, and the matter is serious enough, patiently try to right the wrong done you. If the matter is slight, you will find peace and greater grace in silence. Do not lose your self control in a desire to justify yourself. I judge you according to the facts, not according to what others think of you. Follow the same rule in judging yourself.

THINK:

There is so much pretense in human society, so much "putting on," so much posing. We like to appear better than we are, but we do not always work hard enough to become better. If I were honest, I would admit my many faults and my few virtues.

I would not be afraid to practice this honest self-appraisal when people point out my shortcomings and limitations. Never again would I act as though God owed me something. God loves a man who lives an honest life, a truthful life, not expecting a return of respect or thanks for everything he does. A truly humble man is so conscious of his boundless debt to God that he finds it hard to complain, even when injustice is done to him.

PRAY:

Father of Truth, I desire to prove myself a true son of Yours. I want to be simple, unassuming, and unpretentious in my daily life. Let me not put on airs and act superior to others. I will never make others feel inferior in my presence. I want to think often of my complete dependence upon You for all things. When I am praised, I will thank those who praise me and then thank You for the success which You placed in my hands. I shall never be slow to praise others for their good deeds. Let me live a truthful life, facing facts and admitting them in my actions. Unless I live this way, I shall not be a true follower of Jesus, Your divine Son. I hope to begin at last to be loyal to Jesus by practicing humility in my daily life. *Amen.*

CHAPTER 47

Humility in Action

CHRIST:

M Y CHILD, nothing is more pleasing to Me than to see you truly humble in your daily life. The humble man remains at peace when others find fault with him. His attention is so firmly fixed on Me that he is as conscious of My presence as he is of the people around him. He cannot forget his complete dependence on Me. He is so impressed by his own nothingness that he fights against all forms of pride within him. As a result of this hatred of all pride, he refuses to defend his rights in unimportant matters.

2. People resent the man who seeks to raise himself above them, but no one resents the man who is little in his own eyes. The humble man does not look for admiration. He is as willing to be last, as others are anxious to be first. He does not care what

others think of him, but in all things he is eager to please Me. He is not interested in honors, reputation, or human applause. He knows that I judge without error or misunderstanding, and he seeks only My approval.

3. The truly humble man is not afraid to have others know or correct his faults. He uses these humiliations to prove to himself that he wants no earthly glory, but only self-improvement for My sake.

4. Never compare yourself with those who seem worse than you, but reflect often upon My infinite generosity with you. Remember your enormous debt of gratitude to Me. Humility will convince you that without Me you are nothing. This virtue will urge you on toward greater self-sacrifice for My sake.

THINK:

The man who is little in his own eyes, is truly great in God's eyes, because he is a man of truth. He counts as nothing all the satisfactions, accomplishments, and glories of earthly life because he sees God as his first and highest good. The lower he reaches in self-esteem, so much the higher does he rise toward the God of truth Anyone who attributes any good to himself alone, hinders God's grace from raising him to true perfection. All perfection begins with an honest facing of facts; that is, humility.

PRAY:

My heavenly Father, God of truth, You reveal Your secrets to the humble man. You invite him to a closer and higher friendship with You. Let me abandon all pretense and hypocrisy, and help me be honest with You, with people, and with myself. I must not hide the truth from myself. I want to admit it in my actions, even when it is unpleasant. Only then shall I receive Your peace and joy. Thoughts of death and judgment will not arouse fear within me because my love of truth will be my guarantee of salvation. Let me face what I am, and begin today to improve myself according to Your holy plan. I shall humble myself as often as I can, so that I may never forget my complete dependence on You. I shall look on humiliations as an opportunity to overcome my foolish pride. When praise and honor come to me, I shall pass it on to You, the fountain of all success. My greatest glory lies in living a truthful life, free of self-deception and foolish pride. *Amen.*

CHAPTER 48

Self-Abasement

CHRIST:

M Y CHILD, when you have succeeded in developing the virtue of humility to a high degree, I shall lead you on to a still higher virtue—the virtue of self-abasement. This is the virtue which inspires My followers to avoid all forms of admiration, praise, and honor. In their deep appreciation of Me, they seek the last place among people, preferring to be overlooked, and even mistreated.

2. Through humility, My loyal follower comes to know Me better and better. As he grows in appreciation of My infinite goodness, he seeks to express his love for Me more and more. He realizes that I am constantly giving him more gifts, both natural and supernatural. This realization arouses in him a desire to give Me more and more of himself.

3. This yearning leads him to various forms of self-sacrifice. He seeks to deprive himself of human admiration and praise, since he desires to avoid all earthly rewards for the good which he does. He wants to do more and more for Me alone. Even in giving good example, he strives to do it under the appearance of the ordinary.

4. In his desire to give himself entirely to Me, My self-abasing follower prefers to obey rather than command, to serve rather than be served, to follow rather than lead, to praise rather than be praised. In his own small way he tries to match My generosity with his gratitude. He strives to offer his daily self-sacrifice in return for My boundless love. All this he does by lowering himself as much as possible in his daily life. Of course, this self-lowering does not prevent him from doing his best in his daily tasks.

5. I practiced this self-abasement all through My daily life. I chose a cold and lonely stable as My birth place, a small, unknown town as My home, an ordinary trade as My work. I stood among the penitent sinners who stood in line to receive the baptism

of John. My life and occupation were despised by many. No matter how much you lower yourself, you will never equal the self-abasement of My Passion and death, nor even the self-abasement of the Holy Eucharist, where I dwell under the appearance of bread and wine.

6. Imitate Me in this wonderful virtue of self-abasement. My saints could not practice it enough to satisfy their love for Me. Though they were misunderstood and despised by others, they were happy in the thought that their life was all for Me. They were eager to crowd as much pure love as possible into their earthly life. They did it through self-abasement, the one virtue which excludes all pride and self-deception.

THINK:

If I meditated more often on God's infinite generosity with me, His infinite mercy toward me, and the boundless self-sacrifice of Jesus for my sake, I would make some attempt to practice some kind of self-abasement. Not only would I avoid praise, admiration, and honor, but I would actually desire to be despised and mistreated. This desire would arise from the realization of how very much I owe to God and how little I have given to Him thus far. I would forget the fear of ridicule and contempt which I now have because I would be too impressed by the greatness and goodness of God.

PRAY:

My Jesus, self-abasing Saviour, grant me this wonderful virtue by which You proved Your love for me beyond all question. All the saints practiced self-abasement because they appreciated Your goodness and Your love. I want to share their holy appreciation and their generous love for You. In their determination to serve You without pride or self-deception, they practiced this high virtue of self-abasement. Fill my mind with the sight of Your goodness, and my will with a yearning to satisfy Your all-deserving love. I hope to empty myself of self-love through self-abasement for love of You. *Amen.*

CHAPTER 49

The Virtue of Poverty

CHRIST:

MY CHILD, if you sincerely desire to advance in perfection, free your heart of all earthly attachments. Do it first by breaking away from whatever draws your will toward sin. Then, rise to higher virtue and practice holy poverty.

2. The virtue of poverty is the desire to abandon more and more things in your daily life so that you may have fewer bonds holding you back from Me. This virtue seeks to abandon all that is not absolutely necessary for your daily life.

3. True, you cannot abandon all things in your earthly life. You must eat, work, rest, and provide for the future. However, when the virtue of poverty fills your soul, you will do all of these things more perfectly. Your intention will be to do these things as I did them in My daily life, that you may be a success not only here on earth, but above all hereafter in Heaven.

4. This holy virtue will help you use all things for My sake. You will seek to use these things to please Me. You will see them as helps to bring you closer to Me in your daily life. It will help you think with less prejudice because you will have fewer earthly desires.

5. The virtue of poverty will make you wise in the right use of what you need. It will free your will from its earthly preferences and will lead it on toward Me in your daily activities. Gradually you will become the master of your soul, free from undue distractions and unreasoning attachments.

THINK:

Being poor in spirit does not mean having nothing. It simply means being free from earthly attachments. Such a poor man wants nothing which leads to sin. Moreover, he wants God's friendship so much that he eliminates as much competition as possible within himself. In his eagerness to come closer to God, he turns his back on as many things as he can. By doing this he is able to think more easily of God, speak with Him more often, and please Him more perfectly.

PRAY:

"Blessed are the poor in spirit, for theirs is the kingdom of Heaven." These are Your words, my Jesus. You spoke them long ago, but they are still true. How few have bothered to understand them, much less practice them! We claim to be wise, yet how often we fail to place You first in our daily life. We admit in word that You are our greatest treasure, and yet we seldom think of limiting our earthly interests in order to give You more attention and better service. I am tired of living this illogical life of mine. I want to begin this day trying to have fewer things in my daily life, so that I may have less to draw my attention away from You. Fill my thoughts with You. Direct my intentions to Yourself, so that I may begin at last to live for Your praise, honor, and glory. *Amen.*

CHAPTER 50

The Virtue of Patience

CHRIST:

MY CHILD, I came down from Heaven for your salvation and perfection. Not only did I make reparation for your sins, but I also gave you an example of the virtues which you need in order to gain eternal life. I took upon Myself your daily trials and difficulties, in order to show you how to deal with them.

2. One of the virtues which you often need in your daily life is patience. I had to practice a great deal of patience with the people around Me during My earthly life. I had to bear the same things which annoy and irritate you. I bore these trials with patience. Meditate on My patience and pray for the wisdom and strength to imitate Me in this holy virtue.

3. Consider how I treat My loyal followers. I do not send them an easy life, but one which demands great patience, not many earthly joys, but many trials; not honors, but contempt and hatred; not ease, but endless labors. By their unwavering patience they earn a crown of unending glory.

4. Some are willing to suffer only what they choose to endure. Others can be patient with certain persons, but not with everyone. A truly patient man, however, makes

no exceptions and sets no conditions as to when, or with whom he will be patient. One who possesses supernatural patience, does not consider what kind of people cause his trial; whether they are superiors, equals, or inferiors, whether they are well-meaning or malicious. He is interested only in taking this trial as though I were handing it to him. As long as the matter does not require him to defend his rights, or to correct the people involved, he is willing to bear his trial for My sake.

THINK:

The supernatural virtue of patience is an act of love for God shown by the disregard of one's own convenience or inconvenience. It is another form of self-giving. Jesus could have saved me with far less inconvenience to Himself. He endured much more for me than He needed to. That was His way of showing His love for me. If I fix my eyes on Him, I shall never again say that I can take anything except this or that. I shall be willing to suffer anything for Jesus. I shall lose sight of the people involved, and see only Jesus.

PRAY:

Dear patient Jesus, who can describe the boundless love with which You suffered so many trials in Your daily life? Can I think of this and still refuse to practice greater patience in my own life? Can I see my God and Saviour bearing so much aggravation for my sins, and still go on demanding a smoothly running life for myself? You are still practicing patience with me, as You wait for me to come to my senses and start practicing a bit of humility in my daily life. If I were truly humble, I would find it easy to be patient. I deserve far worse than what I now suffer in my daily life. Therefore, I shall be patient with the trials which come along. Some day I may rise to a higher generosity with You. I may even reach the joy which Your saints had in suffering for You. I must, however, begin today. I hope to face my problems and annoyances with patience, for Your sake, my Jesus. *Amen.*

CHAPTER 51

Daily Need of Patience

CHRIST:

MY CHILD, though you may plan all things and arrange everything with the greatest care, you will still have many opportunities to exercise the virtue of patience. You cannot eliminate the unexpected, the unforeseen, and the unavoidable. In many cases your best remedy and weapon will be an intelligent patience with yourself as well as with others.

2. Every man has his daily share of troubles and trials. Sometimes it may be bodily pain and discomfort. At other times it may be mental or spiritual suffering, some annoyance, disappointment, or anxiety. Sometimes you may feel that I have deserted you. Then again, you may have to bear misunderstandings, misinterpretations, or even bad will from your neighbor. In fact, there are times when you are a burden and a bother to yourself.

3. Everybody would like to be free of these trials, but it cannot be. They are a part of

your earthly life. Wherever you turn, you will always find My cross in one form or another. Patience will help you to bear it more easily. This virtue will help you keep your soul at peace, so that you may continue to walk toward Heaven in time of trials.

THINK:

I see only too clearly how wonderful a virtue patience is. It is the key to peace, and even joy, in time of trouble and suffering. I need never be surprised, resentful, disappointed, or sad when things go badly for me. Wherever I go, I bring with me one of my greatest troubles and burdens—myself, with all my unreasoning desires and endless wants. Through the virtue of patience I can gain greater possession of myself. I shall more easily see how to deal with the trials facing Me.

PRAY:

My Jesus, King of true glory, You embraced a life of suffering and trials for love of me. You mounted a throne of shame and agony for my sins. Can I expect, or even desire, a life of ease, with everything going as I wish? When I consider what You chose to suffer for my sake, the disappointments, hatred, ingratitude, humiliation, injustice, and more, can I want a life of planned successes and pleasant friendships? No, Lord. If I really love You, I shall desire a share of Your cross in my daily life. Teach me patience to accept the heartaches, aggravations, and disappointments which come my way. Make me more like You in a life like Yours. No greater glory is possible to any man. *Amen*.

CHAPTER 52

The Sufferings of Daily Life

CHRIST:

MY CHILD, as you advance in the virtue of patience, I shall draw you closer to My heart. I will show you how great a privilege it is to bear anything for My sake. When you see what I have suffered for you, and when you reflect on the great trials and troubles which My saints suffered for My sake, you will realize how little you are doing for Me.

2. You have not been asked to shed your blood nor to suffer tortures. You will find it much easier to bear your daily burdens and

trials when you realize the agonizing sufferings of My earthly life and the great trials of My glorious martyrs. My loyal followers had to fight violent temptations. Their patience was tested in so many ways, but they passed through all this with the clear vision of unselfish love for Me. If this consideration fails to make you think less of your own trials, this is only a proof that you still think more of yourself than of Me.

3. I will not permit anything in your life which does not help your highest interests. Therefore, learn a valuable lesson from Me. Be less anxious to enjoy this earthly life and more willing to bear your daily trials for My sake. Prepare to face the disappointments, misunderstandings, contradictions, and labors with greater resignation and patience. I will not be outdone in generosity. I shall give you the grace to act more wisely and calmly in time of trial.

4. Do not expect to reach Heaven's eternal happiness by a life of ease and contentment on earth. My heavenly gifts are not given to those who are impatient with suffering and adversity.

5. Patience will help you to think clearly. You will come to look on suffering as a privilege, for it is just that when accepted and embraced for My sake. You will then understand the joy of My Apostles who rejoiced when they were punished for preaching My words. They knew what a privilege it was to suffer for My sake.

THINK:

It is truly a privilege to suffer anything for Jesus' sake. Man's greatest achievement on earth is to forget self and offer all to God, especially when things are contrary and difficult. I must pray for an opportunity to prove my unselfish love of God. The better I know Him, the more will I desire to suffer for Him. I can begin by accepting the ordinary trials of daily life. Later I may rise to greater opportunities and seek more opportunities to prefer His holy, all-wise Will to my own blind, selfish will.

PRAY:

My Jesus, so many people recommend patience and admire it with their lips, but so few are willing to exercise it in their daily life. Please do not allow me to be a theoretical follower of Yours, but an active one. I desire to be generous with You in real life. You deserve so much more than I can ever offer You. It is little enough that I have to suffer when compared with the cross which You embraced for love of me, or compared with what Your saints did for Your sake. Let me at least find joy in embracing, for love of You, the trials, contradictions, disappointments, and labors of this day. I hope to rise higher than this later on, by wishing to suffer more than my ordinary share of daily tasks and trials. All this let me do for Your sake, my all-deserving Saviour. *Amen.*

CHAPTER 53

The Value of Adversity

CHRIST:

MY CHILD, a man's true greatness is seen in adversity. Hard work, disappointments, failures, criticism, misinterpretations, opposition, sorrow, and bodily suffering are the tests which show you what you really are. Your virtues are proved and your faults are revealed during these adversities.

2. Prosperity and success are not always good for you. Your greatest achievement on earth is to be united with Me in all things. You can achieve this union best in time of adversity. When all goes well, you can deceive yourself, but not so when matters go badly. Faith, hope, humility, patience, and the other supernatural virtues can be measured only by their testing in real life. In adversity you cannot deceive yourself, but you see yourself as you really are.

3. I want you to become truly holy. I desire you to offer yourself to Me without reservation or exception. Such an offering is best made in trials and suffering. Your natural self-interest and self-seeking must be buried in My Will. You cannot be sure that this has been done until you accept whatever adversity I send in your daily life.

THINK:

Nothing is more pleasing to God, nor more profitable to me, than to suffer willingly for love of Christ my King. As I grow in the appreciation of this truth, I shall come to prefer adversity to consolation and ease. Within me will grow the desire to do more for Jesus, Who did so much for me. I shall advance in the desire to be more like Christ and His saints. I shall therefore wish to suffer more, endure more contradictions, misunderstandings, failures, disappointments, sorrows, and pain.

PRAY:

My loving and all-wise God, although You allow me to face temptations and adversities, it is for my own good that You do so. You want me to rise to greater heights of goodness, so that I may gain greater eternal glory in Heaven. In the middle of my trials and sufferings I ought to love You as much as ever, realizing that this adversity is a loving gift from You. You know what is best for me, and You send it my way so that I may embrace it and accept it. Grant me the wisdom to bless You in my trials and to love You in my sufferings. *Amen.*

CHAPTER 54

Joy in Adversity

CHRIST:

MY CHILD, this earthly life is not a last-ing home. You were made for an un-ending life of perfect happiness with Me in Heaven. This earth is not a place of rest but of labor. Men often spend a good part of their lives working for some earthly goal. Then, after a brief enjoyment of their success, they pass on into eternity. If they are willing to sacrifice so much for a passing earthly goal, how much more willing should you be to labor and sacrifice for an unending heavenly glory?

2. Do not think that you have found true peace when things run smoothly in your daily life. My peace is given to those who know how to face adversity and endure hardships. Your model is My earthly life. From the hour of My birth until My last breath on the cross, I patiently endured all kinds of adversity. Grief and want were not strangers to Me. I frequently heard complaints and criticism around Me. I bore disgrace and reproach though I lived a faultless life. Ingratitude was

My reward for all the help which I gave to so many people. Falsehoods were hurled against Me after I offered My saving truth to all.

3. My loyal followers had the same experience. Apostles, martyrs, confessors, and virgins—all of My saints bore adversity in their lives. All of them rejoiced at the privilege of suffering something for My sake. They were able to endure so much because they kept their eyes on Me and on Heaven.

4. You too would find joy in adversity if you exercised more faith, more humility, more patience, more love for Me, instead of favoring yourself so much. If you had even a passing glimpse of the indescribable glory of Heaven, you would no longer seek what is pleasant and satisfying on earth. You would easily admit that all earthly trials and sufferings are small in comparison with the heavenly reward. Never again would you complain in time of adversity.

THINK:

There is no comparison between my earthly labors and sufferings and the heavenly happiness and glory which Jesus has prepared for His faithful followers. St. Paul said: "The sufferings of the present time are not worthy to be compared with the glory to come." Jesus gives me an example of the highest wisdom. He embraced a life of adversity with patience and with complete self-possession. He refused to rebel against His Father's Will in any way. He was obedient unto death, even the death of the cross. He wants me to do likewise in my daily life, so that He may one day grant me the glorious reward of Heaven.

PRAY:

My Jesus, model of true holiness, no goodness is worthy of Heaven unless it is inspired by Your grace. To be like You is my greatest glory. I believe this truth, and I desire to follow it in my daily life. Help me to understand You better, so that I may think like You and act like You. The worst thing in the world is not suffering, nor disgrace, nor human failures, but sin. In fact, there must be something great about suffering and trials, since You embraced them in Your earthly life. Let me see the eternal good which lies in earthly adversity. As far as it is good for me, let me desire to suffer more than I now do. If for no other reason,

I desire it in order to be more like You, my suffering Saviour. May I never again look on sufferings and adversity as something to be hated and avoided. *Amen.*

CHAPTER 55

The Perfection of Charity

CHRIST:

MY CHILD, as you strive to center your love on Me. I shall draw you on toward the peak of perfection. I shall show you how to love Me with the purest love possible to man or angel.

2. The perfection of charity lies in seeing My boundless goodness so clearly that you love Me for what I am—simply because I deserve your best attention and your complete self-giving. Your greatest joy will be in turning your thoughts to Me and in living your daily life with the intention of pleasing Me in all things. Appreciation of My infinite perfection will make you turn away from all lesser goodness and perfection, including yourself. Having found the best, you will no longer be content with less. Though you must live a human life, performing many

human activities, your main desire will be to please Me in these activities.

3. Then will I bestow upon you a vivid awareness of My love for you, and an ardent desire to give Me all that you are. In your daily occupations you will do your best for My sake. In your trials and disappointments you will no longer be content with the virtue of resignation to My Will. You will seek to rise to the higher virtue of preferring My Will, refusing to pray for any relief for self. Your petitions will always be for the benefit of others. As for yourself, you will desire only to suffer for love of Me.

4. When you have reached this high degree of love, I shall grant you a foretaste of My heavenly peace and joy. Your self-dedication to My all-wise Will, will bring you My peace. Your awareness of My friendship will bring you My joy.

5. When these graces come to you, earthly trials will seem small to you. They will lose their power to arouse fear, anxiety, and worry within you. You will carry your burdens without being burdened, and all bitterness will be turned into sweetness.

Indeed, you will feel impelled to offer me more and more of yourself, constantly desiring to do what is more perfect for My sake. The very peak of this holy virtue brings with it a yearning to die, so that you may be with Me in the perfect union of Heaven.

THINK:

I cannot reach this high perfection without God's graces, but I can dispose my soul for these wonderful graces by my generous efforts today. If I make good use of the holy thoughts, desires, and opportunities which God sends me today, I will be disposing myself for greater graces. I must earnestly strive to strip myself of all self-seeking by offering my daily activities to God. I shall never achieve this disregard for self until I see how much more I gain in preferring God to myself. My self-offering will be pure only when I am ready to accept whatever God cares to send me, be it pleasant or unpleasant, great or small. Though my unreasoning moods and feelings will still oppose my holy desires, I will rise above them with the strength of charity. Though my external activities will still claim my time and attention, I shall now perform them for God instead of merely natural reasons.

PRAY:

All-perfect God, source of all good, how do I dare aim so high? I am so small, so weak, so sinful, yet You invite me to share Your thoughts, Your desires, Your intentions, and Your power in my daily life. If this were not Your invitation, I would suspect my foolish pride and my blind self-love. I surrender myself to You today. I shall make every effort to use well the holy graces which You send me today. No longer will I be satisfied with avoiding sins, nor even with practicing the necessary virtues of daily life. As far as my daily obligations, my strength, and my spiritual director will permit, I shall try to do what is more perfect. I shall seek to be more God-like by imitating Jesus, my divine Model, in all things. All-wise and loving Father, protect me against all forms of self-deception, all foolish extremes, all spiritual pride, vanity, and self-seeking. May I never forget that the first proof of perfection is obedience to those who have a right to direct and command me. *Amen.*

PART FOUR

The Spiritual Combat

CHAPTER 56

Life's Daily Warfare

CHRIST:

MY CHILD, your daily life is truly a warfare. There is a continual struggle within you and around you. The final purpose of this struggle is to win men for Heaven or for hell. The parties engaged in this battle are My Blessed in Heaven, My Church on earth, and I, on the one side, with the world, the flesh, and the devil on the other.

2. The battleground in this warfare is the soul of each and every person on earth. Too often a man joins his own enemies and helps them defeat My efforts to save him. This is done either through foolish pride, or through blind selfishness, or simply through a blameworthy ignorance.

3. The world fights Me by its false standards of self-respect, ambition, and success. These are merely different names for self-seeking without regard for others, not even

Me. True self-respect, and right ambition are those which direct your eyes to your highest perfection and eternal happiness, above all that is temporary and incomplete.

4. The flesh fights Me with its animal desires, its likes and dislikes, which make it harder for you to think clearly and to strive for what is right. Your blind self-seeking and your stubborn pride offer you many false reasons for doing what is really bad for you. With these influences continually at work, you are open to continual self-deception.

5. The devil makes clever use of the enemies mentioned above. He tempts you through worldly people and through your own weaknesses. Your only defense against these enemies is to become a spiritual man. With My help you must have a supernatural outlook on all things. I shall grant you interior vision which will easily detect the clever camouflage of Satan and quickly recognize sin under its numberless disguises. I shall fill your heart with a firm and constant love for Me, so that you may go on daily, fighting for My glory without self-consideration.

THINK:

The daily battle for eternal life goes on at every moment in every human life. God wants me to be an intelligent and active soldier of Jesus, His divine Son. In His teachings and sacraments Jesus offers me the knowledge and strength to be a loyal follower of His. If I cooperate with His holy plan, His eternal, heavenly outlook will replace my narrow, earth-bound outlook on life. Through my interior and exterior imitation of Him I shall be a spiritual man. Then shall I help spread Christ's victory not only within my own soul, but also within the souls of the people around me. In fact, my prayers and sacrifices will bring many graces to people all over the world.

PRAY:

O Jesus, King of my soul, lead me along life's daily battlefield. Teach me to view all of my daily experiences as one great act of love and loyalty to You. I want to fulfill my daily obligations with a sense of serving You. When temptations face me, I shall fight them for love of You. Help me keep this spiritual outlook on all my daily activities. People must not dim my vision of You. Even in helping others, let it be an act of personal loyalty to You. By my example I hope to inspire others with a keener desire to follow You. By humble and timely advice I shall try to help others see Your holy Will. By my prayers I shall try to obtain for others the graces which they need to fight sin and to practice virtue. *Amen*.

CHAPTER 57

Preparing for the Daily Battle

CHRIST:

MY CHILD, you are to face many trials so that you may practice many virtues. I will send you some consolation and interior comfort at times, but do not look for lasting contentment in this life. For My sake, take courage and be brave in facing things which are disagreeable. I want you to become a new man, another person. You will often have to do what you do not want to do, and give up what you desire.

2. I tell you this ahead of time, so that you may be prepared to fight the daily battle for Heaven and gain a glorious victory. Without a fight there can be no triumph. He who refuses to enter this battle deprives himself of

the final and unending glory. Fight on, suffer patiently, and you will have an all-satisfying crown of happiness with Me in Heaven. Only by labors on earth will you earn an eternal rest in Heaven. Only by this daily combat can you achieve the indescribable victory.

3. I, your King and Model, will march before you and fight with you. Follow Me fearlessly and loyally. Be ready to fight every temptation and all selfishness. He who abandons Me and My standards is his own worst enemy.

THINK:

Today some of my efforts will end in failure. Other things which I neither want nor expect, will happen. People will get on my nerves. My own foolishness in some things will annoy me. These are the trials of everyday life. These are my opportunities for virtue. My spiritual greatness or littleness is seen on these occasions. If I keep my patience, I am on the first level of holiness. If I thank God for these occasions, I am on a higher level. If I am glad to have something to suffer for Jesus' sake, I am on the highest level. How much of myself do I really want to give to Jesus? My daily life is the answer.

PRAY:

Dear Jesus, my divine Saviour, You lived a human life in order to suffer my daily trials. By Your patience, kindness, and self-control, You showed the kind of love that You desire of me. Help me to recognize these occasions for virtue in my own life, and grant me the strength to make good use of them. Let me no longer be content with merely avoiding sin. Make me eager to advance in the virtues which I need most. In this way I shall be putting up the best kind of battle against my faults. I shall also be giving You a higher proof of my love for You. *Amen.*

CHAPTER 58

Self-Conquest in Daily Life

CHRIST:

M Y CHILD, before you can be truly Mine, you must endure a great interior battle. Your blind, unreasoning self-love will not easily surrender itself to Me, nor to anyone else. This lower self of yours will embrace only its own visible advantages.

2. And yet, no earthly satisfaction can compare with Me. In Me you will find your

greatest advantage, your perfect satisfaction. I alone am all-perfect and all-good. For My sake you must be ready to sacrifice all things which draw you away from Me. Of all your earthly needs, none is greater than the need to control your unreasoning desires.

3. When you find it hard to obey your superiors or their representatives, look beyond them and see Me. Obey Me in them. If your present occupations are disagreeable or difficult, fix your eyes on the eternal goal of these present tasks. Think clearly and do not allow your feelings, moods, or blind self-seeking to deceive you.

4. With clear thinking, deep faith in My word, firm confidence in My assistance, and unwavering love for Me, you must control and guide your life according to My Will. This will be your highest achievement; this will be your greatest glory. Of all your daily needs, none is greater, nor more important, than this supernatural self-control.

5. When you have gained full control over yourself, you will have control over everything else. Blessed is he who has learned to be firm with himself, guiding himself with

My commandments and controlling himself with My grace.

THINK:

The more perfectly I die to self, so much the more perfectly will I live to God. Jesus Himself goes before me in all my daily experiences. In loneliness I can join the lonely Christ. In misunderstandings I can turn to Christ misunderstood. Tired, I can rest with the tired Saviour. In all my trials I can see Jesus experiencing the same trials for my sake. No longer will my daily hardships and troubles seem as repulsive and frightening as they once seemed. All the glory of Christian life consists in Christ-likeness. I am most like Jesus when I willingly embrace the daily cross of disappointments, difficulties, labors, and sufferings. Christian self-conquest is the daily answer to the blind, natural self-seeking which seeks to turn me against Christ, my King.

PRAY:

Jesus, divine Saviour, King of the universe, I place my heart and my life at Your feet. Freely I choose to follow You in my daily life. Gladly will I fight my blind, unreasoning self for Your sake. You will lead me through this daily battle, on to an eternal victory. The more perfectly I forget myself for Your sake, the more surely do I walk toward my highest good and most perfect happiness. I wish to follow You in two ways. Firstly, by embracing whatever You choose to send me this day in the way of labors, joys, hardships, failures, and disappointments. Secondly, I wish to follow You by deliberately contradicting my natural desires as often as I can do so without hurting my daily obligations. Let me have such contempt for my blind selfishness that I may never sympathize with myself in anything except Your holy Will and greater glory. *Amen.*

CHAPTER 59

Zeal for Perfection

CHRIST:

MY CHILD, do not be afraid of the daily battle for perfection. If you had even a passing glimpse of the heavenly glory which I have prepared for you, you would joyfully embrace any trial and all sufferings for My sake. But I want you to do so without seeing the eternal reward. Strive for perfection with the best and purest motive. Do it because I deserve such effort and loyalty.

2. Look for opportunities to contradict yourself. This mortification will be your surest sign of spiritual progress. Beware of self-deception. Suspect your motives even in the good within you. Root out all foolish self-seeking by a constant self-contradiction.

3. This supernatural self-contradiction will purify your love for Me. However, even in this self-contradiction you must be ready at all times to obey your superiors. The higher you aim in the way of perfection, so much the more do you need the guidance and counsel of others. He who follows the will of superiors is more perfect than one who follows his own will in these matters. Obedience is the surest proof of generosity with Me.

4. Avoid false virtue. Never do anything which would prevent you from fulfilling your daily obligations. Any form of self-discipline which makes you uncharitable or inconsiderate of others is not from Me. Be eager to have your virtues tested by the experiences of daily life. Do not fear misunderstandings,

failures, humiliations, or sufferings. Fear only to see your day go by without some sound spiritual progress.

5. Few reach this rare perfection because few give themselves to Me without some exception or reservation. They leave some small root of earthly self-love in their soul; and like a destructive weed, that root spreads out and chokes the still-tender, developing virtues. Only by daily self-contradiction can you purify your love for Me. Only by daily self-contradiction can you crush the deadly weed of self-deception.

THINK:

If I desire true spiritual progress without self-deception, I must embrace this sure way of self-contradiction. I can do it in two ways. Firstly, I can willingly embrace the unexpected disappointments and unforeseen sufferings which come to me throughout the day, thanking God for them. In these trials I can renew my self-offering to His divine Will. Secondly, I can seek opportunities to contradict my natural preferences and desires, so that I may offer my will more fully to God. In all this, however, I must always be prepared to obey the corrections and counsels of my spiritual guide and of my legitimate superiors. Only then can I be sure that my desire for perfection is complete.

PRAY:

My God, my greatest Treasure, enlighten my mind to appreciate You more fully. Arouse my generosity to offer You the unreserved love which You deserve. Strengthen my efforts to give myself to You more fully throughout the day. Cast out of my heart all worry about the past, all preoccupation with the present, and all fear of the future. Fix my mind so completely on Your goodness that I may hunger only for one thing—to contradict myself for love of You. You deserve the best that is in me. Let me give it without hesitation. Take my love in whatever way You desire it, whether in sufferings of the body or trials of the mind. I want only one thing—to give You all that I am and all that I have. Jesus is my Model of this self-giving. He was born poor in the stable of Bethlehem, and died poor upon the cross of Calvary. His poverty was due to

His voluntary self-giving for my sake. I hope to imitate Jesus in His self-giving. *Amen.*

CHAPTER 60

Man's True Glory

CHRIST:

MY CHILD, let worldly men seek their success and glory from one another. I want you to seek your glory from Me alone. All human glory, all worldly honor, all earthly splendor—these are empty and bare when compared with the heavenly glory, honor, and splendor which I have prepared for My loyal followers.

2. True greatness is not in the man who is satisfied with himself. It is only in those with whom I am satisfied. My standards for judging people are not like the standards of this world. I shall not estimate your merits by your knowledge, nor by your position among men, nor by your having visions and consolations. I shall estimate your worth by your humility and by your charity. I shall look to see whether you think too much of yourself, or whether you prefer My Will. I shall consider whether you seek My honor

and glory in your daily activities, or whether you seek your own advantage and honor.

3. Your highest perfection and glory lie in loving My truth above all else, in forgetting self to the point of being humbled and despised for My sake. Do not consider your strength, nor even your lack of strength. Fix your attention on My boundless power, wisdom, and love.

4. If you love My truth, you will praise My name, not yours. You will esteem and honor My Will, not your puny human accomplishments. You will bless Me in all things, and you will refuse to let the praises of people turn your head. You will never forget your littleness and your nothingness.

THINK:

If I lack peace and contentment in my earthly life, it is because I have been following a false standard. I judge many things from my own advantage and disadvantage, from my own likes and dislikes. The only proof of goodness is God's approval. When God wants something done, I should consider it a privilege to do it, even though I may dislike what is to be done, or can see in it no advantage for myself. All other standards which disagree with this one, are false and foolish.

PRAY:

O Holy Ghost, my God and Sanctifier, Source of all true wisdom, grant me the light to understand this holy standard in my daily life. Let me think straight and see Your holy Will in all things. What people say, is right only if it agrees with Your holy Word. Only God is great, and man's true glory lies in sharing Your greatness by following Your holy Will in his daily life. By doing this, I will be reflecting Your eternal wisdom, goodness, and holiness in myself. This is the highest glory possible to any creature. I hope for the grace to begin this day to live according to this highest standard—the one and only standard of true greatness and glory. *Amen.*

BOOK THREE

The Way of Union

BOOK THREE

The Way of Union

PURIFIED OF ALL SERIOUS FAULTS and most of his lesser defects, and having proved his unselfish loyalty to his divine King, Christ's loyal follower now finds himself longing for a still more intimate union with God. In an effort to give himself completely to God, he strives to use every actual grace which the Holy Spirit offers him throughout the day.

In due time God rewards such generosity by raising the soul to the highest spiritual level, the way of union. The man in this stage of spiritual perfection finds his thoughts turning more frequently and more easily to God. He is constantly aware of God's nearness. His predominant desire in all his activities, is to give more of himself to God, by whatever form of self-sacrifice his daily obligations will permit. In the joy of giving, his selfish interests are abandoned altogether.

Under the influence of the spiritual gifts of the Holy Spirit, life takes on a wonderful simplicity. The generous follower of Christ has reached the mountain top of spiritual perfection. Now he lives not only *for* God, not only *with* Him, but *in* Him. The soul enjoys a supernatural friendship undreamed of by worldly-minded men. Amid life's daily trials and difficulties, Christ's generous follower finds a peace and joy which are a foretaste of Heaven.

PART ONE

Striving for Closer Union

CHAPTER 1

Union with God

CHRIST:

MY CHILD, as long as you are in sanctifying grace, the Holy Trinity dwells within your soul. As long as you live free of mortal sin, I am with you in a supernatural union. The more aware you become of this union, the more will you be influenced by it in your daily life.

2. Live an active interior life, so that you may gain the full benefit of this close friendship. Through the various methods of prayer, learn to direct your mind and heart to Me often throughout the day.

3. You will rise to great perfection in your daily life if you can center your occupations and activities around Me. With such an interior life you will no longer be disturbed by the people around you, nor by the tasks which face you, nor by the difficulties and trials which come to you.

4. This union is the beginning of heavenly peace and joy. You will know My joy because you will be aware of possessing Me. You will have My peace because you will love My Will and follow it throughout the day. Not only will you live your life for Me, but you will live it with Me. You will be aware of My companionship in all that you do and suffer.

THINK:

As long as I am in sanctifying grace, the Blessed Trinity dwells within my soul. This interior union would affect my daily life much more if I were more aware of it throughout the day. I do not need to interrupt my activities, but I need only develop a habit of prayer. This habit would help my mind turn frequently to God within me. In my spare time I would seek to perfect my friendship with Him by reading, reflecting, and conversing with Him. My daily burdens would be much lighter because I would be more aware that God shares them with me. Human friendships would become more perfect because I would bring God's grace into them. My way of thinking and living would help my friends come closer to God.

PRAY:

Holy Trinity, my God, You have been pleased to make my soul Your dwelling. You came to me in baptism, intending to be my closest companion forever. As long as I do not reject Your love by mortal sin, I can live this life of mine in union with You. My loving God, let me be loyal to You, Who have been so loyal to me. Teach me to increase and strengthen this heavenly friendship more and more each day. Your love for me is shown by a constant giving. Let me give back some of Your numberless gifts by my wise and holy use of them. Throughout the day, let me give You more of my thoughts, more of my desires, more of my pleasures and satisfactions. I hope for the day when this life of mine will be lived in perfect companionship with You, so that I may do all things for the highest reason—to please You. *Amen.*

CHAPTER 2

Union with God through Prayer

CHRIST:

MY CHILD, when people march in a parade, they all keep the same step, the same rhythm, and the same pace. They try to form one single unit with the others. When, however, the parade is over, each person resumes his own way of walking. No two walk quite the same. Due to their bodily structure, figure, athletic development, and other reasons, each person has his own manner of walking. So too is it with prayer.

2. In public prayer all recite the same words, express the same sentiments, and assume the same tone and tempo to form a group-prayer. In their private prayers, no two pray quite the same. Each has his own personal touch in dealing with Me. For this reason different methods of prayer have been developed in the history of the Church.

3. Some people like to pray with the help of prayer books; some prefer to think about My words and apply them to their lives; some prefer to use their imagination,

picturing Me near and conversing with them; some like to contemplate the events of My earthly life and imagine themselves as part of those events. There are people who like to pray for sinners, others who like to examine their lives frequently to see where they may please Me more; and others who simply like to kneel or sit in My presence and enjoy My nearness.

4. Prayer is the raising of your thoughts and your will to Me. In prayer you stand before Me with respect, with gratitude, with sorrow, and with desire. Prayer brings respect for My infinite power and goodness, gratitude for My numberless gifts, sorrow for your sins and for the sins of others, and desire for My mercy, for My assistance, and for My friendship.

5. Some people find it harder than others to attain this spiritual union with Me. Different persons use different means to reach Me. Some need to think a while, others need a certain posture of the body. Still others are dependent upon the place of their prayer. And so, again you see how each finds Me in his own way. However, the prayer itself is the

same for all. It is a union with Me in thought and desire. Whatever one does to reach that stage, is only a preliminary to prayer.

THINK:

By being a prayerful man, I will be letting God share in my life. He and I will be living and acting together. I will be supplying the good will and He will supply the strength. In prayer I unite my mind and will to God. Prayer is a friendly chat with Him. At times it is like a brief look at a friend, a look filled with understanding and love. Prayer is independent of time and place. I can raise my thoughts and desires to God at any time of the day or night, whether I be at play or at work, alone or in a crowd. I can say more to God by just raising my mind to Him than I could say to a human friend in an hour. He alone knows me perfectly, knows my slightest wish, feeling, and thought.

God loves me so much that He actually wants to hear me talk to Him. He is truly pleased with my attempts to converse with Him. His answer comes to me in the form of a holy thought, desire, or resolution. Others may tire of hearing me talk, but God loves me so much that He could listen to me forever. The more I chat with God, the better I come to know Him. The better I know Him the more I will love Him in my daily life.

PRAY:

O Holy Ghost, my God, You Who bring heavenly light to my soul many times each day, have watched me go along hour after hour showing so few signs of gratitude, love, sorrow for sin, and so little respect for You. To You I owe all that I am and have. I must pray. Without prayer I cut myself off from You. Without prayer I become less a man. Prayer makes me a better and greater man because it draws me to You and You to me. Through prayer You will teach me many things which I will not learn from books. By prayer I can draw down upon myself and others many blessings and heavenly help for our daily labors and difficulties. In spite of all my limitations, prayer is the one thing which I can always do and do well. All I need is to tell You whatever is on my mind. I need no introduction to You. I can talk to You as to an old friend, the only friend who understands me perfectly. Lord, help me to pray often this day, be it but a few passing words from time to time. *Amen.*

CHAPTER 3

Intimacy with God

CHRIST:

MY CHILD, learn to converse with Me as a child talks with its mother. Let there be no barriers between you and Me. Why should you find it easier to talk to human beings than to Me? I know you better than anyone else.

2. Nowhere will you find the understanding, sympathy, and appreciation which I have. Nobody else is as interested in you as I am. I love you infinitely more than anyone else does.

3. You are never alone. I am always with you, ready to share your burdens and solve your problems. I walk with you at every step. No human being is capable of giving you the perfect friendship which I offer you.

4. I know you far better than you know yourself. Do not treat Me as a stranger. Come to Me without fear or anxiety. Have

confidence in My love and mercy. I prefer to call you friend rather than servant.

THINK:

If all my friends deserted me at this moment, I would still have the Friend who counts most, my God and Saviour. If my own dear ones on earth became too occupied with their own affairs to give me any attention, I would still get perfect attention from God, my loving Father. Human beings can give me part of their affections and attention, but all the human affection and attention on earth cannot compare with God's attention and love for me. At every moment of my life, God is closer to me than anyone else could ever be. I live in the palm of His hand, always present to Him and dependent on Him for my every breath. When I am asleep or preoccupied with cares or pleasures, when my thoughts are far from myself, even then God is thinking of me, interested in me, and keeping me alive. Truly, if I knew how near God is to me at every step, I would live a more peaceful and happy life.

PRAY:

My God and Father, You want me to be a true child of Yours. You wish me to prove my love for You as You have proved Your love for me; that is, by my daily actions. My Jesus, you have called me friend. Your friends are those who strive to please You in their daily lives. I can never do as much as You deserve of me, but at least I will try to do as much as I can to please You. Frequently throughout the day, I will pause to cast an interior glance at You. You love me more than I could ever love myself. You are my closest companion in my daily journey toward Heaven. *Amen.*

CHAPTER 4

Removing Obstacles

CHRIST:

MY CHILD, strive to love Me so much that in all your activities your main desire will be to please Me. Never let any person or thing diminish your self control. If I am to be your main interest and your highest desire, you must abandon any created thing which attracts you too strongly; that is, anything for which you might sin.

2. When you have arrived at this purity of soul, you will have abandoned the world even though you must continue to live in it. Your thoughts and desires will no longer be influenced by the foolish interests, selfish ambitions, and wrong standards of worldly people. As they strive for worldly satisfactions and selfish goals, so will you strive to prove a full love and loyalty to Me, the Eternal Joy and Perfect Goal.

3. You insult Me if you make Me compete with any created being for your attention and love. All things are the work of My hand. They are a feeble reflection of My boundless goodness and beauty. No man is worthy of Me until he has learned to live an intelligent life, placing first things first. I must be the first and highest desire of your soul because I am the all-perfect Fountain of all goodness. Any other way of living is false and unworthy of Me.

4. To achieve this glorious victory over your foolish and blind self-interest, is a great grace. Many people believe that they

already possess this grace, but their daily
life proves that they lack it in many things.
One who reaches the fullness of this spiritual level, becomes free of all fully deliberate sins.

5. Strive to reach this high perfection.
Then you will think clearly and act intelligently in all matters. Though you will never
be free of all venial sins of weakness in this
life, you must never cease trying to be free
of all unreasonable attachments to created
beings. As often as you are not striving for
this perfection, you will not be taking full
advantage of My grace.

THINK:

St. Ignatius says that we must pray as
though the matter we desire depended
entirely upon God, and we must work as
though it depended entirely upon ourselves.
This is a sound principle to follow because
God always blesses good will, and good will
is always proved by effort. My goal must be
to achieve in fact what I admit in theory;
that is, to prefer God to all created things,
so that if I had to choose, I would be ready
to abandon all for His sake. I must not be

content with eliminating mortal sins from my life. I am not to be satisfied even when I have eliminated the deliberate venial sins over which I have full control. I must strive to prefer God above all else by a positive mortification and a desire to decrease even my legitimate needs. Only then will my quest for God's full friendship on earth be sincere.

PRAY:

All-perfect Joy of my soul, all-satisfying Goal of my life, when shall I cease to let created things distract me from You? Nothing can begin to compare with You. Why, then, do I not see things for what they are? Grant me that freedom of soul which will help me conquer all unreasonable attractions on earth. No other degree of love is worthy of You. Since my love for You will never be full until I have reached this high spiritual perfection, let me at least strive for it in my daily life. When my cowardly human nature shrinks from this goal help me cry out in the wonderful prayer of St. Ignatius: "Dearest Lord, teach me to be generous. Teach me to serve You as You deserve; to give and not to count the cost; to fight and not to heed the wounds; to toil and not to seek for rest; to labor and not ask for reward, save that of knowing that I am doing Your will." *Amen*.

CHAPTER 5

An Important Choice

CHRIST:

M Y CHILD, people are frequently faced with choices in their earthly life. Choices big or small, important or unimportant, are being made every day by everyone. When one chooses one thing, he usually gives up something else. He who chooses to study law, is turning his back on other professions which he might have chosen. You cannot have everything which you desire. At times you will have to choose some things in preference to others.

2. The same is also true in the supernatural life. Some things draw you away from Me. If you choose to save your soul, you must turn away from these things. One who is interested only in avoiding hell, will tolerate many a deliberate venial sin in his daily life. He will not make too much effort

to eliminate these sins, because he does not choose to bear the inconvenience which such an effort would involve. He wishes to enjoy his earthly life as far as he can without endangering his eternal salvation.

3. Then again, some people choose to aim at a higher perfection. They seek to come closer to Me by a serious effort to eliminate venial sin from their life, as far as they are able. They turn away from little pleasures and satisfactions which make them less pleasing to Me.

4. Lastly, there are those who want to make Me their highest goal every moment of the day. They strive to do all things without considering their own convenience or inconvenience. They try to do the better thing, as often as this does not hurt their daily tasks or interfere with their daily obligations. This last group are choosing Me by turning away from every earthly satisfaction.

5. They still take the food, rest, and recreation which they need, but they now do so for a new and higher reason. Before they did so for the legitimate pleasure and enjoyment which they received from these things.

Now, however, they take these things from a sense of duty to Me, because I want them to do whatever is necessary for a good day's work. These are the men who have succeeded in choosing Me in preference to all things. They are not content with giving Me glory in their life, but they seek to give Me the highest degree of glory possible.

6. He who seeks Me thus completely, finds My perfect peace, My firm and lasting happiness, and his own highest perfection. I am more than any earthly accomplishment, more than any human praise, more than any worldly satisfaction. Only cowardice, or misguided self-interest can make you aim lower than this high perfection.

7. According as you limit your love for Me, will you have self-deception, spiritual poverty, and discontent. The less you seek My love and friendship, the more do you harm yourself. You yourself will be limiting My generosity with you, because you will not use all of the wonderful graces which I desire to give you.

THINK:

No man can enjoy all the good things on earth. He has to choose some things in preference to others. I have the glorious privilege of making the greatest choice possible to man. I can prefer the close companionship of Jesus to many other good, but imperfect, friendships. Every other achievement and success has its day and passes away, but the friendship of Jesus will endure forever. Not even death can dissolve it. How much do I really appreciate this priceless treasure? My answer lies in what I am willing to abandon for it. How great a price am I willing to pay for it?

PRAY:

O Jesus, King and Treasure of my soul, show me how I can make this highest of all choices in my daily life. Give me the good sense to avoid all foolish extremes and impractical judgments in following You. Let me not follow my own ideas in this quest for perfection. Make me humble enough to follow directions, unselfish enough to keep trying and generous enough to abandon my own petty satisfactions. Without pretense and without seeking to be noticed, let me offer You as many of my natural pleasures and satisfactions as I am able. With balanced judgment and good taste, help me prefer Your company to all other company whenever I may do so. In all this, however, let me never neglect my duties, impede my ability to do Your work, or offend against true charity. *Amen.*

CHAPTER 6

Coming Closer

CHRIST:

MY CHILD, when I am present to you, all is well and nothing seems too difficult. When speak to you, you need no human consolations. When I am silent, no human words can console you. Seek to realize how truly I am your All. Whatever helps you in this life is only an instrument of Mine.

2. It is a great accomplishment to know how to speak with Me. My conversation is with the humble and the simple. I speak to those who do not have a false idea of their own importance. My message is easily understood by those who do not complicate their lives with too many interests and useless activities.

3. Show Me a true purity of soul. Refuse to depend too much on worldly consolation and do not look overanxiously for earthly remedies. In using natural remedies, you must still see My hand leading you on. You please Me very much when you put your confidence in My understanding, interest, power, and love.

4. When you have learned to concentrate on Me, no achievement or occupation will distract you too much from Me. You will refuse to let your desires become too strong, no matter how good they may be. At all times you will be ready to give up whatever you are doing if I so wish. In all things, you will aim at nothing and desire nothing except My Will.

5. As far as you can control your earthly interests, only so far can you be united with Me. As freedom from worldly desires brings you My peace, so does freedom from worldly self-seeking bring you closer to My heart.

THINK:

No matter how good a work may be, I must not desire it so strongly that I lose my peace of soul. No matter how hard I may work on something, I should not become over-eager for success. God will bring success in His own way and in His own good time. My human nature is always looking for self-satisfaction. I can guard myself against all unreasonable self-love by abandoning myself to God's divine providence in all my undertakings. By accepting the results as His holy Will, I shall be giving Him the kind of glory which He desires of me. I shall eliminate all self-deception and shall attain true purity of heart. God will find no obstacles in me and He will draw me into a lasting friendship with Him.

PRAY:

My Jesus, true center of my life, let my attention be so fixed on You that I may be aware of You in everything I do. I will never separate myself from You by undue anxiety or over-eagerness for success. In the good works which I perform, I want You to take charge. I desire to surrender myself entirely to You in all my occupations. No longer shall my will lead me on, but Yours. I shall always strive to make my best efforts. The results are Yours to decide. My greatest joy from now on will be to work for love of You. *Amen.*

PART TWO

Union Through the Holy Eucharist

CHAPTER 7

Christ's Loving Invitation

CHRIST:

M Y CHILD, come to me when you labor and are burdened, and I shall refresh you. There are many ways of coming to Me in your earthly life. You can approach Me in prayer, meditation, reading, reflecting, in the confessional, and in the various sacraments. The most excellent way of coming to Me, however, is Holy Communion.

2. I invite you to receive this heavenly privilege, so that I may give Myself to you in a very special way. In Holy Communion you receive Me in person. I do not merely come near you, but into your very soul. I make Myself as food for your soul, and grant you a greater share in My life. I give you greater strength to live My way.

3. The bread which I give you in Holy Communion is My flesh. Take it and eat. This is My body, which was delivered for you. He that eats My body and drinks My

blood shall dwell within Me as I dwell within him. During those precious moments we are together in a special kind of union, unknown to worldly men.

4. These are My words, though I did not speak them all at one time nor in one place. The words which I speak are the words of eternal life. Meditate on them often. You will find life, wisdom, and peace in them. You will never exhaust their richness.

THINK:

When Jesus first began to tell His followers about Holy Communion, some of them objected. When they heard that they were to eat His body and drink His blood, a number of them left Him. Jesus sadly looked on, as they walked away from Him, but He did not restrain them nor call them back. If He had meant those words in some symbolic or figurative way, surely He would not have permitted those loved ones to leave Him. He would have kept them with Him by simply explaining His words. But no, He did not give any explanation because He meant those words literally. He was really going to offer them, and to me, His body and blood, which in some mysterious way were to act upon our souls as food and drink act upon the body. All the other sacraments are signs of grace which God grants through them. Holy Communion, however, is more than a sign of grace. It is the living body and blood of Jesus. In a word, in Holy Communion Jesus comes to me in person.

PRAY:

My God and my Saviour, of all the wonderful gifts which You have bestowed upon men in this earthly life, none can begin to compare with the wonderful gift of the Holy Eucharist. Under the appearances of bread and wine, You come to me in person, with Your body, blood, soul, and divinity. Your love for me is so deep that You could offer me nothing less than Yourself. This You did in a manner which reminds me of Your death upon the cross for my sake. In the appearance of bread and wine I see You ready to be consumed in order to give me eternal life. This holy sacrament is truly the most perfect image of Your boundless love for me. Lord, let me make full use of this divine gift so that I may learn to give myself to You in my daily life. *Amen*.

CHAPTER 8

Effects of Frequent Communion

CHRIST:

MY CHILD, I offer many special graces to those who receive Me often and devoutly in Holy Communion. Those who take advantage of these graces make rapid strides toward Christian perfection. I draw them closer to Myself throughout the day.

2. I make their minds more alert to occasions of sin, more awake to opportunities for virtue, and more aware of My nearness throughout the day.

3. I teach them to think more often of Me, and less often of themselves. They gradually learn to judge matters My way rather than to follow their own natural preferences and prejudices.

4. Though many at first seek their own advantage in pleasing Me, as they progress, they forget their own advantage and think only of pleasing Me.

5. They eventually find so much joy in My company that they are content to be without human company as often as their daily obligations will permit. Their greatest consolation and happiness is to have My friendship and to offer Me whatever they do throughout the day.

6. Their prayer becomes more perfect because it loses much of the natural strain and effort which came from earthly distractions and worldly interests.

THINK:

Frequent communion, well prepared for and well made, brings me my most perfect union with Jesus in this earthly life. During these precious moments He works wonders within my soul. I must go forth determined to make full use of Christ's graces throughout the day. He will teach me how to go about my daily occupations without losing interior contact with Him. Then shall I reach the wonderful heights of holiness which Jesus has prepared for His truly loyal followers.

PRAY:

My sacramental King, holy Lamb of God, unworthy though I am of Your attention and love, I cannot turn away from this heavenly privilege of Holy Communion. It is Your wish that I enjoy it. In it you bestow on me the highest dignity possible to man or angel. As I kneel there, joined to You, I wield my greatest power and exert my greatest influence before the throne of God. Though this sacramental union lasts only a matter of minutes, grant that its influence may be with me throughout the entire day. Let my mind think as Yours, and let my will choose as You chose in Your own earthly life. I desire to live my daily life as though I were sacramentally joined with You all day. Grant that I may place no obstacles to the wonderful graces which You offer to me in Holy Communion. I shall do my best to avoid all unnecessary distractions, I shall try to fulfill my daily tasks as well as I am honestly able. Finally I desire to please You more by doing whatever extra good I can do today. *Amen.*

CHAPTER 9

Tepidity Toward Holy Communion

CHRIST:

MY CHILD, a number of people travel back and forth to visit the remains of My saints. With admiration and interest they view the magnificent buildings erected in honor of the saints, and they kiss their sacred bones, which are held in gold and silver. My saints deserve all of this honor and more. Too often, however, people are drawn to these relics and holy places by curiosity or some form of self-interest, rather than by contrition for sin and a desire to draw closer to Me. The highest honor which you can pay the saints is to imitate their virtues in your daily life.

2. Here upon the altar you will find not a relic, nor a monument to someone's memory, but Me, alive as ever, all-powerful, all-loving, all-perfect. All the treasures and wonders of this world—whatever can attract the human heart—these things are nothing compared to what you find upon the altar. You will not be drawn to Me by

any curiosity or shallow virtue. Only a firm faith, a steady hope, and a burning love will draw you to Me and keep you loyal to Me.

3. Consider how great must be the tepidity and negligence of this world, since so many fail to take advantage of My gift of Holy Communion. It is sad to see how few are drawn to Me with tender affection and wordless gratitude. In this sacrament I offer Myself, in Whom lie all human hopes and merits for salvation.

THINK:

I should never cease to express my sorrow for the neglect and coldness which is shown to Jesus in the Blessed Sacrament. How great must be His love for us, since He does not become disgusted with so much ingratitude. People go to such trouble to see various objects of beauty, curiosity, or entertainment. Yet, here upon the altar is the grandest, greatest, most magnificent of all beings. How dull can the human mind be! How hard can the human heart become! This is our all-loving Saviour, our God! In Him we live, and move, and exist. Truly, without Him we are nothing. In Him alone shall I find perfect peace and all-satisfying happiness.

PRAY:

My Jesus in the Blessed Sacrament, how can I ever express the sympathy and sorrow which should be expressed for the unbelievable foolishness which we show in our daily neglect of You. The church is so crowded on Sunday with men and women who are ready to do what they must do to save their souls. But on weekdays the same church has but a handful of people who rise a little earlier to come and kneel at Your feet. Others will rise earlier for a number of other reasons, but for an extra half hour with You, they will not do so. You offer us so much in the Mass and in Holy Communion, yet we do so little to deserve Your generosity and love. Lord, place my heart in Yours for a moment and inflame it with the fire of Your love. Let me grow in appreciation of Holy Communion, so that I may come to You more often. You desire to come to me that You may grant me more graces and blessings. In Holy Communion the privilege is all mine. I shall never forget this again. *Amen.*

CHAPTER 10

Preparing for Holy Communion

CHRIST:

MY CHILD, in order to gain as many blessings as possible from Holy Communion, make a careful preparation for this glorious gift.

2. Brighten your soul with holy thoughts—thoughts on what I said or did in My earthly life or what My loyal followers said about Me. Raise your will upwards with holy desires, desires to please Me more in your daily life by avoiding this fault or practicing that virtue.

3. Such efforts open your mind to greater light and dispose your will to greater generosity. When I find these dispositions in you, I bestow greater graces on you than I would otherwise have granted. I never miss a chance to draw you higher in holiness and perfection.

4. Each Communion holds unlimited opportunity for your soul. The limits are set by your degree of interest and eagerness to follow Me wherever I invite you.

THINK:

One Communion well made can make me a saint. Yet, after so many Communions I am still very far from sanctity. This shows me that I have not taken advantage of God's great gifts. I ought to use prayer books if they help improve my prayer. I should use whatever can help me make a better preparation for Holy Communion. In this way I shall not regret my carelessness later on. The more I prepare myself for Jesus, the more shall I profit by His visit to me.

PRAY:

Lord, the more important an occasion, the more carefully do people prepare for it. No event in my earthly life is more important than receiving You in Holy Communion. Let me approach You often but let me never fail to do my best to prepare for this heavenly privilege. I may not always have as much time, energy, or mental alertness as I would like to have for You, but at least I can do what little is possible under the circumstances. I sincerely wish to avoid the dullness of routine or laziness. I shall always use whatever means I have to help me receive You humbly, reverently, and lovingly. *Amen*.

CHAPTER 11

A Diligent Preparation

CHRIST:

MY CHILD, let Me show you the best preparation for Holy Communion. Do not act mechanically, saying the words, but thinking of other things. Do not act with fear, as though I were coming to find fault with you. I come to you because I want to come, because I love you, and because you need Me. If I do not come to you, you will not enter into eternal life.

2. Let your preparation be an intelligent consideration of what you are about to do. Meditate on your daily life, how it could be better for My sake. When you tell Me that you are unworthy of Me, think of the different faults by which you fail Me, and resolve to do something about them at once. With Me, love means action, definite action where it is needed. Make your love for Me a love of action, and you will be best prepared for Holy Communion.

3. There are no words to describe the privilege which I grant you in Holy Communion. Avoid routine. Never become so accustomed to receiving Me that you lose your appreciation of this privilege. Try to make every reception a grand occasion. Do it by putting variety into your preparation and thanksgiving. Do not always say the same prayers, nor always follow the same method. One day meditate on My words or your daily life. On another day say vocal prayers or read prayer books. At another time sing hymns within your mind. Use variety and you will never fall into the dull rut of routine.

4. Do not let the thought of your unworthiness hold you back from Holy Communion. Think only of this, that I want you to receive Me because you need Me. For this reason I command you to come to Me. If it were strictly a matter of worthiness, no one could ever receive Me.

THINK:

My daily life should be a continual preparation for Holy Communion. I ought to be ready for Jesus any morning in the week. It will be so if my loyalty to Him is firm throughout my daily activities. In spite of the aggravations which come along, I can keep a reasonable amount of clear thinking and self control. To help me achieve this, I can make use of religious articles, holy pictures, and pious habits. At various times during the day, I ought to take a quick glance over my activities in order to see where I have failed or where I may improve. Never should I come within distance of any church without making a visit, be it ever so brief. As far as my duties will permit, I must try to make contact with Our Lord every so often, praising Him, thanking Him, expressing sorrow for my sins, and asking for the spiritual and material assistance which I need. If I really try to make my daily life a preparation and a thanksgiving for Holy Communion, this holy Sacrament will work miracles within me.

PRAY:

My Jesus, unappreciated and unloved by so many, let me give You some small part of the honor and love which You deserve in the Blessed Sacrament. Frequently throughout the day I shall express my desire to receive

You. I want to show You my gratitude for this divine gift. I wish to lay my needs before You, together with the spiritual and material needs of others. I long to express my sorrow for my sins and the sins of the world. Never again will I receive You through dull, thoughtless habit. Each reception will be an intelligent and loving approach to You, my God and Saviour. Though I cannot prepare as You deserve, I shall at least do my best to receive You more worthily. *Amen.*

CHAPTER 12

CHRIST Spiritual Communion

CHRIST:

MY CHILD, receive Me in Holy Communion as often as you are able. Try to purify your motives, so that you may eventually come to Me without any selfish consideration, but only from a desire to please Me and to be with Me. When you have risen to this high spiritual level, I shall grant you many special graces which you have not yet experienced.

2. One of these graces is the thirst of supernatural love. Your desire to be united

with Me will grow stronger and stronger. You will reach the point where you will wish to receive Me more than once a day. Not being able to do so sacramentally, you will turn to spiritual communion as a remedy for your spiritual thirst.

3. With faith and love you will turn to Me frequently throughout the day, asking Me to come to you as though in Holy Communion. Through spiritual communion you will seek to imitate My sacramental visit in some small way. For the brief moments at your disposal you will speak to Me, listen to Me, and act as though I had come to you in Holy Communion.

4. Though spiritual communion can never replace nor equal My sacramental presence, it is an excellent method of prayer. It is very pleasing to Me and will bring you many extra blessings throughout the day. I shall teach you to shut out the world around you for a while. You will learn to be more aware of My nearness in your daily activities. You will appreciate My friendship more deeply because you took the trouble to come closer to Me.

THINK:

Though there is no real substitute for the Blessed Sacrament, I can make frequent spiritual communions to satisfy my spiritual thirst in some small way. When I ask our Lord to come to me in spiritual communion, He is pleased and grants me many extra graces. Spiritual communion will help me come closer to Jesus in my daily life. Yes, through this method of prayer I can join my heart to Christ's as often as I choose. This is one desire with which Jesus will cooperate every time.

PRAY:

My Jesus, close companion of my soul, I am tired of forgetting You in my daily activities. Though you are present in Heaven, here on earth You are also present in various, less perfect ways. In the Blessed Sacrament You are supernaturally present in Your divine and human natures, just as when You walked the earth. Then, by sanctifying grace you are present in my soul in a different manner. When You come to me in Holy Communion, Your union with me becomes stronger and more active. Your human nature binds me more securely to Your divinity. Your precious body and blood act like food within my soul, helping me live Your life more perfectly. Though spiritual communion is a very imperfect and incomplete substitute for Holy Communion, You are pleased at my wish to be united with You once again. Since You also desire to see me live in constant union with You, You will grant me wonderful graces each time I make an effort to come closer to You through spiritual communion. I hope to make this effort more often as I go through my daily occupations and activities. *Amen.*

CHAPTER 13

Visits to the Blessed Sacrament

CHRIST:

MY CHILD, if My true presence on the altar were limited to one place alone, many people from all parts of the world would try to visit that place at some time or other in their lives. Yet, now that I have made it easy for all to come to Me, see how many visit Me only when they are obliged!

2. Many people are so cold toward Me. Like children they are impressed only by what they can touch and see. I have given them their greatest treasure in the Blessed Sacrament. Through My Apostles and their successors, I have promised to be personally present wherever the Blessed Sacrament is. Make every effort to be deeply impressed by this greatest of all earthly gifts.

3. It is not enough for you to believe in My real presence upon the altar. I placed Myself there for love of you. I wanted to be near you in some visible way, so that you might visit Me as often as you wished. You should wish it as often as possible.

4. People come to Me for different reasons. Some come only on Sundays and holy days, through a sense of obligation. Either they do not want to lose Heaven, or they desire My help in their daily life. Then there are those who come to Me through mere habit. They act automatically, without any particular devotion to Me. There are, however, a certain number who come to Me for the best reason. They come because they are glad to be near Me. These people please Me

best of all. They receive many extra graces which are not granted to the others.

5. Consider how devoted My saints were to Me. They seized every opportunity to visit Me and stay with Me. They desired to abandon all useless interests so that they might have more time with Me. In return for this generosity with Me, they received a clearer understanding of My boundless goodness and a deeper appreciation of My infinite love.

6. You, too, have the opportunity to give Me more of your time and attention. Make a greater effort to come closer to Me in friendship. You have the privilege of kneeling before Me like the simple, wonderful shepherds; the tired, admiring Magi; the suffering, begging leper; the penitent, hopeful Magdalene; the convinced, converted Thomas. How are you taking advantage of this privilege?

7. How much easier it will be for you to face Me in your judgment if you have loved to face Me often during your earthly life. Each visit to Me is an act of faith, of love, and of self-purification. Come to Me often,

so that I may shower more of My gifts upon your soul.

THINK:

One who neglects Jesus in the Blessed Sacrament hurts himself more than he realizes. By frequent visits I come closer to that wonderful union with God which He desires to grant me in my daily life. Each visit can bring me nearer to Him in true friendship. I need no special formula, no particular prayers, no unusual requirements. All that I need is to present myself before Him, talking if I so wish, listening if I am so disposed, or simply staying with Him. He is more interested in me than anyone else. Though I may feel very dull, He is interested in my thoughts, my desires, my needs, hopes, ambitions, efforts, and labors. My daily life is a matter of the highest importance to Him. He is glad to see me come because each visit gives Him another excuse to grant me more blessings. He is there for love of me. I ought to visit Him often for love of Him.

PRAY:

My Jesus, truly present in the Blessed Sacrament, I have not shown You half the appreciation which I owe You. Grant me the grace to grow in this appreciation. You deserve far more attention than I have shown You. How often could I come to You with a slight effort or even inconvenience to myself! Yet, I fail to do so. I do not treat my human friends half so neglectfully as I treat You. This sacrament is a living proof of Your love for me. I hope to show my love for You by a greater devotion toward You from now on. You will see me more than just once a week. As often as I am reasonably able, I shall visit You. I want to give You more of my attention, my time, my interest, and my life. *Amen.*

CHAPTER 14

The Meaning of Self-Oblation

CHRIST:

MY CHILD, self-oblation is another name for self-offering. When you offer yourself to Me, it means that you place yourself at My disposal, so that I may do as I please with you. It means that you will try to direct your thoughts, desires, and actions as I desire. It means that you will never deliberately contradict My Will in any detail.

2. Self-oblation necessarily involves the offering of whatever you possess, whether it be talent, occupation, opportunities, friends, and everything else. True, such an offering does not necessarily mean that you are to deprive yourself of these things. It usually means that you will now deal with them and use them only to please Me.

3. Everyone is obliged to abandon whatever leads him into sin. However, the man who makes an act of self-oblation aims higher than simply avoiding sin. He seeks to please Me in a positive way, by practicing as many virtues as he can in his daily life. In his desire to belong more surely to Me, he tries to use things more from necessity than for personal satisfaction. In order to avoid all self-deceit, he would rather have less than more of this world's good things, he prefers to obey rather than command, he would sooner follow than lead.

4. In all of these desires and efforts my loyal followers desire only My greater glory. They are ready to change any of their plans or intentions, if I should so wish. In their self-oblation they are no longer interested in

acquiring anything for their own honor or earthly satisfaction. Their main purpose in life is to please and honor Me. They strive to center their life around Me. Many more people would reach this high level of perfection if only they would pause long enough to think of it, desire it, and try to reach it.

THINK:

Many people fear self-oblation because they think that it would make them slaves in mind and body. Yet this high level of perfection would actually lead them to true interior liberty and perfect peace of soul. In seeking to follow God's holy Will more perfectly, I am following my own highest good, my greatest perfection, my most enduring peace and happiness. Only in self-oblation am I living my daily life most fully, most intelligently, and most profitably. I shall have the highest purpose possible to man, to give eternal praise to God and to obtain eternal life with Him. This is the purpose for which God Himself made me. Can I aim at anything less?

PRAY:

Eternal Father, my Creator, to You I owe absolutely all things which make my daily life worth while. From you I receive each moment of life as a personal gift. I ought to offer myself to You because You own all that I am and have. Jesus, Your divine Son, has given me a perfect example of self-oblation in delivering Himself up as a victim for my sins. Every thought, word, and deed of His, from the crib to the cross, was offered to You for my sake. Can I hesitate to return such generous love in my own small way? Even today I can see the self-oblation of Jesus in every Mass and in every tabernacle, where He resides in the Blessed Sacrament. He is there for love of me. What shall I do to repay such unbounded love? Grant me the courage to make my daily life a self-oblation. I hope in You for the strength to continue this effort all of my life. *Amen.*

CHAPTER 15

Self-Oblation Through the Mass

CHRIST:

MY CHILD, every moment of My earthly life was an act of self-oblation. As man I had a human will, and as God I have My divine Will, which I possess in unity with

My heavenly Father and the Holy Spirit. As a victim for your sins, I submitted My human will to the divine Will. By My obedience and self-sacrifice I made reparation for your sins, opened the gates of Heaven to you, and earned the graces which you need in order to enter eternal life.

2. On the cross I hung in agony, the perfect victim for sin. By My self-sacrifice the divine justice was completely satisfied. As man I represented all men, and as God I was worthy to blot out the offense which sin hurled at the Holy Trinity.

3. I instituted the holy sacrifice of the Mass to remind you of My self-oblation upon Calvary. In it I continue the work which I began upon Calvary. In each Mass My body and blood are offered to My Father as an act of perfect adoration, thanksgiving, reparation, and petition for your needs. As I once represented you upon the cross, so, now in each Mass, do I represent you upon the altar. As the Mass is Mine because I am the victim and high-priest in it, so, too, is it yours because it was instituted entirely for your salvation.

4. In each Mass I am still performing My supreme act of love for you. I am there for your sake, doing what you yourself should be doing; namely, begging pardon for your sins, adoring the Divine Majesty, thanking My heavenly Father for His numberless gifts, and asking for your daily needs. You should be devoted to Me in the Mass, because in the Mass I show once again My devotedness to you.

5. Your devotedness to Me will be proved most perfectly when you have learned to join your daily life to the holy sacrifice of the Mass. Attend Mass as often as possible. Then go forth and prove your love for Me by transforming your daily life into your Mass for Me. In other words, as I offer Myself upon the altar for love of you, so should you offer yourself for love of Me in your daily occupations and activities. Thus there will be a close bond between My work for you and your daily work.

6. This will make your daily life a perfect self-oblation. No longer will you seek what you like, at any price. For My sake you will guard your patience, your generosity, your

confidence in Me, and your desire to please Me in all things. In your disappointments, difficulties, fears, failures, efforts, and labors, you will unite your will to Mine. You will seek to belong ever more perfectly to me by practicing greater self control and mortification. As I offer Myself to you in Holy Communion, so must you learn to make each act of yours an act of self-offering to Me.

THINK:

Many important activities are taking place today in the lives of individuals and of nations. Of all the activities and events occurring this day, the greatest and most important by far is the holy sacrifice of the Mass. This is the central action of all salvation. It is the main source of God's grace. The greatest blessings and benefits of Calvary are brought to us today through the Mass. As each second of my life is a continuation of God's creation, so does each sacrifice of the Mass continue Jesus' redeeming sacrifice on Calvary. In attending Mass I behold the loving self-oblation of Christ as truly as the mob which stood at the foot of the cross. Will I be content with assisting at Mass only when I am obliged to do so? Should I not be eager to attend as many Masses as possible?

PRAY:

My loving Saviour, truly active in each sacrifice of the Mass, I have not appreciated You enough in this wonderful act of love. No one on earth does as much for me as You do in each Mass. This is the central act of Your Church, just as You are the center of Your religion. I hope to make the Mass the main activity of my daily life. My union with You throughout the day will be strengthened through the holy sacrifice of the Mass. I shall act most perfectly for You when I have learned to make Your Mass a regular part of my daily activities. Lord, I will do my best to learn more about the Mass in order to grow in appreciation of it. Help me become devoted to You in the Mass, where You are so devoted to Me. *Amen.*

PART THREE
Union Throughout the Day
CHAPTER 16

Seeing God's Hand in All Things

CHRIST:

MY CHILD, what I said to My disciples, I also say to you: "As the Father has loved Me, I also love you." All men receive life and strength from Me, be they great or little, rich or poor, talented or dull. I am the fountain of all good.

2. I know what is needed by each individual. For good reasons of My own, I decide who shall have more and who shall have less. He who has little ability need not become sad because of it, nor should he envy the man who has many talents. Fix your eyes on Me. Leave your life in My hands, and you will find it easy to avoid all envy and complaints.

3. It is My love for you which makes Me treat you as I do. Your present trials and sufferings are as much My gift as the satisfaction and consolations which I send you. Some day you will understand why I

dispense My gifts unequally among people. You will then praise and thank the wisdom which now puzzles you.

4. Too often you see only the natural and human causes which disturb you. Look beyond these and see My loving hand guiding you on toward your perfection and eternal glory. In your difficulties and real needs I am ever near to assist you and protect you from harm. Not all that you fear is bad for you, nor is all that you desire, good for you. Seek Me above all else. I shall lead you to your unending happiness in Heaven.

THINK:

One of the consequences of genuine union with God, is that it makes one think clearly and correctly. When I have attained this union, I will find reason to praise Him when life seems dark and unbearable. Knowing that God's love rules every moment of my life, I shall seek his honor in all things. Whether I am a success or a failure in my plans and efforts, whether I experience joy or sorrow, my only wish will be to please and honor Him in every thought, word, and deed.

PRAY:

My Lord and loving God, You manage my life with an all-wise providence. You take care of me at every moment. If I were the only person on earth, You could not give Me more attention, nor more love than You give me at present. I need not look at others, despising those who have less than I, or envying those who have more. I need only keep my eyes on You and let You govern my life. When I see You face to face, as I hope to do some day in Heaven, I will see how wise and loving You are in Your care of me. Then will I understand how all-deserving You are of my perfect confidence and loyalty. Then I shall wish that I had spent all of my time on earth praising and thanking You in all my accomplishments. I shall realize at last how completely I depend on You for all things, and how helpless I am without Your blessing. Let me not wait until then, when the truth will be easy to admit. Grant me the grace to do so now in my every action. *Amen.*

CHAPTER 17

Gratitude to God

CHRIST:

MY CHILD, all things were made by Me, and without Me nothing can exist. I am the center of all existence and the source of all truth. In your daily life you must love truth. I am pleased with the honest man, the man who lives his life according to the truth. Face facts and admit them in your thoughts, words, and actions.

2. The truth is, that you are the work of My hands, dependent on Me for every moment of your existence and for everything in your daily life. This truth demands that you be grateful to Me. I cannot allow you to act as though you deserved the talents, opportunities, and good things in your daily life. Such an attitude would be a lie. I owe you nothing, while you owe Me everything, absolutely every good thing which you have or enjoy.

3. In every breath, in every heartbeat, in every thought, word, and deed, you receive My assistance. In many ways it is I who

serve you, rather than you who serve Me. Unworthy as you are, My generosity never ceases to help you. My goodness never turns away from you. My love cares for your needs every second of the day and night.

4. I have given you the intelligence to realize this truth, and the free will to admit it in your daily life. Be true to that intelligence and make good use of that freedom by often showing your gratitude to Me. Your gratitude will be imperfect if it is in words alone. You must perfect it by action. Be humble in your attitude toward others. Be patient with those who cannot live up to your expectations. Be kind and generous with those who need your help. Your good example will help others please Me more in their own lives. This is your daily proof of sincere gratitude to Me.

THINK:

Can I ever forget my complete dependence on God? Yet, do I not forget it in my daily life? How often I am guilty of foolish pride, shallow vanity, blind self-seeking, and childish self-satisfaction. Without God's loving support I am nothing. My true greatness lies in accepting this fact and living according to it. How differently I will treat those around me, when this truth has become a part of my ordinary thinking. Only then will I be a man of truth. Only then will I be a man after God's own heart.

PRAY:

My God and my All! Dear Lord, make this the frequent cry of my heart! Let me never forget how very truly You are my All. All the good things which have made my life worth while, not only those which I know, but also those of which I am unaware, every one of these things is a loving gift from You. No matter how much I think of my welfare, no matter how much I desire my own good, You think of my good and provide for my welfare far more than I ever could. Lord, let me prove my deep gratitude, not just with words, but as You desire. I wish to prove it with a daily life which seeks first and foremost to please You. I want to take each gift of Yours today and return it to You by my intelligent and unselfish use of it. In my dealings with people, I hope to treat them with some of the generosity, love, and consideration which You have shown to me. In all my thoughts, in all my words, in all my actions today, I hope to shout a heartfelt "Thank You" to You. *Amen.*

CHAPTER 18

Peace and Joy in God Alone

CHRIST:

MY CHILD, when you have risen so high in virtue that you seek comfort and satisfaction from Me before all earthly remedies, I shall bestow on you the grace of knowing Me intimately and of enjoying My friendship as never before. Your interior peace will no longer be disturbed by daily events. No more will you be attached to what you have, nor complain about what you lack. You will place yourself entirely in My hands. I shall be your main interest, and nothing will ever again take My place in your life.

2. I am the fountain of true peace and lasting joy. Keep close to Me in your daily life. The man whose main interests are on earth, does not know the meaning of true peace. His joys are temporary and rapidly

passing. No person or thing on earth can fully satisfy the thirst within your soul. You were made for Me, and I alone can bring you the perfect, all-satisfying happiness which you seek.

3. This supernatural friendship requires that you give your heart entirely to Me. This simply means that you will give due attention to every person and every duty in your daily life, without giving them any more attention and time than they deserve. Your main desire must be to give Me all the attention and time possible each day.

4. If you make reservations in your self-surrender, if in anything you seek your own desires rather than My Will, you will be hindering Me from giving you the special graces which I want to bestow on you. Your union with Me will be imperfect, and you will not be ready for My higher gifts. Offer Me the actions of your day. Repeat your offering at different times, and renew your intention to shut out all worldly self-seeking. In due time, when you have proved yourself, you will receive My most wonderful graces.

THINK:

Peace and joy! For these does every man strive all through life. Whatever people do in their daily life, they do it to gain some measure of peace and joy. Since created things are only a reflection of God, they can give me only a small share of the all-satisfying peace and joy which my soul craves. In God alone shall I find that perfect happiness which will set my heart at rest. No matter how hard it may be for me to surrender myself to God's holy Will, I should never forget that it is a very small price to pay for so perfect a reward. When I have succeeded in giving myself to God without any reservations, then will God give Himself to me so completely that I shall neither need nor desire anything else.

PRAY:

My God, I feel attracted to this person at one time and to that one at another time. Sometimes one thing interests me, and sometime another. Yet, in all of these persons and things, what really attracts me is a reflection of Your own unlimited goodness and beauty. Without realizing it, it is really You that I seek. Since these created beings are so imperfect, they cannot give me the complete, all-satisfying happiness that I desire. This yearning for perfect happiness is in my very nature, and I cannot destroy it without destroying myself. Grant me, therefore, the wisdom to advance each day closer to You, by a well regulated life. Let me find my true peace in the fulfillment of Your holy Will. Fill my soul with the joy of possessing You more consciously in my thoughts and in my every act. *Amen.*

CHAPTER 19

Looking Forward to Heaven

CHRIST:

MY CHILD, in your daily life think often of Heaven. Do not let earthly desires dim the vision of your last and highest goal. This vision will bring you peace in adversity and joy in time of trial.

2. In Heaven you shall have more than you have ever desired, more than you ever imagined. You will never know the end of your joy, nor will you be tormented by the fear of losing what you love. You will always

have what you want, and you will always want what is best. You will share My knowledge, and My happiness will fill your soul.

3. In Heaven no one shall ever have reason to complain about you. No one will resist you nor spoil your plans. You will enjoy at one and the same time all the things you love. I shall give you a glory undreamed, as a reward for your victories over temptation on earth. You will receive an all-satisfying praise for your patience and for your loyalty to Me in your earthly trials. My infinite love for you will be shown in gifts unmatched on earth.

THINK:

Human language could never describe Heaven. Why? Because in all human experience there are no words which can tell us what Heaven is like. St. Paul was granted a vision of Heaven, and yet he could not tell us what it is like. All he could say was that we have never seen, nor heard, nor even imagined what Heaven is like. This thought of Heaven's greatness should impress me very much. Every moment brings me nearer to this all-glorious life. How small and insignificant are my earthly sufferings and trials when compared with this all-satisfying, never-ending reward!

PRAY:

O Jesus, King of Glory, the thought of Heaven arouses within me the desire to practice more virtues in my daily life. It gives me a firm determination to despise whatever hinders my spiritual perfection. You made me for eternal glory, and in this earthly life you have granted me the opportunity to prove my sincere desire for that glory. Even though I seek peace and happiness in everything that I do on earth, I shall never know the perfect happiness which my heart seeks until I have entered into Heaven. Help me see this earthly life through Your eyes. Let me never lose an opportunity to resist evil and do good in this earthly life. May my love of good works grow. I wish to do more and more for love of You. If You love me enough to grant me the perfect reward of Heaven, should I not love You enough to give myself to You for the rest of my life on earth? I hope to imitate Your boundless generosity in my own limited, human way from now on. *Amen*.

CHAPTER 20

The Nature of Love

CHRIST:

M Y CHILD, love is the greatest virtue in any man. It makes him resemble Me most closely. Love brings many other virtues into the soul. It makes a man devoted, sincere, patient, loyal, long-suffering, courageous, sensitive, prudent, unselfish, pleasant, and strong.

2. Where love reigns, there you will always find generosity. Love desires only one thing, to please the loved one. The love of Me makes a man humble, honest, serious-minded without strain, careful to avoid sin, eager to practice virtue, obedient to superiors, unselfish with equals, kind to inferiors.

3. The pure love of Me makes a man willing to suffer anything for My sake. He carries his burdens without feeling the weight. He seeks to do more rather than less. He never complains nor gives up hope. He is willing to try anything, even the impossible,

for My sake. He accomplishes many things which selfish people fear even to attempt.

4. When pure love fills a man's heart, he is always looking for more to do for Me. He finds joy in fatigue, because he looks on this as a proof of his love. His love for Me makes him eager to do great things for Me. It helps him see the incompleteness of worldly satisfactions. He seeks Me, the all-perfect Good, the all-satisfying Goal.

5. Nothing is sweeter than this pure love for Me. Nothing is stronger, nothing is higher, nothing is more far-reaching, nothing is more complete, nothing is better in Heaven or on earth. Such love is My gift to the generous. It will never be perfectly content until it possesses Me in Heaven.

THINK:

True love consists in wanting to give. It is a reasonable thing. It sees the worth of the loved one, and seeks to please him. God deserves my purest love because He is all-good. He deserves my first and highest love because He is the Highest Good. I can never do too much for Him. In fact, I can never do enough for Him. The better I come to know

Him, the more clearly shall I see that He deserves the best within me at all times.

PRAY:

My God and my All! To one who understands You, those words mean a great deal! My God and my All so much truth is contained in those few words. When You are near, life means so much, but when I lose sight of You, I become tired and disgusted with myself and with everything else. Teach me to love You in all things and above all things. Let me see You near in all that I experience. Make me glad to do things for love of You. I want to do ever more and more for Your sake. In looking at You, I desire to forget myself. I wish to abandon my own desires and do only what will please You. Grant me light to see how this may be done in my daily life. Grant me also the generosity to follow Your light. *Amen.*

CHAPTER 21

Loving God Above Creatures

CHRIST:

MY CHILD, whatever is not God, is a creature. Every person and thing which I have created, is a creature. You must prefer Me to all creatures. No creature can compare with Me. Whatever goodness you see in any creature, is only a reflection of My boundless goodness. Nothing on earth can bring you the perfect joy which I shall one day give you in Heaven. When this earthly life is over, you will realize how little and imperfect all creatures are in comparison with Me.

2. If your main interests are on earth, you will always prefer to think of earthly things or people. You will always want what is pleasant and you will even sin to avoid what is disagreeable.

3. If, however, I am your main interest, you will prefer Me to all creatures. You will prove this preference by striving to please Me ever more in your daily life. You will give Me more of your time and attention.

You will seek to come ever closer to Me by reading, reflecting, prayer, and spiritual guidance. Your chief desire in all your daily activities will be to please Me, whether the matter at hand be pleasant or unpleasant.

4. As long as any person or thing has power to draw your will away from Me, I am not your main interest. Creatures may attract your feelings, capture your imagination, and arouse your unreasoning desires, but they have no real power over you until they influence your will. As long as you do not follow unreasonable earthly attractions, you belong to Me.

5. Seek to simplify your daily life more and more. Get rid of all unnecessary interests. Concentrate on the things which make you more like Me. Strive to think more like Me, to be more helpful to those around you, and to keep both your attention and your intention centered on Me. As you advance in this simplicity, creatures will have less and less power over you.

THINK:

It is not wrong to love people and to desire the good things which will improve my earthly life. In fact, since these are all reflections of God's goodness, they should be loved and desired. I do wrong, however, when I love any person or desire any thing more than they deserve. This happens whenever I am ready to sin for their sake. At such times I prefer these creatures to God. My dealings with all persons and things should be reasonable and sinless. God wants me to live an orderly life, placing first things first. Only then can I say that I love Him above all creatures.

PRAY:

Dear God, Creator of all things, You have made a beautiful world. I find myself constantly attracted to different persons and things. They attract me because they reflect some perfection of Yours. However, they are imperfect reflections, and they are not always as good for me as they seem. Help me to please You by using these things or abstaining from them, according as they deserve. Whatever brings disorder into my life, is bad for me. Whatever makes me more pleasing to You, is good for me. I sincerely desire to love You above all things created. I hope to do this by pleasing You every hour of the day. No person nor created thing shall ever again induce me to sin. I shall strive to be more like Jesus in my use of creatures. *Amen.*

CHAPTER 22

Transforming Love

MY CHILD, how great a man is, depends on how much he loves Me. You will understand this truth clearly if you understand My saints. They wanted the best, labored for the best, and lived only for the best. *I am the best.* Compared with Me, all earthly goodness and beauty fade away.

2. This desire and love for the best, raised My saints above themselves, raised them high above all earthly things. They saw the best in Me and devoted their lives to Me. Nothing on earth could turn their thoughts and desires away from Me. Their love was purified like the finest gold. They underwent all kinds of sufferings in soul and body, but they continued to choose My Will in these trials.

3. I showered My graces upon these generous souls. As they made good use of these

graces, a wonderful transformation took place within them. Their minds became sharper, so that they could see ever more clearly the highest value of their daily activities. Their will gained strength, so that no temptation or adversity could draw them away from My Will. As their generosity with Me grew, self-interest faded. Their love for Me became entirely selfless.

4. Self is forgotten only when one has found a higher interest, a more perfect good. I revealed Myself in mysterious ways to My saints. In their pure love for Me, they lived above worldly attractions and earthly joys. They knew a peace which worldly men do not even suspect. Theirs was a happiness unknown to the earthly-minded.

THINK:

What miracles the love of Jesus can work within me, if only I will surrender myself to it! Such a surrender is no great mystery, nor is it a straining effort which will destroy my health of body or mind. It consists firstly in trying to know Him better through reading, reflecting, and praying; secondly, in trying to imitate Him more perfectly in my daily life. As I come to know Him better, I shall love Him more fully. By my daily effort to imitate Him, my love will be purified of selfish motives. He will put me to the test, so that I may see myself as I really am. When I have proved my readiness to give Him all, He will raise me up to new heights of knowledge and love. Then shall I know by experience the transforming power of supernatural love.

PRAY:

Jesus, King of my soul, in You alone shall I find the greatness for which You made me. My greatest glory on earth is to surrender myself to You. With St. John the Baptist, I want my motto to be: "Jesus must increase, while I must decrease." Yes, Lord, I want You to take over my life, and live it as You please. Grant me the privilege of being in Your hands, directed by Your thoughts, Your desires, Your Will. I shall reach my greatest glory on earth when I can exclaim: "It is no longer I who live this life of mine, but Christ Who lives it within me." Only a great love for You can achieve this heavenly transformation within me. Grant such a love. *Amen.*

CHAPTER 23

The Fullness of Love

CHRIST:

MY CHILD, how much you love Me, is seen in your willingness to sacrifice yourself for My sake. You love Me only as much as you are willing to suffer for Me, no more and no less. If in any matter you disagree with My Will, you are setting a limit to your love for Me. True, there is a limit to all human love. In the generous lover, however, that limit is set by Me rather than by him.

2. Those who have a full love are ready to bear anything in their daily life. Their eyes are so fixed on Me that they do not look at the people who cause their sufferings, but at Me. Since I govern all things on earth, they patiently and graciously accept all difficulties and trials for My sake. In all things I am their motive, their strength, and their goal.

3. When you love Me with all your heart, you will no longer hold back anything. You will make no reservations for yourself, but you will strive to live fully for My sake. When you have learned to love Me in this degree, I will

give Myself fully and entirely to you. You will then know a peace and joy beyond all telling.

THINK:

God wants no competition in my heart. He is the Highest Good, the Source of all Joy. No created person or thing can compare with Him. Therefore, it is sheer foolishness for me to place any created being before Him in my desires. The only kind of love worthy of God is a full love, a love which is ready to give whatever He may ask of me. His greatest wish for me is that I become daily more like Jesus, His divine Son. My self-surrender will be complete when I try to live this daily life of mine as Jesus would if He were in my place. How full my love for Him is, is seen by how fully I cooperate with this wish of His.

PRAY:

Father in Heaven, You gave Jesus to me not only as a redeemer, but also as a model. In Him I can see what it means to love You fully. He lived each moment as an act of love for You. He so embraced Your holy Will in all that happened to Him, that His life was a continual act of self-sacrifice. Let me imitate this holy example so unselfishly that I may offer You a full love. With Your help, I will never again turn my back on what is unpleasant and disagreeable. Do with me as You wish, dear Father. Only this full love is worthy of You. Therefore, with all my heart I proclaim: "Take, O Lord, and receive all my liberty, my memory, my understanding, and my entire will. Whatever I have was given to me by You. I return it all to You and surrender it entirely to be governed by Your Will. Give me only Your love and Your grace. With these I am rich enough, and I ask for nothing more." *Amen*.

CHAPTER 24

The Test of True Love

CHRIST:

MY CHILD, many an affection is mistaken for true love until it is put to the test. Only time and trials prove how genuine your love for Me is. Both the time and the trials are given to you in your daily life.

2. Do not fail Me in your daily activities. Keep up your good resolutions. Do not allow your good will to grow cold, but as the day progresses renew your intentions.

Otherwise, when adversity comes you will look for relief, instead of accepting it and offering it to Me as a sacrifice.

3. Today will bring you a number of occasions to prove your love for Me. When disappointments, difficulties, and failures come, do not let them frighten, sadden, nor discourage you. Do what you can to solve your problems intelligently, and if they are beyond your control, accept them as My Will.

4. As you were pleased when I sent you pleasant things, so too should you willingly accept any unpleasant things which I may send. Keep your eyes on the Giver, not on the gift. See My love for you, My wisdom, and My eternal purpose for you. Refuse to feel sorry for yourself, or even to consider yourself. In all things let Me direct your life.

5. Do not be ashamed to serve others for My sake. I want you to live each moment for Me. Keep your eyes on Me in all things. Bless Me as much when life is disagreeable as when it is pleasant. If you know Me well, you will never stop praising Me, even if I give you no more gifts.

THINK:

Am I a fair weather friend of Christ's, or am I a true and loyal friend? My daily life is the answer. My attitude, my desires, my actions when things are difficult and unpleasant—these prove how much I belong to Jesus. I need to keep this fact before me throughout the day, especially at the very moment when my self-love tends to rebel at the people who make my life harder. Instead of resenting my unpleasant circumstances, I can prove my true self-surrender to Christ. When I must bear the unexpected and undesirable, then do I prove beyond all doubt, my degree of love for God. I show either a partial, compromising love or a pure, selfless love.

PRAY:

My God and Saviour, all things that occur today, are under Your guidance and control. Even the evil which others will do to me, even this You permit for Your own good reasons. In accepting life's daily trials, I cooperate with Your all-wise providence and I help fulfill Your eternal plan. To the worldly-minded, I will seem a fool, but it is great wisdom to be such a fool. This is the foolishness of God which will overcome the wisdom of this world. I therefore offer to You all that I am and all that I have. Grant me light to see how this offering may be put into practice today. Give me courage and generosity to follow Your light in all that happens. *Amen.*

CHAPTER 25

Generosity with Christ

CHRIST:

MY CHILD, many desire My heavenly kingdom, but few desire My cross. A large number of people seek My consolation, but few care for My trials. All wish to rejoice with Me, but very few are willing to suffer anything for My sake.

2. I see so many people follow Me as long as they experience no trouble. They bless Me while I send them pleasant things, but when I send them any hardship or suffering, they quickly become resentful, and murmur against Me.

3. A mercenary is a soldier who serves for pay rather than for any patriotic reasons. Should I not call these selfish followers of Mine mercenaries? They are devoted to Me,

not for Myself but for My gifts. They follow Me for what they can get, not for what they can give. They love themselves more than Me. If they realized what I mean to them, they would love Me above all else, even above themselves. How few are those who serve Me without self-interest!

THINK:

It is so true. How often I have done good deeds with a selfish motive. Too many times I do things for Jesus, but with a selfish reason. He was completely unselfish in His self-sacrifice for me. I should never rest content until I have succeeded in serving Him for His own sake. He is all-good and all-lovable. No matter what I may do for Him, whatever it may cost me, He deserves that and more. I owe Him my loyalty even when loyalty is difficult and disagreeable to me. True, I cannot do anything for His sake without gaining many blessings for myself, since God will not be outdone in generosity. Still, I should strive to purify my motives by an honest desire to please Him without any gain to myself.

PRAY:

Jesus, my Lord and King, even if I got nothing from my labors and self-sacrifices, I ought to serve you loyally because You deserve it. I wish to remember this truth in everything I do. I yearn to live the words of St. Ignatius of Loyola which he wrote in his "Prayer for Generosity." In all my daily actions let me say with him: "Dearest Lord, teach me to be generous. Teach me to serve You as You deserve; to give and not to count the cost; to fight and not to heed the wounds; to toil and not to seek for rest; to labor and not ask for any reward, except that of knowing that I am doing Your will." My God, I hope to say this wonderful prayer over and over again throughout the day. Grant that I may fulfill it in all that happens today. *Amen.*

CHAPTER 26

The Pure Desire for Heaven

CHRIST:

MY CHILD, I made all men for the perfect happiness of Heaven. He who strives for Heaven, pleases Me because he is fulfilling the purpose of My creation.

True, people want Heaven for different reasons. Still, no matter what the reason, if one shows any degree of love for Me, he shall enter into eternal life.

2. The love which I require is not a feeling, nor a sentiment. It is a love of appreciation, an intelligent act of the will, based on the first truth. This first truth is that I am God, the beginning and end of all creatures. All men are obliged to live their daily lives according to this truth. They do it by surrendering their self-will to My supreme and all-wise Will. In this self-surrender they show the love which I demand of all intelligent creatures. There are numberless degrees of perfection in this love of appreciation, but they may be conveniently divided into three degrees.

3. Some love Me only as much as they are obliged. They desire to avoid hell, since they dread all harm and inconvenience to themselves. They surrender their self-will to Me only enough to avoid serious sin. They disregard venial sins because they want to please themselves as far as possible, without losing Heaven. Though these people are blindly and

foolishly selfish, they are, nevertheless, offering Me the love which I require of them. If they die in the state of grace, they will eventually enter into Heaven, after they have been completely purified of self-love in Purgatory.

4. Others rise to a higher degree of love for Me. They desire to be more generous with Me. They seek to surrender themselves to My Will, not only in serious matters, but also in lesser things. They make an honest effort to eliminate all venial sins from their daily life. As they embrace My Will more fully, they die to self more completely. Much of their Purgatory is fulfilled in their earthly life. They shall receive a higher heavenly glory than the first group.

5. There remains the highest degree of love for Me. Those in this class are not content with opposing all sins, big and small. Their appreciation of Me rises higher still. They desire to offer themselves entirely to Me by imitating Me in their daily life. Even where there is no question of sin, they strive to abandon their natural preferences and to follow My example of self-sacrifice.

They have seen My goodness and have preferred it to all created things.

6. These generous souls are known as the "pure of heart." They seek to live only for the highest reason—My eternal plan. I made man that he might become God-like on earth, fulfilling My wisdom, growing in My goodness, and finally sharing My heavenly glory. The pure of heart have only one desire—to please Me as much as they can in all things.

7. After a period of devoted and selfless love for Me, they feel a growing desire to be with Me in the perfect friendship of Heaven. They want Heaven with a pure desire, a desire which looks entirely to Me. They are not content with the incomplete friendship which they enjoy with Me on earth. This interior yearning to be with Me completely and perfectly, is My crowning gift to their souls. They shall receive the highest and most wonderful share of Heaven's glory.

THINK:

Even holiness has its degrees, and further degrees within those degrees. People's generosity with God varies with each individual. How far am I God's own and how far am I holding on to my natural self-interest? Is there still a bit of self in my heavenly desires? God offers me the very heights of holiness. How far am I willing to go with Him? These are very important questions. Yes, when I feel eternity's door opening to me, I shall consider these the most important of all questions. I can find the answers in my daily life and in my own intentions for the future.

PRAY:

My God and my All! That should be the motto of my earthly life. You really are my God and my All! Shall I refuse to make You my All in this life of mine? The greatest thing I can do for myself is to forget self and follow Your holy Will in all that happens to me throughout the day. Even in my yearning for Heaven I ought to let Your Will for me reign supreme. I desire at last to make this earthly life of mine what You have always intended it to be—a daily walking toward eternal life. *Amen.*

Outline

BOOK ONE
The Way of Purification

BOOK THREE
The Way of the Union

A. M. D. G.